The Irish Peacock

THE

Irish

Peacock

The Confessions of a Legendary Talent Agent

by

BILLY GRADY

ARLINGTON HOUSE   *New Rochelle, N.Y.*

Library of Congress Catalog Card Number 72-77636

ISBN 0–87000–174–4

MANUFACTURED IN THE UNITED STATES OF AMERICA

The Irish Peacock

One

*I*RVING BERLIN said it better than anybody else. He said it in a song he wrote for his hit musical, *Annie Get Your Gun.* Ethel Merman was the star, and she belted out the song for all the world to hear, "THERE'S NO BUSINESS LIKE SHOW BUSINESS."

I'll echo my friend Berlin. Show business, every facet of it, has been my life for nearly seventy years. I've dreamed it and lived it, never knowing any other line of endeavor. There is no profession more fascinating, no profession more frustrating, on that trip up the ladder to hoped-for success. It is all-consuming and one cannot make a convenience of it. To succeed, one must devote his life to it. The rewards are great, but one must always be aware that many are called but few are chosen. Lady Luck has a hand in all careers. I know she did in mine.

For me it started at the tender age of seven, as an actor, if you please. I was an altar boy in a one-night stand melodrama, *The Fatal Wedding.* An uncle played a priest and was my guardian on the road. My young career was short-lived. The juvenile authorities caught up with the show on a Saturday night in Maine. Their edict? "Get that altar boy back to school or else."

The "back to school" sounded ominous to the manager and he

wasted no time putting me aboard a Boston-bound train with a note attached to my jacket. It read: "This boy's name is Willie Grady, put him off the train at Lynn, Massachusetts, where he will be met by the police." The train conductor put me in the baggage car under the watchful eye of the baggageman. Mr. Baggage read the note, saw the mention of police, and evidently thinking I was a felon, watched my every move on the hundred-mile journey to Lynn.

When the train stopped at Lynn, my baggageman guard was astounded to see the young felon leap into the arms of a smiling policeman, who hugged and kissed the new arrival. The lawman was my father, John P. Grady, a Lynn policeman whose beat included the Boston and Maine depot. John P. and my mom, Nellie, lost no time arranging for their thespian son to start school the next morning.

I was a lousy student, each year getting no more than passing grades. I think my teachers graded me just enough to get me out of their sight. Seven years of it and John and Nellie were finally convinced it was a hopeless task trying to make a scholar out of their offspring. I went to work.

John P.'s brother, Nat, was boss stagehand at the Lynn Theater, the home of the Lindsay Morrison Players, a stock company that changed its show each week. Uncle Nat took me on as assistant property man; my immediate boss, a skinny redhead named Brick Cunningham. Brick moonlighted as a steeplejack and when he was "steepling" I was in full charge . . . until a fateful day in September.

It was hot and humid, typical Indian summer. The Morrison Players, under the direction of a fussbudget of a little man named Walsh, were rehearsing a beautiful love-story drama. They requested ice water and Walsh ordered me to provide same. These were the days before air-conditioning and ice-making machines. Ice was a scarce commodity around the theater. I filled a bucket with water from the tap in the property room, and asked Brick about the ice. Property men are noted for their resourcefulness, and Brick was no exception. Taking the bucket of water from me, he crossed the alley to Corcoran's Undertaking Parlor.

Also because of the lack of air-conditioning, the deceased were packed in ice awaiting final arrangements for burial.

Brick sneaked in the back door of Corcoran's, scooped ice off the nearest stiff, and made it back to the theater. I served ice water to the Morrison Players and they were very grateful.

In the midst of a very intense love scene between Miss Valerie Valaire, the leading lady, and Wyrley Birth, the leading man, old man Corcoran came storming into the theater.

"Where is the sonofabitch who stole the ice off Mrs. Carmody's body?"

All eyes turned to me. The actors turned first green and then yellow. Miss Valaire fainted and fussbudget Walsh came running after me, yelling at the top of his vocal capacity that I was fired and never to darken the doors of the Lindsay Morrison Players again. Cunningham, the coward, ran for the nearest steeple and waved goodbye to me as I ran down the street.

I began a succession of jobs—actor, midway spieler, circus ticket-seller, lecturer in an amusement park at Rochester, New York, booker of vaudeville theaters throughout New England and Nova Scotia, working for B. F. Keith's Vaudeville Exchange in Boston, Massachusetts.

It was here in 1908 that I first met Louis B. Mayer, owner and operator of a small vaudeville house, the Colonial, in Haverhill, Massachusetts. Mayer was unknown outside New England at that time. I serviced his theater with three acts of vaudeville biweekly. Louis B. Mayer, in my opinion, was one of the great showmen of our time, and to a great degree he must be given credit for the motion picture industry's rise to world importance. He was to become a big factor in my future.

It was at Mayer's suggestion that I was transferred to the Keith New York office, there to try and recruit vaudeville acts for the New England territory, replacing the Boston coast-defenders, as we called them. These defenders seldom left New England, and as a result managers were complaining about the lack of new talent. My New York try at replacements was not a success. New York acts would not accept the salaries that Boston managers could afford; I resigned to take a fling as a Broadway agent and found my immediate future bright.

I was fortunate to be associated with the greats, near-greats, and soon-to-be greats, and today it gives me an inner pleasure to feel that I had a small part in their success.

Some of my clients were W. C. Fields, Al Jolson, Ruby Keeler, Cary Grant, Busby Berkeley, and Patsy Kelly.

As early as 1912 I had seen Bill Fields, the comedy juggler, in big-time vaudeville theaters. I was a pushover for his type of comedy and went to see his act at every opportunity. We had never met.

In 1916 he was a star in Florenz Ziegfeld's Follies. Two clients of mine, Gus Van and Joe Schenck, were in the Follies. They took me to see Fields in his dressing room. The introduction was a doozy. Fields gave me a "wet-fish" handshake, looked me in the eye, and said, "Grady—I hate Catholics and agents"—and I was both.

The laughter that followed roused me from my shock and I realized that this was a sample of Fields's off-the-cuff humor. In spite of the remark I liked the guy, and from that time on began a friendship that lasted for many years. It was sometime after our meeting that I learned the why of the Catholic and agent dislike.

Some years earlier Fields had married a lady of the Catholic faith. It did not work out and because of the lady's deep religious beliefs, plus a son born of the union, she would not consent to divorce. Fields was very bitter. In all the years that Bill and I were together he never mentioned the son. Bessie Pool, Fields's girlfriend in the Follies chorus, told me about him.

The aversion to agents stemmed from the fact that he could not see paying 10 percent of his salary for any service they might render. Fields was a very selfish man who lived for Fields and Fields alone. Any expenditure that did not contribute to his personal comforts was unthinkable. He would initiate all his own deals with producers, arranging every detail of a contract. An agent could relieve him of these important details and in many instances do better money-wise, but Fields had the aversion, and stubbornly adhered to it.

I was not Fields's agent in the complete meaning of the term. I functioned as his representative in disputes with managers, and there were plenty. There was stubborn Pennsylvania Dutch in Bill and he was very difficult to reason with once he had made up his mind. His disputes with Ziegfeld over comedy material in the Follies were frequent. Florenz Ziegfeld had no peer when it came to the selection of beautiful girls to grace his productions, nor were there more beautiful stage-settings, but to him comedy was a necessary evil, to be used as change of pace whilst his girls changed costumes and the stage crew the settings.

Bill Fields's inventive comedic mind was such that at every performance he was constantly trying out new gags on the spur of the moment. He never gave the same performance twice. Ziegfeld would okay a scene at dress rehearsal and expect it to remain that way. In the actual performance there would be changes, and, I might add, for the better.

From his office above the theater, Ziegfeld would send long Western Union telegrams of protest to Fields's dressing room backstage. The messages would insist that Fields refrain from using any material other than what Ziegfeld had okayed at the dress rehearsal. There would be a confrontation and Fields, having no taste for arguments, would agree with Ziegfeld and promise not to do it again. The very next performance the great Fields would be doing things his way again. There were continual arguments and protests.

It was my function to intercede in all the many disputes with management. Ziegfeld was as stubborn as Fields but I was lucky to have an ally in Gene Buck, Ziggy's number-one assistant. Gene knew comedy and was an ardent admirer of anything that Bill did. With Buck's great help I invariably won all disputes with Ziegfeld.

Fields never paid me a dime for my services—again the agent phobia. All moneys that were due, Fields was to let accrue and leave to me or my estate in his will. I knew there was such a document because our mutual insurance agent, John Kemp, had witnessed it and congratulated me on its content. Gawd, I would be rich if I survived Fields.

In later years, while I was under contract to MGM and doing all right, Fields had me investigated financially. The findings were that I was doing all right, so I was eliminated from the will. I didn't mind; the good times we had together in the old days were ample compensation. Just an insight into Fields's peculiarities.

If Bill Fields's first concern was his money, next in importance was his stage material. Woe to him who dared appropriate any for his own use without permission. Fields would go to any extreme to avenge pilferage. One occasion concerned Ben Blue, the comedian.

Blue was playing the Palace Theater, New York. Opening matinee he used a couple of Bill's gags. A Lambs' Club friend phoned Bill at the Astor Hotel and told him about the incident. Monday night Bill went to the Palace, observed the piracy, and planned revenge.

Tuesday evening Bill and I dined at Dinty Moore's. Finishing, he said he had an errand to do and I was to meet him at the stage-door alley of the Palace at ten o'clock. I thought it a strange meeting place.

At about ten minutes to ten, Bill drove up in his open Lincoln, bundled up in his oversized raccoon coat, a slouch hat pulled down on his head. I started across the street to meet him, and he yelled at me in an excited voice, "Stay away—stay away!" with no reply to my "What's going on?" In a few moments Blue emerged from the alley and I heard Fields yell, "There's the sonofabitch—get him!"

Two hoodlums came out of the shadows and gave Blue a good going-over. They belted him to the sidewalk and were about to give the foot-stomping routine when Fields yelled, "Hold it— that's enough." The roughnecks ceased their belaboring of Blue and disappeared as quickly as they came.

Fields yelled for me to get into the car, then drove along 47th Street and turned up Sixth Avenue to Central Park. It was several moments before he spoke: "That'll teach that sonofabitch and all the others."

When Fields observed the theft of his gags on Monday evening, he had immediately gone to a hoodlum hangout on 41st Street and hired the two strong-armers for $50 to do the Blue job.

Two

*T*HE BLUE AFFAIR should be a convincer that Fields was a
fanatic when it came to the protection of his stage material.
One more example of this obsession concerned Ed Wynn and
a Fields specialty in the Ziegfeld Follies.

Fields had a trick pool table. It was so constructed that no
matter in which direction the ball was hit, after several trips
around the table it would wind up in a pocket.

To make his fantastic shots, Bill used comedy cues. Long
ones, short ones, cues for hitting around corners. One was a
Scotsman's crooked staff with a tip on the end. Typical Fields
gestures and mannerisms made the act a comedy masterpiece.

The finish to the pool table act was a belly laugh. Ed Wynn
was Bill's assistant in the act and it was his chore to rack up the
balls after each trick shot. After racking, Wynn would take a
seat under the table, facing the audience.

In the middle of the Follies run, Fields discovered that the act
wasn't getting the usual laughs. It was a mystery. Bessie Pool
and Fields's dwarf assistant, Shorty, were sent out front to see
what was the matter. Perhaps he was doing something wrong.

Bessie and Shorty reported to Bill that Ed Wynn, after each

racking of the balls, was sitting under the table making faces, thus detracting from the action on the table.

As usual, Fields kept his plan of action to himself; during the evening performance he kept sneaking glances at Wynn, who was under the table making faces. Those seated in the first few rows could hear Fields's salty remarks. If they couldn't hear, they could read his lips.

The finishing trick of the act was a big laugh. Bill would pocket the fifteen balls with one stroke of the crooked cue. The balls would circle the table from cushion to cushion, and one by one drop into a pocket.

As our Willie prepared for the finishing trick, he took a good look at Wynn, still under the table making faces. Just as Fields was about to stroke the cue ball, he stopped, reversed his hold on the cue to the tip end, and BOOM, belted Wynn over the head, knocking him cold.

"That'll teach you, you face-making sonofabitch," and a few more remarks about Wynn's ancestry accompanied.

Years later I heard Wynn tell what great pals he and Bill Fields were, but he did not mention that he was a vice president of the Ben Blue Club, with the scar on top of his noggin to prove it.

Two things Bill Fields considered inviolate, his stage material and his money. He never did admit that he pirated his best comedy act, "The Family Ford," from Harry Tate, the Englishman, who originated "Tate's Motoring," an act Bill had seen in England. Tate and Fields were bitter enemies over the situation.

Bill Fields had a lot of money, cash, and he meant to keep it. He would wine you and dine you, but if you tried to borrow money from him you were off his list forever.

At one time Bill had a very valuable assistant who acted as his property man and general assistant. The young man traveled with Bill all over the world and, I might add, at very short wages—a habit of Bill's.

The assistant fell in love with a chorus dancer during a Follies engagement. They planned marriage, but because of Bill's lack of generosity there was little to start married life on. Bill was asked for a loan of $300. The assistant of so many years' standing got the money and was promptly fired.

Charlie Mack, of Moran and Mack, the Two Black Crows, was once in jail in Syracuse, New York. He and Bill were close pals; they had dressed together when they were in the Follies. Mack was in jail for nonpayment of alimony to his second wife. He had plenty of money in the bank, but his wife had tied it up. He needed $1,500 desperately to get out of jail, and wired his pal Fields. His pal answered immediately by sending a case of Gilbey's gin and a note which read, "Drink your way out."

Several afternoons a week, Bill and I would go to the New York Athletic Club and play handball. During one of our games he sustained a slight ankle sprain. The club's trainer suggested epsom salts bathing and curtailing of activities.

Back to the Astor Hotel, and after two days in bed and off the foot he was as good as new. Fields carried compensation insurance for incapacitation. It paid him $300 a week for the period of inactivity. The Follies had closed and we were in process of weighing offers for next season. The sprained ankle was reported to the insurance company and the compensation would be forthcoming. An insurance doctor confirmed the club trainer—stay in bed and off your feet for a few days.

The ankle healed quickly and Bill seemed disappointed. It would stop the insurance money. He would prolong the incapacitation and still continue the handball.

The Fields suite at the Astor Hotel had a large living room adjoining the bedroom. Bill ordered all the furniture removed. In this limited-size court, we resumed our handball games.

The insurance doctor always seemed to come for an inspection of the patient when we were in the midst of a hot rally. The doc would be announced by the hotel desk, and Bill would dash into bed in the other room. Here the good medical man would find his patient dripping with perspiration. The ankle, when touched, called for a cry of pain from Fields. It was a mystery to the doctor how a slightly sprained ankle could produce such high fever. The patient was advised to stay in bed and take some prescribed medicine that the doctor left on the night table. The doctor gone, we were back to our handball.

A third visit and the doctor was still mystified by the profuse perspiration. He was going to call an associate for a consultation and return the next day. Once he was gone, we went back to our handball.

Did you ever sense that something was wrong? In the midst of a very fast handball volley, we both suddenly stopped and turned. There was the good insurance doctor standing in the doorway keeping score. He had forgotten his thermometer (he said). We felt pretty sheepish. A look of disdain from the medic and he was off. Naturally, there was no compensation and Fields was so mad he canceled the policy.

On the spur of the moment after a performance in New York, he would call me to take a ride. Our favorite spot was in Upper Manhattan, a grove of trees overlooking the Hudson River. The trees, on moonlit nights, would form silhouettes that we named . . . Ed Wynn, Groucho Marx, and Mae West. We really led a happy life.

One such spur-of-the-moment ride was a lulu. Fields was between shows and had time to play. It was during Prohibition, and though Bill had an ample supply of spirits on hand, he had an idea. He had heard that a friend of ours living out on Long Island, Henry Young, manager of Dillingham's Globe Theater, had a supply of Irish whiskey in his cellar. Young was going to have a couple of visitors.

After arriving at the Young abode in a blinding snowstorm, we got him out of bed and went to the cellar. The Irish "holy water" was wonderful and I'm afraid Bill and I overindulged.

Several hours later, after wild tales about Zulus and Pygmies, we left Young, offering grateful thanks, and went to the car. It was covered with snow and there was a foot of it on the back seat. Fields was all for more driving, but I was for the sleep routine, so I wrapped myself in blankets and in no time was dead to the world.

Several hours later, Fields roused me. I awakened and couldn't believe my eyes. Instead of New York's tall buildings and the noise of traffic, we were in Williamsburg, Virginia. How he'd made it never will be known. Gawd, I'd have some explaining to do when I got home. Fields was also in trouble; Bessie Pool would be waiting for him at the Harriman Bank to get money to pay the movers for an apartment change. The long drive back to New York had two "hungovers" thinking up excuses.

Any time you traveled with Bill Fields you had to be prepared for the unusual. In the first place, he always traveled by open automobile. No matter the weather—rain, snow, hail, or sleet —he was prepared. He carried a tarpaulin with five slits for the passengers' heads, three in the rear and two in front. As for passengers in the bucket seats, they didn't see the light of day until we arrived at our destination. It was an eerie sight seeing Fields's car go through a town with just the heads showing through the slits. Many times he would be stopped by gendarmes asking for an explanation.

The Ziegfeld Follies, in which Bill was appearing, had closed its New York run. Next stand Boston, opening on Monday night. Some of Bill's show material was not getting the expected laughs. He asked me to go to Boston with him to find the trouble. W. C. Fields was a perfectionist as far as comedy was concerned, hence his anxiety.

For the Boston trip, we met at the Astor Hotel at ten o'clock, Sunday morning. In the party were Bessie Pool, Bill's gal, and Arthur Rosenbaum, the Follies stage manager, with his wife, a chorus girl in the show with Bessie. Fields and I completed the passenger list. In the trunk of the car Bill had installed a bar, and I can assure you it was well stocked. Fields was at the wheel of the car, I rode beside him.

It was a cold, miserable day in December. Fields and Bessie were in oversized raccoon coats, the Rosenbaums coated and wrapped in blankets. Grady was in mink, if you please. I had just purchased a mink-lined fur coat from Al Jolson. We were all hunky-dory for the elements.

As we drove towards New Haven, Bill found it necessary to inspect the trunk many times. Bessie and the Rosenbaums accompanied him. I wasn't a daytime imbiber and I knew that the way Fields was going, it was only a question of time before I'd have to take the wheel.

We were nearly six hours making New Haven, ordinarily a three-hour run. On the outskirts of the city I heard Fields say, "What a helluva place to put three trees—right in the middle of the road!"

I strained my eyes. There was no sign of trees, so I knew it was time for me to take over. I suggested we stop at the Taft Hotel for a snack. By this time the rain was coming down in buckets.

Fields drove the car across the sidewalk, right to the hotel door. I thought he was going to try and make the lobby.

"No use getting the tootsies wet," said he.

Cocktails preceded lunch, red wine with the lunch. My companions were feeling very little pain. With six hours yet to go, the trip to Boston should be interesting.

Outside, the weather was the sort for which the Coast Guard puts up small craft warnings. Fields spread the tarpaulin over us and it was a peculiar-looking craft that left New Haven with just five heads sticking up through the slits. As I drove, my passengers slept, interrupted by numerous stops, "to feed the rabbits," as Bessie Pool described it.

Between New Haven and Springfield, Massachusetts, the snow came down, not in the usual flakes but in chunks. I suggested putting up at the Kimball Hotel, Springfield, and proceeding to Boston the next day.

Fields would have none of it. "No," he said, "the family that drinks together stays together."

As we were en route through a small town, with hills on both sides of the highway, a boy on a sled ran into the side of the car. Fortunately, I was driving slowly because of the elements. The boy was stunned, more frightened than hurt. I pulled to the curb some yards ahead. I didn't want the curious to see my loaded passengers.

The youngster was all right, but a policeman who saw the incident insisted we go to the nearby police station to make a report. I insisted that I go alone, because Bessie Pool was pregnant and could not be excited. The Rosenbaums were her doctor and nurse, and Fields her worried husband. I got away with it, despite Bessie's protest that she was not pregnant.

I whispered to Fields that under no circumstances were he and the others to leave the car, and of all things they were not to show up at the police station.

When the officer and I arrived at the station, the boy and his father appeared. The father insisted I had been driving recklessly. The policeman came to my rescue and declared otherwise, but I read the father's mind. My passengers were dressed in expensive raccoon coats, me in mink, and the car was a brand-new Lincoln convertible. We must be stinkin' rich. The father had his hand out. He insisted I be cited. The policeman could not do otherwise. I was booked. I blew my top and asked for the captain in charge. There was no captain, but there was a Sergeant Kenny. The Sarge had a brogue you could cut with a knife. He listened to Fogarty, the policeman, and then said to me: "Rosie O'Grady—what do you say to this?"

"The father is wrong, Captain Kenny. Because of the storm I was driving very slowly. This boy came from nowhere. The policeman will confirm this." I now got an inspiration. Rosie O'Grady and that brogue. I'd try a little schmooze.

"By the way, Captain Kenny. Are you any relation to the Kennys of Salem, Massachusetts?"

"Why do you ask?" the Sarge asked curiously with his brogue.

"Well, that was my mother's name, and a very illustrious family name it is. I am proud of them, as I am of all people with the Kenny name."

Kenny smiled, threw back his shoulders and relaxed in the chair behind the high desk. I knew he was mine.

"Tell me, Mr. O'Grady, are you any relation to Sweet Rosie O'Grady?"

"Well, now that you mention it, sir, that song was written as a tribute to my grandmother."

"Was it now?" said the Sarge. "Between the Kennys and the O'Gradys, we're pretty famous."

Now my pal, the sergeant went to work on the boy's father and talked him out of the complaint. I gave the kid and his father $10 each, and it was over, or so I thought.

Out of the blue and into the station staggered Fields in the big fur coat. "You Irish so-and-so, what the hell are we going to do —stay out there and freeze? Come on, let's get out of this jerk village. Let's get going!" It was Fields at his best.

Sergeant Kenny was stunned. "And who is this?" he bellowed.

"Who am I?" said Fields, leaning toward the desk. You could smell his breath at forty paces. "I own the car that hit that kid. This is my chauffeur," pointing to me. "I want to get out of this goddamn milk stop. Come on, you goddamn Catholic!"

"Wait a minute—wait a minute—you ain't going anywhere. You're drunk. Lock him up, Fogarty."

Now I stepped in, after vainly trying to shush Fields.

"This is my friend, Mr. Kenny. He's had a few drinks to protect him from the weather. We have an open car."

Fogarty whispered in the sergeant's ear.

The officer here tells me his wife is out in the car and she's pregnant."

"She's liable to have the kid any minute," yelled Bill.

"You shut up, Mister. I'm talking to Mr. O'Grady," yelled Kenny.

"O'Grady—O'Grady—why, he's nothing but a Presbyterian from the north of Ireland. That's not his right name."

Now Kenny took off on me. "That makes you worse than he is, O'Grady, or whatever your name is. Who are you, anyway? Lemme see your license, and as for you, Mister, I don't like the tone you used when you called him a goddamn Catholic. What about that?"

"I don't want people to know I'm riding with a Presbyterian, that's why I called him a Catholic." Bill was having a helluva time at my expense.

Now all hell broke loose. Bessie Pool staggered in with the Rosenbaums. Fields hurried to her side and went into the worried father routine.

"Are you all right, my little chickadee?"

"No, I'm not all right. I'm damned cold, and you so-and-sos left us out there to freeze."

"Now who is she?" inquired Kenny.

"She's his pregnant wife," said Officer Fogarty.

"Who's pregnant?" blasted Bessie. "I ain't pregnant, never was pregnant, and never will be pregnant—I hate kids."

No amount of persuasion by the Rosenbaums and myself could keep her quiet. Kenny was steaming himself. He charged everybody with being drunk and disorderly, excepting me. He had seen my right name on the license. Because I was in the clear, Fields was furious . . . called me a bloody renegade.

"Lock 'em up, Fogarty," yelled Kenny, banging on the desk.

Fields, Bessie, and the Rosenbaums were locked in an anteroom. Everybody had to go to the bathroom. It was bedlam. If they didn't stop their language, which Kenny could hear through the door, they would get life.

I talked with the sergeant over the noise from the anteroom. I explained who Fields and the others were, as well as my position. Kenny smiled, but he could do nothing about the disorderly conduct charge. He must save face in front of Fogarty. A judge would have to arrange matters, but it was Sunday and we were in trouble.

Kenny was as anxious to get rid of us as we were to get out of there, but there was nothing he could do under the circumstances, and besides, that Presbyterian thing had riled him. I was given permission to use the telephone.

Bill and I had two close friends in Boston who might have influence enough to get us out of the jam. One was Joe Kennedy, *the* Joe Kennedy, and the other was his partner in a liquor business, Ambrose Dowling. I found that Joe Kennedy and his family were in Palm Beach, but I did contact Dowling who, in turn, had a lawyer appear in our behalf. We left $50 appearance money for the following Wednesday morning, and the gang was dismissed.

I went into the anteroom to bring out my friends. Bessie was quieted down, as were the Rosenbaums, and Fields was sound asleep on a table. He did not want to be disturbed. He was about to make a crack about police in general when I clapped my hand over his mouth. The lawyer and I had to practically carry him out.

We made Boston at 4:30 A.M. Another dull day with the great Fields.

Fields was a one-gal guy. I never knew him to two-time. An amazing thing, though; he had a change of heart every seven years. I could always tell when a seven-year amour was ending. He'd call my attention to some gal he had eyed. I remember one gal. Bill asked me to meet her in a restaurant where he and I used to do some late evening imbibing. I was to sit with the girl whilst he took Bessie Pool home. I was warned to watch my language in the lady's company. I was told she was a Southern first-family belle, a college graduate who dripped with degrees. I don't know where he met her but she was a doozy.

As I walked into Haas's Restaurant, the belle sat at a rear table facing the door. I took one look. I thought there were three of her. She was wearing a big black fur coat that covered a pair of shoulders that could tote a half-ton cake of ice without strain. As I approached her table, a fat hand removed a cigar from her mouth.

I introduced myself and she said, "Yeah, Pokey told me a little old 'Arishman friend of his would sit with me until such time as he completed his errand." (Note the spelling of 'Arishman— it's just the way it sounded.) I didn't like this dame, and figured there is no accounting for tastes.

When I asked her what the Pokey name was, she replied it was her pet name for Mr. Fields. I got up the nerve to ask what Bill called her and she replied, "Putsie." The cow. Just then our Lothario, Willie, showed up. I couldn't get away fast enough. Yup, the seven years started that night.

At this time, Bill was rehearsing a new show called *Poppy*. It was being produced by Philip Goodman and costarred Bill and Madge Kennedy. It was Bill's first book show or play. One week of rehearsing and he hated it and wanted to quit because he had to stick to the written lines. Fields liked to invent his own dialogue and also to ad-lib. Several times he called me to the Apollo Theater where they were rehearsing so I could give Goodman notice that he was quitting. I had attended several rehearsals and he was wonderful in the part. It was a new W. C. Fields. The last time he threatened to quit, I warned him I'd beat his brains out with a baseball bat.

Poppy had its tryout in Atlantic City. Opening night Fields wrote out his notice that he was resigning after the Saturday night performance. I was to deliver the note to Goodman, the producer. I pocketed the letter, and did not deliver it.

Opening night was a triumph for Fields. The audience gave him a standing ovation and when I arrived backstage his dressing room was overflowing with well-wishers. Bill took me to one side. I knew what he wanted. I handed him his notice of quitting. He kissed me on the forehead. The show ran nearly a year in New York, and during the run was made into a picture by D. W. Griffith. Here was Bill's new medium and his start toward immortality as a great comedian.

Following the close of *Poppy* and the making of Griffith's picture, there came an offer from Paramount to make a picture in Florida. "Miss Southern Comfort" and I motored down with Bill.

In a remote section of Alabama, I got lost in a detour and wound up on a lonely country road needing gas. Ahead I saw a one-pump gas station on the side of the road, stopped the

Lincoln, and awaited the attendant. No action. I honked the horn for someone to appear and gas us up, but nothing happened. Bill, in the back seat with the belle, got impatient and started yelling in language that would unleaf the trees for miles around.

"Anyone here to run this goddamn thing?"

The pump platform was at the foot of a hill and high up, on a house porch, sat a man in a rocking chair. He was so unshaven you could hardly see his features. In answer to Bill's yelling, he yelled down, "I run the goddamn thing. Why?"

"We need some gas," said Bill.

"How much?" asked the whiskered one from his seat on the porch.

"Does it make any difference?" yelled Bill.

"Well, mebbe I ain't got that much."

"Give us what you have."

"I need some for myself." The man never moved off the porch, just sat there and rocked.

The dialogue that followed wouldn't pass censorship in a Hong Kong bordello. Fields was at his most vituperative and used expressions that I had never heard before. He stood up in the open car and started to menace all and sundry with a cane he was carrying. The belle was soothing him as though he were a kitten.

"Now, now, Pokey, listen to Putsie." The guy on the porch was one of her people.

"Do we get gas or not?" yelled Bill. "If we don't, we'll go somewhere else!"

"Where'll you go?" said the man, rocking complacently.

"Oh, we'll find some somewhere."

"You-all will hafta ask me, and I ain't of a mind to tell yuh."

I could see that this was getting us nowhere and Bill had been doing a martini routine. He might say something that would really foul us up. I stepped in.

"See here, Mister, we need gas to get to Florida. Will you please sell me just enough to get me to another gas station?"

"Well, I'll give some to you, young feller, but that Yankee in the back seat I don't like." And for the first time the man got up from the rocker and stood surveying the scene down the hill, as much as to say, "God, have I gotta walk down that hill?" I yelled my thanks to the man for his anticipated help. It was now nearly a half-hour since we had pulled up to the pump.

Now comes the slow, and I mean slow, descent from the porch. Slowly he walked to the pump and from his pockets took a bunch of keys. From its size it looked like he had a hundred on the ring. It took some time to find the right key and unlock the pump.

Now came the slow process of pumping with a creaking noise that was like pulling a knife along a piece of glass. It annoyed Bill. The man kept staring at Fields in the back seat and at Putsie, who was giving the guy cow eyes. Now Fields called to me, as I stood with the man at the pump.

"Hey, Irisher, ask the old sonofabitch if there's a lady's room around here."

I returned to the pumper and his creaking handle. "Is there a lady's room around here?" and I nodded my head toward the belle with Bill.

The old guy stopped pumping so he could hear better.

"What's that thing you wanted?"

"Have you got a toilet for a lady?" Bill yelled.

The man yelled at Fields as though he were stone deaf. "What's she want to do?"

Bill was now furious at the man. "What d'ya mean, what's she want to do? She wants to go to the toilet." You could have heard him in Atlanta.

"She does? Well, let her do what everybody else does around here. She can go in the bushes, or she can climb the hill to the shed. Most people use the bush there. They ain't been looked at yet."

Through all this dialogue, the man hadn't pumped a pint of gas and we'd been there nearly an hour. Again Bill bellowed, the gal was in the bushes, and the dialogue got choice.

"Hey, Mattress Face, will you hurry up with that gas and let us get the hell out of here?"

"Just for that language, Mister, you get no more gas. You and that lady in the bushes can get out o' here just as soon as she's finished."

No matter how I pleaded he wouldn't pump another drop. I checked and we had three gallons aboard. It came to sixty-four cents. I tendered a five dollar bill. The man looked at the bill, at me, at Fields, toward the bushes, held it up to the sun, and then the long trek up the hill for change. I was for leaving to save time, but not our Willie. "I wouldn't give that old bastard the time of day. We wait for the change."

We waited and down he slowly shuffled. He was a dollar short, and again up the hill. I wanted to leave now more than ever, but Fields said the guy was purposely acting this way. After a long wait, the man came down the hill again, the dollar change counted out laboriously in nickels and pennies.

The dame came out of the bushes with a torn dress. She was crying and Fields, the lug, was trying to soothe her as one would a four-year-old child, and at the same time, out of the side of his mouth, he was calling the pump man every name he could think of, and he had quite a list. We were over an hour getting three gallons of questionable gas. It was a relief to drive off. To cap the climax, just around a bend of the road we passed the largest gas station we had seen since leaving New York. That guy in the rocker . . . what a stinker!

The evening of the episode with the bewhiskered gas-pump man, the Lincoln developed a leak in the radiator water hose. We would have to stop for the night. We found a hotel—if you could call it that—on the main street. As you entered your room, your eyes rested on a "thunder mug" in the open door of the commode. A water pitcher and matching basin were on top. A sign said, "Toilet Down The Hall." The mattresses had corn shucks for filling, and when you turned over it sounded like the cracking of walnuts.

My room was in the front. Fields and the belle took rooms in the back overlooking the rear of the sheriff's office next door. Baying hounds took voice lessons throughout the night. Even while sleeping I was aware of an occasional crash and a yelp from the hounds. Nevertheless, I slept well.

At about two in the morning Fields came to my room. He couldn't sleep because of the baying hounds. Would I mind changing rooms with him? Sure, I'd be accommodating. I was no sooner in bed in my new quarters when there was a knock at the door. It was the hotel clerk accompanied by the sheriff.

"Git you clothes on, Mister. Ah tol' you I'd come and git ya fer messin' with my dawgs."

I looked. The water pitcher, basin, and thunder mug were

missing. That stinker, Fields. He had known the sheriff was coming and had changed rooms, leaving it to me to either take the rap or get out of it. I explained I must have done it in my sleep, and with a promise to pay the hotel for the crockery, plus a five dollar bill to the cop, I was allowed to finish the night in the hotel. That Fields was a cutie.

A service station attendant fixed the water hose on the Lincoln and we were again on our way. Bill and I sat in the back, dozing. The belle was at the wheel. In mid-afternoon the car stopped with a jerk, the motor dead. Fields and I, aroused from our sleep, looked around and, to our amazement, discovered we were smack-dab on a railroad track.

Bill, when excited, had a voice midway between a tenor and a soprano. He was then W. C. Fields at his excitable best. There was a rapid-fire, staccato run of short, to-the-point phrases: "What the hell is the matter? What the hell are you doing on this road, anyway? Goddammit, do something, somebody!"

Looking around, we saw that we were on a one-lane country road off the beaten track. How the dame ever found it I'll never know.

Fields again: "Get out of the car. Mebbe a train is coming. Hey, Catholic, go down the track and wave the train down. Putsie, you go the other way."

He was running around like a chicken without its head. The belle and I started out in opposite directions, she yelling . . . she had nothing to wave.

"Take off your dress, take off your bloomers, wave something, goddammit it."

I was taking off my shirt as I ran.

Fields began tinkering with the motor. No results. Looking up the railroad bank he saw a man staring at us over a rail fence. He was holding the reins of a pair of horses attached to a plow.

"In trouble?" inquired the onlooker.

"Well, that's the silliest goddamn question. Certainly I'm in trouble. Is there a train due along here?"

The man slowly reached into his overall pocket and took out a large thick silver watch, snapped the case open, and looked at the time as he came down the bank. He said calmly, "It's about time for the 4:40."

From my vantage point up the track I could see Fields suddenly get panicky and start removing things from the car. True to the Fields tradition, the first thing removed and carefully placed under a bush out of harm's way was the booze. He handled the bottles like they were newborn babies.

In the car were our traveling bags and clothes, a typewriter, plus a case of valuable camera lenses, recently brought from Germany to be used in shooting the picture. The booze taken care of, the rest of the car's contents followed. Fields was screaming like a banshee to the man from up the bank.

The man stood in the middle of the tracks, looked to his right and to his left. He wet his forefinger and touched the tracks. Not satisfied, he knelt and pressed his ear to a rail, and then came the announcement that stopped all announcements, "Yup—she's a-comin'."

Fields, now more panicky than ever, yelled and waved to the belle and myself to get off the tracks, and started to turn to the man.

"Can't you get those goddamn horses down here to pull us off?" Pointing to us up the track, he said, "Mebbe they can stop the train. By the way, which direction does the train come from?"

"What's the difference—you gonna get hit anyway," said the man, and Fields blew his top.

"Will you get those goddamn horses?"

"Well, it'll take a little time. I gotta take 'em down to the gate. It's down the road a piece."

"The hell with that. Rip the goddamn fence down and bring 'em down the bank," yelled Bill.

"I don't think Mr. Cartwright would like me to tear down his fence."

"The hell with Cartwright, tear down the bloody fence," screamed Bill. "This is a matter of life or death."

"Don't talk like that about Mr. Cartwright—he's our preacher."

"I wouldn't care if he was your mother—tear the goddamn fence down. Here," and Bill handed the guy a twenty dollar bill and then ran up the hill to rip out the fence. Halfway up, he stubbed his toe and discovered he was in his stocking feet. Good thing the Rev. Mr. Cartwright wasn't within earshot.

Fields removed the two top rails, leaving the lower one. The horses started through the opening. One horse made it, but the second balked—wouldn't move. The horse already through got turned round facing the second horse. The harness got all fouled up. Time was a-wastin', with foul statements spewing from the great Fields. The horseman wondered if he was safe with this wild man.

At last the horses were straightened out and at the car. Now the decision as to whether to pull it from the rear or the front. "What the hell's the difference?" cried Fields. "Goddamn it, hurry up!"

The man hitched the chain to the rear spring, but before moving the horses he again went to the tracks, knelt, pressed his ear, and said, "Here she comes."

"Will you, for Chris' sake, get going?" And Fields jumped behind the wheel to guide it.

The car finally off the tracks; there was a sigh of relief. Bill went to the bottle of brandy.

"By the way," said Bill to the man, "is the 4:40 a passenger train or a freight?"

"I dunno, I never have seen it. I live over in the woods and only hear the whistle."

With the car free, Fields now got fresh. He said to the man, "Well, I'll be goddamned. You're the most stupid sonofabitch I ever met."

"Yeah? Well, I ain't so goddamned stupid that I let my car get stuck on a railroad track," and he was off with his horses.

Bill and I laughed and he said, "You know, I like the sonofabitch."

We heard a klaxon auto horn. It was a Ford wanting to get past. A man approached and asked if we needed help. I explained the motor failure. Whatever the man did under the hood of the car I'll never know, but soon he straightened up and said, "Step on the starter." The engine purred like a kitten.

"Thanks, stranger. We had a pretty narrow escape. The 4:40 must be late."

"No," said the man, "she went through on time. You see, this is a storage track; the main line is over about a mile," and he was off.

We reloaded the Lincoln and Bill took the wheel. As we

crossed the tracks he looked up at the man with the horses and yelled at him, "What I said about liking you doesn't go. You're still a stupid sonofabitch," and we were off for Florida.

Ocala, Florida, and the hotel . . . it would be good to sleep on a mattress that wasn't made of cornhusks, and without the sound of baying hounds in the background. There had been a wind and rainstorm before our arrival that damaged the sets to be used in the first few days of shooting. There would be a delay.

It was Bill's first trip to Florida and he elected to sight-see. A trip to the Gulf via Homosassa was selected. Homosassa, at that time, was hardly more than a cleared swamp with two buildings to attract homesteaders. One building had a high stone wall. There was an ornate, curving gate, and antique carriage lamps stood atop the posts. On nearing the wall and giving it close inspection, you discovered that the whole wall was made of cardboard with the bricks painted thereon. This was at the height of the Florida real estate boom.

We had a laugh as we passed the Ocala hotel newsstand and saw a local paper with a big headline: "Floridian Run Over By Tractor." In those days if a tractor went over five miles an hour, they were speeding. How a pedestrian was dumb and slow enough to get run over was a mystery, and it made me think of the gas man in the rocking chair.

When we left Ocala, our way was barred at a railroad crossing. The protective gates were lowered and the crossing tender waved a greeting. Bill, who was driving, stopped the car. He returned the friendly greeting. We sat and waited for the train to pass. Several minutes—no train. Our Willie was getting restless. A ten-minute wait and still no train. Bill stood up and yelled to the gate-tender.

"What are we waiting for?"

"The regular," said the gateman.

"Where is it?" yelled Bill.

"Dunno—should be here," as he looked up the track.

"What regular is it?" inquired the impatient Fields.

"Oh, the Florida East Coast regular comes through every Tuesday, Thursday, and Sattiday," said the man.

"Well, goddamn it, this is Friday," yelled Fields.

"Is it, sho' nuff?" said the man as he slowly walked into his shack without raising the gates. He checked the calendar against the Ocala newspaper for the date. Satisfied, he reappeared and raised the gates, and as we passed we heard, "Well, bless my soul."

As we drove on Bill said, "Now I know how that sonofabitch was run over by that tractor."

Fishing in the Gulf was dull. No action. A passing boat was hailed and Bill bought a pail of crabs. We would have them cooked at the hotel for dinner. We started home.

At Homosassa, Bill got a brainstorm. We would park, belt some Manhattans from the thermos, and boil the crabs.

While I gathered firewood, our Willie and La Belle went to the river for water. They were gone about five minutes when I heard the most terrifying scream and yell. Fields had stepped on the back of an alligator thinking it was a rock. The reptile hissed and snapped his jaws, and we nearly lost Fields. His usually florid face was as white as a sheet—all but his nose. That stood out like a red doorknob. Two thoroughly frightened and begrimed people, shaking like aspen leaves, sat on the running board and hit the brandy bottle. After a bit, things were seminormal and we set out for home again.

As we approached Ocala, La Belle got a brilliant idea. "Ah think it would be just beautiful if we drove into town with the little ol' car covered with those beautiful, little ol' dogwood blossoms."

Fields, as usual, agreed with her, and while I removed the now smelly crabs from the front seat where I was sitting to their portion of the car in back, Bill and the lady gathered dogwood blossoms. They covered the whole car.

"Now, Pokey honey, don' that look just beautiful?" I must confess it did.

They double-crossed me; she wanted to drive the decorated car into town with Fields beside her. I won the smelly crabs again in the back seat.

On the main street of Ocala, La Belle got a great idea; the car looked "so peachy" she would attract attention, and to that end she loudly blared the horn. We attracted attention, all right. In front of the courthouse we were arrested. It's agin the law to pick dogwood blossoms, and to the tune of a $50 fine, plus an assessment of $5.00 per blossom for 105 blossoms, Bill parted with $575.

WOW! And to top it off, the crabs spoiled in the hot sun. Never a dull day in the life of Fields.

Palm Beach, the ultra-ultra of winter vacation spots, was the second location spot for the Fields picture. Shorty, Bill's dwarf valet, errand boy, prop man, and "packer-upper" when he was on the move, met us at the hotel.

Shorty was four feet tall. He looked as though someone had started pushing his head down and someone else his feet up, much like an accordion. They stopped when they got halfway. This was the little man who walked across the stage with squeaky shoes when Bill was doing his golf specialty. He handled the electric fan that blew the tissue paper into the ball and clubs throughout the golf game. Putting the trick Ford together after each performance was an important function. Shorty was darn near indispensable, but he could rile Fields more than anyone I ever knew.

The little man had a penchant for getting into the booze trunk, removing a bottle of gin, and peddling it, drink by drink, to the chorus girls. He would then refill the bottle with water, and put it back in the trunk. On being accused, he would deny it. Shorty had a memory as long as his stubby fingers.

I booked the W. C. Fields and his Family Ford act into the New York Hippodrome. Shorty played Fields's father-in-law. Marjorie Main played Bill's wife. Our Willie had a cold and elected to stay in the theater dressing room between matinee and night show. His favorite snack dish was a turkey leg and potato salad. Shorty was dispatched to a delicatessen four blocks from the theater for Fields's turkey leg—cold—and potato salad. Bill sat with mouth watering in anticipation. It was 4:30. Shorty was supposed to return in about twenty minutes.

Bill and I discussed some business while awaiting Shorty's return. It was 5:15 and no Shorty. Fields was getting mad. At 5:45, still no Shorty. The paint on the dressing room wall was beginning to peel; Fields' language was getting hotter. Came 6:00 P.M. and still no Shorty. If everything happened to Shorty that Fields wished, he'd never live through the night. Finally, by 6:30, Fields was famished, and in came Shorty empty-handed.

"Where the hell have you been and where the hell is my dinner?"

"I couldn't find any. I went to eight places, and everywhere I went and asked for them, people laughed at me."

"Listen, Shorty, what—did—I—send—you—for?"

"You sent me for turkey eggs and potato salad." A typical result to a Shorty errand. Fields had to put up with a stale ham sandwich from the backstage lunch counter.

The picture location was the beautiful Stotesbury estate on the Palm Beach Gold Coast, a showplace. Spacious lawns, gardens of rare flowers . . . a rainbow of color. Throughout the grounds were beautiful statues, Italian imports. The Stotesburys were leaders in Eastern society, and their home was the gathering place for notables.

The picture script called for Fields and his family to start out on a picnic in the family Ford. They were to drive the ocean-front road looking for a picnic spot. Everywhere they would encounter signs: "Private" . . . "Keep Out" . . . "No Trespassing" . . . "No Dogs Allowed."

Fields was to rebel against the rich and their private estates that deprived him and his family of a recreation spot. At the high iron gates barring his way into the Stotesbury estate, his rebelliousness would be at fever pitch; the script called for him to storm the gates with the car in high gear and drive in. So far, so good. This was all prearranged with Stotesbury.

Joe Pasternack, fresh from Budapest, Hungary, was the second assistant director on the picture. In his very thick Hungarian accent, Joe gave Fields his directions. Bill listened politely. He had an idea as to what he was going to do.

Joe said there were papier-mâché and plaster-of-Paris statues posted throughout the spacious lawns. Bill was to drive in through the flower beds, knock down the fake statues, and generally wreck the place.

Fields really did a wrecking job. The flower beds were a shambles, broken statues all over the place. Just one thing went wrong. Pasternack didn't tell Fields which were the fake statues and which were the real ones. All hell broke loose.

I thought Stotesbury would sue Paramount, Fields, Pasternack, the crew, and even Shorty, but I looked and there was old man Stotesbury holding his sides with laughter. He was having a helluva time, and no complaint. Fantastic.

It would take the crew some time to clean up the mess, so Bill and I went back to the Royal Danelli Hotel. In the lobby there was a young hoodlum from New York whom I knew slightly. He was from a bootlegging syndicate.

It seems his outfit had 300 cases of Gilbey's gin stashed in a hiding place down in Miami. They had hopes of delivering the gin to New York speakeasies, but there were so many Florida roadblocks set up by the state police looking for Cuban rum smugglers that the syndicate could not get a truck through with the gin. They would have to sell their product in small-case lots. Would we be interested?

If the gin were the real McCoy, Bill would take six cases, but our Willie wanted to be sure. The hood said, "No dough until you get back to New York. I'll see you guys in Moore's and collect." That gave me an idea. Dinty Moore was at his Palm Beach home four blocks away. If there was good gin around, Moore would know about it. To Jim "Dinty" Moore we went.

Jim okayed the gin, in fact took twenty-five cases for himself. Fields would take six cases, but we had to go to Miami to get it. Price? Only $80 a case—cheap for the real thing. The mob must really be in trouble.

The hood gave us directions for the pickup. Fields and I were to drive to a certain street corner in Miami, park, and await instructions. It seemed cloak and dagger. Fields was packing his thirty-eight.

Miami and the designated street corner. I parked and waited. Twenty minutes later an old Chandler limousine pulled alongside. The driver beckoned me to follow him. Fields had his thirty-eight at the ready. There was no need for it.

The Chandler pulled up on a dark side street. The driver came to our car. "Where d'ya want the gin?" It would have to be put in the rear seat, as the trunk had the bar and there was no room there. The gin was loaded, four cases on the floor and one each side of Bill on the seat. The man also loaded two chairs and a small table, covering everything with a blanket. If we got stopped in a roadblock, we'd say we had attended an antique sale in Miami. This guy thought of everything. If all small-lots buyers got the same attention, there wouldn't be an antique left in Miami.

The night was chilly and Fields was wearing his big raccoon coat. He looked like Queen Victoria, seated with the ends of his coat hiding the gin, and he erect and regal, staring straight ahead.

We started north for Palm Beach. No inspections as we drove through two roadblocks, though Fields did get a bawling out from the state troopers. They said it was insulting for him to wear a fur coat in Florida. We were saluted and waved on.

After the third roadblock, I heard fidgeting in the back seat. I didn't pay much attention, though I did have an idea what was going on. Fields was cold and was trying to pry open one of the gin cases, and he succeeded. In the rear-view mirror I could see him guzzling.

As we drove through the main street of Hollywood, Florida, we came to a square lighted by an overhead arc. A man stepped into the street and raised his hand. I roused the sleeping Fields with my sudden stop. I noted he was feeling no pain. Bill saw the man approach and grabbed his thirty-eight. The stranger looked at Bill in the back seat.

"I beg your pardon, would you-all be going to Palm Beach?"

"We would," said Fields, fondling the pistol.

"Sir, I have missed the last bus and I would deem it a great favor if I could ride with you gentlemen. I am speaking at a luncheon in Palm Beach and it's imperative I get there."

Fields did a bit of bowing and emitted some drunken old-world charm as I reached across the seat to lower the window and release the lock on the door. The newcomer put one foot on the running board, hesitated, and directed his conversation to Bill.

"I am an ordained man of God. I travel the highways and byways, lecturing on temperance and the blessings of prohibition. I . . ."

That's as far as he got—no farther. Fields brandished the thirty-eight. He yelled like a banshee.

"OUT—OUT—OUT—you lily-livered so-and-so before I fill

you full of holes. OUT—OUT—OUT!" Bill tried to balance himself on the gin cases and furniture. He was weaving from side to side, trying to keep his balance. He looked like a giant standing there in his fur coat. The man was about to say something when Bill raised his foot and pushed it into the man's face. He went sprawling in the street. I took off.

I felt a little sorry for the ordained man of God, but of all people to ask for a ride at 4:00 A.M., William Claude Fields—the chief advocate of the benefits of the grape.

Bill and I were tired from the Miami trip and the bed felt good. It was our intention to sleep late and breakfast at noon. No such luck. Our slumbers were interrupted in the early A.M. by a phone call from Bill LeBaron, Paramount producer of Bill's picture. They were delighted in New York with the films they had seen from Florida. He also advised us that sets were ready at the Paramount Long Island studios for the interior scenes.

LeBaron asked Bill to assist in a Paramount Company matter. Their very important star, Miss Bebe Daniels, was en route to Palm Beach by train to start her new picture. LeBaron asked if Fields would arrange a suitable reception for the star's arrival at the railroad station. Miss Daniels's star magnitude was such that perhaps some local celebrities and city officials would act as reception committee. Bill agreed to help and went to work on the arrangements in typical Fields fashion.

The star was scheduled to arrive the middle of the next afternoon. Pullman car number and the location of her drawing room aboard the train were supplied. Bill made his plans over a few martinis. After cocktails, he was always inspired.

Shorty, Bill's dwarf valet, would be the great "celeb" to meet the Paramount star. We scurried around and obtained an old pair of striped formal trousers, together with a swallow-tailed formal coat, ascot tie, silk hat, and "yaller" gloves. Bill cut the trouser legs off just above the knees with a razor blade. It was a hasty job, and when we tried them on Shorty for length, we found that the seat trailed the floor, but luckily the long formal coat covered that scene. Shorty had to wear special shoes of his own, and his resplendent outfit was finalized by the yellowest pair of brogans I have ever seen. All was in readiness with the exception of music.

I went over to Palm Beach and hired a five-piece Dixieland jazz band that worked in a local honky-tonk. These Negro gentlemen doubled as wrestlers in the local arena. I have never seen a more motley collection of broken noses and gaping mouths with no teeth.

The arrival hour and Shorty was decked out in his reception finery. He looked like a professional baby frightener or lease breaker. A tired bouquet of flowers was held in a yaller-gloved hand. The little man was seated in the rear seat of a rented open car—a Packard—with a 300-pound chauffeur at the wheel. They parked at the station platform.

Miss Daniels's train was an hour late, but the Dixieland boys made things merry for the curious that had gathered.

The train arrived. Miss Daniels, from her drawing room window, heard the band and saw the crowd. She waved and blew kisses. Little Shorty was out of sight.

The great star hurried to the Pullman car door for her regal exit, got one look at Shorty and the tired bouquet, let out a shriek, and ran back to her drawing room. It took a few moments for her to regain her composure and she proved what a good scout she was by returning to the scene of action and entering into the spirit of things.

We loaded the Dixie boys into a car and escorted Miss Daniels's car, Shorty beside her, through the streets to the hotel.

Fields's reception was a humdinger and I will always have a great admiration for Miss Bebe Daniels—a star of stars in my book.

The Florida jaunt behind me, I returned to seminormalcy in New York, if one could call the life of a Broadway agent in the twenties even closely related to normalcy.

During my first week, I had a call from Earl Carroll, producer of the revue, Earl Carroll's Vanities. He wanted to talk to me about Fields.

Carroll had just finished a very unpleasant stay as guest of Uncle Sam at the Federal Penitentiary at Atlanta. The resulting publicity didn't help his image or his Vanities productions. He planned a new Vanities and figured that if he had a star like the great W. C. Fields, it might restore his Vanities to its former degree of popularity, as well as ease himself into public acceptance.

I went to Carroll's office. He was my friend and I had to level with him. Bill Fields had always expressed his dislike for the man and for any Carroll operation. As a star of the Ziegfeld Follies, he had gone as far as he could go in theatrical importance. A Vanities would be a come-down. I felt it hopeless for Carroll to seek Bill Fields's talents and told him so. I also said that Fields's demands would be such that the Vanities could not afford him.

Carroll would not take "no" for an answer. He insisted that I see Fields for a final decision. To that end I went to see Bill at the Astor Hotel. His reaction was as I had anticipated. "I wouldn't work for the sonofabitch if he gave me his theater."

I looked at things realistically. The W. C. Fields picture, via Paramount, would be flooding the country. To my mind, the movies were his future, if he would bide his time and await the public's reception of his pictures. If the reaction was favorable, it would put him in a better bargaining position with Paramount, but there must be an interim engagement. The Vanities, perhaps? Use it as a stopover?

When Fields wanted to think something out, he would take three tennis balls into another room and juggle for a spell. He left to juggle and in a short time returned.

"I never did like that guy's setup. He's a sensation- and publicity-seeker. All he knows is to put a lot of bare-fannied dames on a stage. Just look at what he did last week at the Central Park Casino."

What Fields was referring to was a spectacle that Carroll had made of himself at a large charity function at the Casino in the Park. All of New York's social, theatrical, and café society had attended a dinner there for some worthy cause. O. O. "Odd" McIntyre, the famous Hearst columnist, was the master of ceremonies. I, for some unaccountable reason, was seated at Earl Carroll's table. Walter Winchell, whom Carroll blamed for his government difficulty and subsequent imprisonment, was at a table across the aisle.

There was a lull in the proceedings and Carroll rose and addressed himself to O. O. McIntyre. In essence he said, "Mr. McIntyre, this room is filled with a gathering of very nice people," and turning to Winchell, he hissed, "Walter, you don't belong in the company of nice people. Why don't you leave?"

If a bomb had been dropped on the building, it would not have had more effect. There was complete silence. Carroll sat down amidst an embarrassed group of people at his table. He left early.

Winchell, the country's most important columnist, just sat and ignored Carroll. Everybody present was in Winchell's corner and was appalled at Carroll's action. Ooooh, what a situation!

In those days either you liked or disliked Winchell, and I must say he handled himself admirably that night and gained many new friends. It was the opposite for Carroll. Even the papers that didn't carry Winchell gave him all the best of it the next day.

After Fields's reference to the Park Casino episode, he continued, "I can see the logic in what you say, Catholic, but if, and I repeat, IF, I go to work for the sonofabitch I'd want so much money he couldn't afford me, and he'd forget it. You tell that guy I want $6,500 a week. I'll furnish four sketches for myself and I want $150 royalty a week for each. I must have my name advertised in all publicity, and in lights over Earl Carroll's name and over Vanities. My name must be in larger type."

I said, "Bill, he'll never go for that. Besides, he can't afford it."

"Good, then I don't have to work for the sonofabitch."

Back to Carroll with the news. He was a soft-spoken man, always trying to convey the impression that he was a nice guy but that the world was against him. He was a shrewd operator. As I enumerated the Fields terms, he put the tip of his long bony fingers under his chin and seemed on the verge of tears, a mannerism I was wise to.

He said, "Billy, I am terribly disappointed."

"Earl, as I told you earlier, Fields doesn't want any part of the Vanities. I tried to help the situation, but those terms are the result. It looks like it's down to take it or leave it."

"Well," again the tapping of fingers under the chin, "as I said, I am greatly disappointed and under the circumstances I guess I'll have to say no and forget Mr. Fields."

Back at the Astor I related Carroll's reaction and answer. Bill said, "Good. Putsie and I will drive to California for a vacation." That was that.

The Fields-Carroll thing behind me, I became busy with a new project, the Silver Slipper night club. One morning, to my amazement, I read in the theatrical section of the newspaper the announcement: "W. C. FIELDS TO BE THE STAR OF EARL CARROLL VANITIES." You could have knocked me over with a kumquat.

Carroll, in his usual slimy manner, had called Fields at his hotel. He asked for an appointment, and it was made. When Carroll arrived, Fields had a back-slapping friend, a lawyer, present. The outcome of the meeting? The trio closed the deal that I had outlined. I was out in the cold. I was hurt, but knowing Fields's dislike for agents in his affairs, it would be useless to protest. I told Fields and Carroll, whom I telephoned, that I thought it pretty shabby of them both. From Carroll I'd expect it, but not from Fields. And his explanation didn't excuse him: "What the hell do you care? You'll be in the will anyway."

I found out later that the Southern belle had a hand in the proceedings. The lawyer was a friend of her family and for a small retainer closed the deal with Carroll. My original feeling about the chitlin' eater was confirmed.

Bill and I, so close over the years, were estranged. I missed the companionship but it was more bearable when, at the end of the Vanities engagement he left for California and the Paramount Studios. I remained in New York as MGM's studio representative, and did not see Bill for several years, though I did get a letter once in a while.

After my transfer to the California studio as casting director, I'd run into Bill at Chasen's or visit him at his home. That close companionship never returned. Good friends, yes, but it was different. Everytime I ran into him I noted a deterioration physically, and it was not long before physical handicaps had him on the sidelines.

Shortly after my arrival in California, I bought a ranch in Corona. Fields was an occasional visitor. I was shocked at his appearance. He was no longer the fastidious dresser that I had hung around with in New York. He had an unsightly skin infection. Walking laboriously, he was accompanied by a driver who helped him navigate. It was obvious that there was serious illness in the offing.

In Los Angeles, Bill had leased the beautiful De Mille estate on Los Feliz Boulevard. This was the gathering spot for his drinking companions and was furnished according to his newly developed tastes. There was a pool table in the ornate living room, gymnastic equipment in the dining room, and a steam cabinet and rubbing table in the library. His personal quarters were an office and bedroom on the second floor. Burglar alarms and intercom buttons were everywhere. Two young women were in constant attendance. His deterioration was more apparent every time I saw him.

My last call on him at the De Mille place was a lulu. I had volunteered to drive a spinster lady named Stockhouse to the Naval Hospital at Corona where she was volunteer organist in the chapel. When I called and told him of my intended visit, and filled him in on Miss Stockhouse, he told me to bring the old gal along. Arriving at the Los Feliz gate, I pressed the intercom button. Fields answered.

"Who's there?" answered Fields.

"The Catholic."

"Come on in, you silly sonofabitch—got the organ grinder with you?"

Miss Stockhouse was shocked and seemed disinclined to accompany me. I assured her everything would be all right. After a long walk through the grounds to the door—another button.

"Come on in, you silly Catholic, and let the dame in first—don't show your ignorance."

More wavering by the spinster lady. As we entered and she saw the strange layout, she must have thought she was in the home of a lunatic.

"Goddammit, come upstairs. What's keeping you?"

I took the knee-shaking lady by the arm and helped her up the stairs. Arriving at the office door I looked in. There was Fields seated at his desk fanning himself in the July heat. He was bare to the waist. I presented Miss Stockhouse. Fields extended his hand in greeting and stood up. Good God, he was as naked as a jay bird. Miss Stockhouse took one look, shrieked, and ran for the door, taking the stairs three at a time; she shot out the front door, and we could see her, skirts flying, running for the gate.

Under the circumstances I cut my visit short and he apologized for his "fox pass," as he called it; he'd just forgotten he was unclothed. When I finally got to my car, there was Miss

Stockhouse talking and pointing hysterically to a motorcycle policeman she had flagged down.

I explained matters to the officer; he laughed and was off— he had been to the Fields house before. I don't think the lady spoke two words to me all the way to Corona; she kept dabbing at her eyes with her hanky. It was her first meeting with a movie star, and by gad, it would be her last.

Bill was in a sanitorium in Pasadena. I'd visit him when it was allowed. Very few visitors, no alcohol, and a strict diet. For him it was torture. At Christmas time he was very ill. Dave Chasen and I donned comedy costumes, he as a fireman and I a tramp. We secreted Scotch and bourbon in our clothes and carried a roast turkey. Our friend was to have what for him would be an offbeat Christmas.

Christmas morning, as we approached the cottage at the hospital, a nurse came down the steps. We were greeted with: "Are you here to see Mr. Fields?"

"Yes, Ma'am."

"I'm sorry, Mr. Fields passed away about ten minutes ago."

Dave and I sat on the grass and blubbered like children. A great man had died, but he had left his permanent imprint on a changing world.

All his pals were at the funeral at Forest Lawn. It was a sad occasion. After the services, we all went to Jack Dempsey's home on Los Feliz Boulevard and drank to the memory of a man who would always be a star.

Three

*N*OT TOO LONG ago a loudmouth made the remark that
"good guys finish last," a statement with which I heartily disagree. One of the finest gentlemen in the motion picture industry
is a "good guy." His name is James Maitland Stewart. If only
many of our other top-ranking picture personalities would pattern their public and private lives after his. James Stewart is
one actor who will not appear in a picture if it does not reflect
credit on the industry, his family, and himself.

Over the years Jim Stewart and I have been very close. The
"movies," as he calls them, have given him wealth and fame,
but he is still the retiring, unobtrusive man I first met, quite by
accident, when he was a student at Princeton.

My friend George M. Cohan had invited me to attend the
opening of his new play in Atlantic City. Driving down, I
stopped at Princeton for lunch. While waiting to be served, I
telephoned my office in New York and was informed that the
Cohan play, due to a production difficulty, had been postponed
one day. In order not to waste the day, I decided to attend the
annual Princeton University Triangle Show opening that evening.

Princeton shows were always interesting; this one was no

exception. It got off to a good start with a line of thirty-two male undergraduates in female chorus garb, trying to emulate the Radio City Rockettes. They were a motley group, and like all amateurs, accentuated their ridiculous appearance with excessive mugging and gestures. All but the skinny guy on the end. He was six-foot four, towered over the others, and looked uncomfortable as hell. While the others hammed it up, the thin one played it straight and was a standout.

Later in the show the thin one did a specialty, singing a song to his own accompaniment on an accordion. He could not seem to coordinate the lyrics and the instrument. First the accordion was a bar ahead, then the lyrics would be behind the instrument. The audience thought it a comedy routine and rewarded with loud applause. I noted that the singer had an ingratiating personality, an asset in my scheme of things theatrical.

The show over, I sought the young man backstage for a talk. He was a senior, his name was James Stewart, and he lived with his parents, Alexander and Daisy Stewart, and two sisters in Vinegar Hill, a suburb of Indiana, Pennsylvania. Alexander Stewart, a Princeton alumnus, owned the local hardware store and was a bit of ham—some of it rubbing off on his son James, who had been sent to Princeton to learn business administration but decided to try for a stage career when the acting bug got him.

I'll take license and reveal that in later years, Stewart's hardware store had Jim's Oscar prominently displayed in its window, surrounded by stills from his latest picture. Indiana was proud of its native son. Alex Stewart had befriended an inmate of the local almshouse and took him on as handyman around the store. He was known as "Irish," a short, chunky man with a head of matted hair that was trimmed on Thanksgiving Day and at Easter time, and a scraggly beard to match his several tobacco-stained teeth. The year-round, be it hot or cold, Irish would be attired in a hand-me-down suit, heavy wool socks, and brogans. A very oversized winter coat completed the picture. When Irish finished his mopping up chores, he would retire to the rear of the store behind a pot-bellied stove and there go into a snorting and snoring sleep, slouched in an overstuffed chair.

The display of the Oscar in the store window had passersby

stopping, looking, and getting the idea that movie star Stewart was in the store. They would enter and inquire of the clerk (Alex) if the young Mr. Stewart was in town, and were informed that James Stewart was in California. The visitors would then ask for Jim's father. This is where the ham really came out in Alex. He would hesitate, wipe a tear from his eye, and almost sobbingly inform them, "This is a very sad case. I dislike to tell you about it, but follow me."

The group would be led to the pot-bellied stove; pointing out the snoring Irish, Alex would whimper, "Jim's father." Alex had many laughs. Jim didn't relish the gag at first; his mother and sisters were mortified. I loved Alex.

Back at Princeton, young Stewart informed me that after graduation he was going to take up residence in New York City and make an attempt at an acting career. I wished him well and took my leave. In my office file it was recorded, "James Stewart, Princeton student, a type of no particular interest."

In New York Jim moved in with three pals in Greenwich Village—Henry Fonda, Myron McCormick, and John Swope. Each day they would visit producers' offices, seeking the job that would start them on their pro careers. Hank Fonda and McCormick were lucky; they got jobs in a little theater, the Provincetown on Cape Cod.

One week after their arrival at the Cape, Hank and Mac telegraphed Jim. "Get up here as quick as you can. Josh Logan has found a spot for you." Bags and accordion packed, he was on his way.

Jim was met at the train on arrival by Logan, Fonda, and McCormick. Logan led him to the "spot"—accordion player in a tearoom. Jim was lower than a duck's bustle, but he took the job.

The old gal who owned the tearoom was in Boston when Jim was hired. When she returned home and saw the new tearoom setup, she advised all and sundry that she hated accordion music and all that went with it. James Stewart, entertainer, got the heave-ho and went back to New York for the daily rounds.

I saw him in his first Broadway show in December, 1933. It was a short-lived thing, *All Good Americans*, and Jimmy played a bit. Next came *Yellow Jack* in March, 1934. This was a dramatization of Major Reed's war on malaria-carrying mosquitoes. Jim played an Irish soldier, and though I couldn't give him much for his brogue, he did a very creditable job. My file said he was still just a type.

Next came a tryout of *All Paris Knows* at the Red Barn Theater, Locust Valley, Long Island. This was a stock company of which Jim was a member, and quite a favorite in Locust Valley. I liked to see plays there. Next door was a wonderful restaurant, the Stagecoach Inn. Good food and a drink specialty called a stirrup cup, brandy with other good things. Three stirrup cups and you wanted to marry a horse.

The Red Barn Theater was just over the fence from the Long Island Railroad tracks. Coal-burning locomotives hauling freight and passenger trains noisily rushed through during every performance. If, at rehearsal, it was discovered that an important scene would be in progress as the 9:12 freight passed, the starting time of the play would be changed. It made no difference with inconsequential scenes.

In this play Jim had a big love scene scheduled to begin after the 9:12 went through, but the night I saw the play the 9:12 was late—it came roaring by just as Jim went into a clinch and a kiss with the leading lady. Undaunted by the noise, Jim held the kiss and ninety cars of freight passing helped make history. It was the longest kiss in the history of the American Theater. Heh—my man is sexy. The file now said, "A good type."

Next, *Page Miss Glory*, his fourth show in less than a year. This meant sixteen weeks of rehearsals with no salary and about four shows, giving him about ten weeks' work at short wages. Not very profitable; he was learning his trade the hard way. Hank Fonda had already made it in *The Farmer Takes A Wife*. McCormick was making a name for himself in important roles in Broadway plays. Josh Logan was a stage director. Though Jim did a good job in *Glory* he was still just a good type in my records.

About this time I had been transferred to the California studios of MGM as casting director, making monthly trips to New York to review new plays and see new talent. On a visit in November, 1934, I saw Jim in *Divided By Three*, starring my favorite actress, Judith Anderson. He was in fast company that included Hedda Hopper and James Rennie. My man really held his own. My file now read: "James Stewart.* This man has finally arrived. Unaffected and sincere in everything he does. We should send for him and talk contract."

The New York office finalized a contract with Stewart while I returned to the studio. It was my intention to start Jim in a "Thin Man" picture, a series that starred William Powell and Myrna Loy, but the next one was at least four months away. I promised to look for a picture for him to fill the interim.

At the studio was a script that needed casting. It was called *Murder Man* and was to star Spencer Tracy and Virginia Bruce. Incidentally, this was Spencer's first picture under the MGM banner, after an unfortunate experience at Fox. The producer of *Murder Man* was Harry Rapf, a close friend of L. B. Mayer. In the script was the part of a police reporter called Shorty for obvious reasons. I thought it would be a good part for our new contract player, though he was far from being a Shorty physically. I had a talk with Rapf, made my pitch but got nowhere. He insisted he wanted a jockey-sized actor, nothing else would do. I was accused of trying to rewrite his script. Our talk wound up with a loud and definite "NO" on Stewart.

Tim Whalen, a friend of mine who was the director of *Murder Man*, had started shooting on Stage 18. I went to see him and told him all about Stewart. Whalen and I always did see eye to eye on talent. Tim's answer was "Bring on your man, the hell with Rapf, I'll start Stewart and say nothing to Rapf."

A phone call to Jim at Vinegar Hill found him mowing the lawn. He let out a whoop and dropped the mower, and two days later was at the studio. The third day he was Shorty and did a helluva job. Whalen was delighted, as was Spencer. I now had Rapf to contend with.

When my producing friend Rapf saw the film with Jim and not a jockey-sized reporter, he raised hell and went immediately to L. B. Mayer's office. Though I knew Rapf back in New York in his struggling days, he insisted to Mayer that I be fired for disobeying orders. This didn't worry me as I had just signed a new five-year contract. The expected call from L. B.'s office summoned me. I received the first of the many bawling outs I was to get from him over the years. I waited for him to finish and asked that he withhold judgment until he had seen the film.

The three of us went to the projection room and reviewed the

Stewart first-day's shooting. At the finish, Mayer turned to Rapf and bawled the hell out of him; I got a pat on the back and was complimented by Mayer. My man Stewart was on his way, and with a succession of good roles in top pictures in no time he became one of MGM's important personalities.

We jump several years and find a madman named Schicklgruber, former paperhanger, the head man in Germany. He has the world in a turmoil, a war is on, and the United States is in it. Motion picture star Stewart wants to be part of it. The father, Alex, had come out of World War I as a captain; the son would carry on the tradition.

A visit to an Air Corps recruiting office and disappointment. Jim is turned down because he was underweight. For six months there would be a rigid body-building campaign. Never did a man work so hard at it. When he finally achieved the necessary weight, he received "Greetings" from Uncle Sam; he was drafted.

Burgess Meredith, a pal of ours, was living with Jim at his home in Brentwood and came up with a good idea. Unbeknownst to Jim, Buzz and I would arrange a going-away surprise party, inviting twenty of his pals. Hank Potter suggested we all dress as Knights of the Round Table. I was to arrange for the food and the refreshments and a place to hold the shindig. Meredith would round up some gals to decorate and lend class to the festive board.

Dave Chasen was to do the catering, and though we always used his second-floor private dining room for our parties, twenty men dressed as Knights parading through the usually crowded restaurant would look a little silly. More so, with Meredith's gals tagging along.

Franchot "Doc" Tone offered his home situated back in the hills of Brentwood. The Doc would be on location with a picture and his mother would be in Palm Springs. I knew the Tone place and it would be ideal for our purpose, though a little difficult for our friends to find. I suggested to Dave that he have his men place direction signs along Sunset Boulevard approaching Tone's, and up the street to Tone's house.

Chasen followed the suggestion to the letter. Every other pole along Sunset Boulevard had a red lantern hanging on it. A cruising deputy sheriff might run into an interesting situation. Whitey Hendry, our MGM police chief, would take care of that. We would be safe.

I thought the guest of honor should have a beautiful dinner companion. A gal who played extra in pictures would just fill the bill. Around the studio she was known as the Belle of the Ozarks. Tall and willowy, she dripped you-alls and sho'-nuffs.

A visit to MGM's wardrobe department and the Belle was outfitted in a used Greta Garbo gown. Man and boy, did she fill it, leaving nothing to the imagination. It took quite some persuasion to have a wardrobe woman cut the seat out of the all-revealing dress. With no undergarment, the opening would reveal quivering Ozark Hills as she walked. An extra twenty-five dollars would compensate for any embarrASSment she might have. She would wear an evening wrap until the unmasking time. At Tone's house, she would sit on a divan at the end of the room and await the guest of honor's arrival. A studio limousine would deliver her in style.

When I arrived at the party the guests were all there, the goddamndest-looking Knights ever assembled with their cutlasses, sabers, wigs, and feathered hats. I don't know where Meredith found the dames, but they looked like parolees from a detention prison. I had misgivings when I saw several of them finish their drinks and place their empty glasses in their purses. It promised to be an interesting evening.

The Belle of the Ozarks arrived, clad in an evening wrap over the Garbo gown. I escorted her to the divan at the extreme end of the room, where she sat and held court. Every Knight went on the make, the parolees looked daggers at the newcomer.

A phone call from Meredith at Stewart's house. Jim was very appreciative of the surprise party, but could we get along without him? He had to be up at three in the morning so as to meet the induction center trolley at four. It would be a trying day and he thought it best to go to bed. I was all genuine sympathy, but I asked wouldn't he please come up for just a moment to greet the gang and have a quick snort, then he could return home. Okay, he would come.

When Jim arrived he was startled to say the least. A quick

survey and his eyes rested on La Belle of the Ozarks, looking
very regal seated on the divan.

"J . . . J . . . Jeez . . . who . . . who . . . who is that?"

"It's your dinner partner, Jim. Come and meet her."

At the introduction Miss Ozark offered her gloved hand. Jim
stammered an acknowledgment. In answer to his question,
"Yeah—Ah'm enjoyin' it immensely, but Ah would like to have
a li'l ol' drink at the bar. Would you escort me, suh?"

The ever-gallant Stewart offered his arm. She stood up sans
the evening wrap and then those li'l ol' Ozark Hills rippled like
Jello as they walked the length of the room to the bar. The gang
went wild. Jim was mystified at the laughs, thoroughly unaware of the reason as he stood at the bar with La Belle. When
I thought the gag had gone far enough I called Jim to one side
and turned him around so he could see the "hills." One fast look
and he yelled, "CRIPES!" and made a dash for the door out of
the house.

In his mad scramble he collided with two new arrivals,
Jimmy Cagney and Spencer Tracy. Stewart grabbed them, took
them to a window, and screamed, "LOOK!"

The three, remembering the red lights along the way, ran
like a bat out of hell down the hill.

As I came through the door in pursuit, I was nearly felled by
a bundle of bed linen thrown from an upper window. The parolees were looting the house. Articles were stashed in bushes
and hedges for a later pickup. I returned to the house and had
the Knights go into action. Looters were caught and frisked.
Chasen sent his men to take down the red lanterns. A visit from
a nosy deputy sheriff and we'd all be in trouble.

With the guest of honor gone, the dames figured the party was
over and started screaming for their money, Miss Ozark among
them. Meredith had paid the "den mother" in advance, but the
girls didn't know it. There was hell to pay. Chasen caught a
dame walking through the kitchen attired in one of Tone's
suits. That did it. Dave pulled the main light switch and the
party was over. It cost us $803 for damage and lost articles. A
night to remember. Eventually the dames and La Belle were
paid off.

Next A.M. Meredith and I planned to drive Jim downtown to

the induction center, but he would have none of it. He would go in the trolley with the rest of the draftees, eighty of them.

At the center, two men waited in the corridor silently praying all would go well with their pal. Suddenly a door flew open and a tall skinny guy in his shorts, carrying his clothes over his arm, ran past us, screaming like a banshee.

"I'M IN—I'M IN—I'M IN!" He waved a goodbye and was off to Fort MacArthur.

I had to have important studio papers signed by Stewart, so I went to Fort MacArthur and received the C.O.'s permission to talk to Jim. He was playing volley ball and I waited nearly an hour for his signature. I felt that I was intruding, and no doubt he did also. This man was going to make a helluva soldier.

Next an Air Corps training field in Northern California. (Jim was an experienced pilot, with his own plane at Clover Field, Santa Monica.) Here his ability was recognized and he won corporal's stripes. One minor difficulty. The brass at the field had many social gatherings, and Corporal Stewart, the movie star in their midst, was expected to be in attendance, a chore he hated inwardly. It seriously interfered with his training. He was offered a cushy desk job but turned it down. A few words of complaint in the right civilian channels and word came from Washington.

In essence it said, Corporal James Stewart shall not be deterred in any way, shape or form in his efforts to be an outstanding airman. It had the Presidential signature. There were no more social obligations and he drove himself relentlessly. Soon came orders to transfer to four-engine bombers at Kirkland Field, New Mexico.

I was at my ranch in Corona, California, when the Corporal drove up on his way to New Mexico. He was driving an ancient Chevy held together with wire, safety pins, and button hooks. How in all that's holy he made it from the north I'll never understand, and he still had 500 miles to Kirkland Field. We sat and reminisced until 2:00 A.M. He was off to bed for a three-hour sleep and off on the road to his next stand. He had about twenty hours more to go in that egg crate. I prayed that he would make it.

I didn't hear too often from my man of the four-engine bombers. Kirkland would be his last stand before going overseas. I did hear from the willowy La Belle Ozark.

La Belle was now a stripper in a Los Angeles burlesque house; she was going to be married onstage during a performance and that it would be right nice if Jim would give her away at the ceremony. I thought it right neighborly of the girl to want to share her happiness with a future United States general. Ozark thought it right unpatriotic of the military not to give its four-bomber trainee a twenty-four hour pass to fly a bomber down to L.A. and give her away. I thought it inconsiderate; after all, she was a taxpayer. I could have named a dozen guys who would do a better job of giving her away, but I kept silent.

Jim's letters from overseas were infrequent; when they did arrive they said nothing of his bombing missions or experiences. Even after his arrival back in the states he was reluctant to talk about them. The only time I had firsthand information came at a very embarrassing moment for Jim. It was during a golf game at the Bel Air Country Club.

As we were about to drive from the fifteenth tee, Stewart saw four young men in uniform approaching, and recognized them as former members of his bombing crew.

"Here come four guys from my crew. I gotta look good in front of them."

The young soldiers and Stewart greeted one another warmly for a few moments, then their former skipper teed up his ball. As we watched, Colonel Stewart took a lusty swing and an "empty" was the result. He missed the ball by nearly a foot. God, he was embarrassed. His second shot went out of bounds into Alfred Hitchcock's garden. Embarassing moment number two. The third try was the redeemer—down the fairway about 275 yards. The crew kept their silence on the first two tries but applauded the third. My drive, a stout 150 yards down the middle. I talked with the boys out of Jim's hearing. It all summed up with them declaring Stewart the best pilot they ever flew with, and as a commanding officer? There was none better. It was the only information I ever received about his doing a helluva job overseas.

Jim's family and myself were in New York to welcome him home. Alex, with his World War I button signifying he was a captain, looked a bit envious of Jim's eagles denoting the rank of colonel. It was a happy group, proud of the soldier who went from draftee to colonel in three years, a soldier who earned every award the hard way.

I had a chore to do for MGM. Stewart had three years left of his studio contract, suspended during his time in service. I was to try and persuade him to come back to us and take up where he left off, but I was knocking my head against a stone wall. Leland Hayward, Jim's very astute agent, had advised him of a new order of things in the picture business. Stars were taking a minimum salary and a percentage of either gross or profits of all pictures they appeared in. It was a procedure that Nick Schenck, president of MGM, would have no part of. All artists under MGM contract would be salaried, and no participation. Stewart, under Hayward's guidance, went for the percentage arrangements in all contracts. MGM was without the services of one of their top stars.

Jim and I shared a drawing room on the Santa Fe Super Chief for the trip to California. He said he was through with flying. They all said that. Gable, the King, Bob Taylor, and all the other airmen, but in no time they were back in the air as of old. To pass the time en route, I introduced Jim to gin rummy. From Chicago to Pasadena he didn't win a game. I wound up with 8 million matches.

It didn't take long for Jim to get back to making pictures. The new contractual arrangement proved a bonanza for him. Forty weeks under MGM would net about $125,000 yearly for two and sometimes three pictures. The new order of things meant a minimum of $750,000 per picture and some in the $1,000,000 class. The income would be spread over a period of years, a tax advantage.

Between pictures it was Chasen's every night for dinner and gag happenings now and again. One of the gags backfired on me. Stewart had several movies in release. Hayward, his agent, was worried about overexposure, so it was soon announced that Jim was to do the stage play *Harvey* in New York. This was the story of the invisible rabbit that Frank Fay originated. Stewart would take over. I came up with a crazy idea.

Very hush-hush and unbeknownst to Jim, I asked anyone who had so much as a nodding acquaintance with him to deposit some rabbits at his door in Brentwood in the dark of night. The gag caught on and soon there was a scourge of the beasts in the area around the Stewart home. He could offer no explanation to complaining neighbors. I thought I would top the rabbit routine.

In Culver City there was an establishment that raised rabbits for the meat markets. I went there and bought six. They were nearly the size of Shetland ponies. Stewart was at home and I could not drop them lest I be discovered. I'd have to wait.

I went to Chasen's for dinner and just as I finished, Stewart joined me. To get away, I said that I had to go to the studio to see a picture.

Outside, in a secluded area of the parking lot, the fat, sassy beasts were feasting on lettuce and carrots; they were very unmannerly and not housebroken. The stench was overpowering. Three blocks and I had to give up; I couldn't stand it. Parking on a side street, I opened the windows and walked home.

The following A.M. I came back. The rabbits had escaped but they had left their mark and it would be permanent. Disgusted, I called a dealer and traded in the car for a new one. Luckily I only lost $300 on the deal, but it was fortunate the dealer had a head cold.

On Christmas Eve, Jim and I, as was our habit, hired three broken-down musicians, loaded them in the car, and stopped at homes in Beverly Hills to sing Christmas carols. Some of the occupants recognized us and invited us in for some Christmas cheer, but we only had one drink to a customer. One of our stops was at a house in Brentwood. By this time we were feeling no pain. The lady of the house invited us in, and while we were imbibing, a maniac attired in pajamas came down from a bedroom. He raised hell because we had disturbed his slumbers and threw us out of the house with a few very choice exit lines. The maniac was Pat O'Brien; pals of his or not, out we had to go. Such an unappreciative host with no Christmas spirit. Spirits, yes, it was almost spilling over.

Another stop at a well-lighted house. There was a party. In we went and found Keenan Wynn pouring for his guests. As we entered I noted a beautiful young lady seated on a staircase. She seemed a bit on the down side. I recognized her. It was Gloria Hatrick, the daughter of a great friend of mine, Ed Hatrick, a Hearst executive. Ed and I had adjoining offices in the old days in New York, and he was loved by all with whom he came in contact. He had personality to spare and he did all right by his daughter—she inherited it.

Jim stopped to talk with Gloria. That was the beginning. They saw much of each another in the ensuing two years and then came the announcement of a wedding. I was Jim's best man and still carry his gift, a money clip inscribed, "You are the best man of all time—your friend, Slats. August 9th, 1949." Slats was my nickname for the thin guy I first saw at Princeton.

It was now a trio for capers. We didn't miss a trick when it came to laughs. Our favorite hangout was La Quinta, a desert resort near Palm Springs. One dull Sunday afternoon we drove to Palm Springs and browsed through a novelty shop. Some hideous masks caught our attention. We bought three of the frightening things.

On the return trip to La Quinta in an open car, we donned the masks. Jim and Gloria hid their heads under the instrument panel and I drove. When a car approached, my masked friends would raise their heads, and the horrible spectacle would frighten the pants off the occupants of the other car.

Pulling up at the hotel in La Quinta, we noted a young man bending into a car window, evidently trying to get the girl occupant to stay at the hotel with him. Maybe it was for hanky-panky, maybe it wasn't, but the guy was making quite a pitch. I called Gloria and Jim's attention to the man and made a suggestion. "Let's go in the back entrance, get rid of the desk clerk, and take over." No sooner said than done.

With the clerk dismissed, we three donned the masks and hid under the counter. Our young man came to the desk, saw the sign: "Ring For Attendant." He rang the bell, and we raised our hideous heads from under the counter. I have seen frightened men in my time, but this guy literally turned an ashen white, staggered out the door into his car, and was off. He couldn't have had any thoughts of hanky-panky for weeks afterwards.

With the passing of not too many years, Jim Stewart and I are not the constant companions we once were. His extensive business interests occupy much of his time, together with his great devotion to his family. I was doing a lot of world traveling for a spell and I guess we just got out of the habit.

I have been fortunate in having Jim Stewart as a friend, and this country of ours can be proud of Brigadier General James M. Stewart, ret., as one of its foremost citizens.

Four

*W*HEN JIM returned to movie-making after the war, there was a period when he and Hank Fonda were nightly guests at party after party. Several weeks of this, and Stewart and Fonda wanted to reciprocate by throwing a bash for their male hosts. There would be twenty-eight men and I was called in for suggestions. There was some thinking to do.

Invitations were sent out, each one stressing that the party would start promptly at 7:00 P.M. at the Beverly Hills Club, Roxbury Drive. To a man the guests came on the dot, which was unprecedented in Beverly Hills social circles.

There was a very beautifully appointed private dining room. Place cards in place on a table that was a work of art. The finest in china, crystal, and silver amidst an array of fresh-cut flowers. A decorated bar at the rear was also a bower of flowers, but there was no liquor in sight, nor a bartender to cater to the wants of the guests.

Twenty minutes of just standing around and the guests got restless. Jim and Hank were asked, "What about a drink? Where's the bartender?"

Stewart asked me about the drinking arrangements and I professed ignorance. He went to the club desk and came back astonished. He was told that if he didn't like the way things were going, he could take his party the hell out of there.

Hank Fonda blew his top, went to the desk, and got the same answer. Several of the guests, including the very proper Jules Stein of MCA, had found their place cards and were already seated.

It was up to me. I went to the desk and returned with great indignation. We had been ordered out of the place. Stein felt disgraced. Where could we go?

I suggested that we all go to a friend of mine's place. It was a Swedish smorgasbord. Fonda protested that no restaurant could take care of thirty people without notice, but I insisted my friend could. A few very uncomplimentary remarks about the Beverly Hills Club, and we filed out.

At the curb in front of the club was a large school bus. I instructed Jim and Hank to enter; the rest followed like sheep. Aboard was a saxophone player with a battered old instrument. He had been hired to play one tune, and one tune only, under penalty of not being paid. The tune was "Annie Laurie." It would be funny for a while . . . but wait.

The bus took off to the musical accompaniment. The driver crossed Wilshire Boulevard and into Bedford Drive. As we crossed Santa Monica Boulevard, a motorcycle policeman stopped the bus. The driver was driving in Beverly Hills without a Beverly Hills license. All the boys aboard started to pull rank, Jules Stein in particular. They got nowhere. The policeman was adamant, the driver was instructed to follow him. Yes, "Annie Laurie" was in full swing throughout.

One half-block and the policeman turned left, one more left turn and we were in an alley. Mid-alley the policeman stopped the bus. Over the cycle radio an accident had been reported on Wilshire Boulevard. All units were ordered to report. The bus was ordered to remain where it was until the policeman's return.

Fifteen minutes of an alley wait and the occupants of the bus got restless. I noted a light shining under the door of a garage. Alighting from the bus, followed by the others, I lifted the garage door and discovered a weazened little old man sitting in an old-fashioned rocker. His hand was cupped to his ear while he listened to a recording of the worst prima donna I have ever heard. The dame was singing an aria, and so flat and so badly that it was unidentifiable, but the old man was in raptures, paying no heed to the intruders. Beside his chair was a pail of beer, and with his free hand he was guzzling to his heart's content.

In a corner of the garage was an antique dresser, and beside it a keg of beer ready for drawing. Jules Stein, curious, inspected the dresser, opening the drawers. To his amazement, the top drawer contained bourbon, the second Scotch, the third a thermos of cocktails, plenty of ice. With a cheer, drinking was in order for parched throats. Between "Annie Laurie," which hadn't stopped, and the lousy prima donna, it was bedlam.

Some barber shop harmony started. The little guy started spouting original poetry at the top of his voice. Things were going pretty good until two motorcycle policemen arrived on the scene. Neighbors had complained about the drunken revelry in the garage at 518 North Roxbury. This was no gag, it was on the level. It was my garage and I took the rap; they warned me to stop the din "or else." I stopped the racket. I was afraid of the "or else."

I didn't reckon on the little guy. He was a once-famous comic by the name of Sweeney, and a friend of Dave Chasen's. He was loaded to the gills and wanted to lick a cop. Sweeney said it was his home and he could do as he pleased, and "no so-and-so flatfoot was going to stop him!" The police shut him up fast, took him by the seat of the pants into my house, where a church bridge party was in session. Sweeney's language was not for tender ears. The police were directed through a side door to my room, where the little guy was to change his clothes and be on his way.

Ah, but he didn't change his clothes, and ah, he wasn't going on his way. He elected to sleep in my bed fully clothed, all the time spouting poetry that he had written. You could hear him in Pomona, thirty miles away. The police were called again by the women folk and Sweeney was taken to the jug. I had hired him for the garage bit, but he went overboard. When I got home that night I caught hell.

Back to the bus, but more trouble. During the confusion with Sweeney, the bus driver got loaded on bourbon, and one of the guests had to take over. I think the "Annie Laurie" routine drove him nuts. We took off.

Next stop was Romanoff's Restaurant. There we were to have snacks and salad in a private dining room. We were just about to be served when Dave Chasen appeared on the scene. Dave was mad because we were supposed to be at his place an hour before, and he accused Mike of trying to steal his business. There was an argument between the rival restaurant-owners, and Mike drew himself up to his Imperial Highness, five feet, five inches, and with that imperial tone ordered us all out of the place, at the same time brandishing a cane at the poor slob playing "Annie Laurie." God, this "Annie" was getting annoying.

Next stop was Chasen's. It was to be the last in our progressive party. We filed in through the crowded restaurant, the "Annie Laurie" guy leading the way to a private dining room on the second floor.

The saxophone player took me to one side and told me that Jules Stein had offered him three times what I was to pay him if he would stop with the "Annie" thing. He refused the offer because he was also a bit player in pictures and didn't want to disobey my orders. Good man.

Our dinner at Dave's was to be his blue ribbon roast sirloin of beef. It was served in a very large, over-sized platter with cover, carried in by four waiters. Dave advised that it was to be served via an old English custom. The hosts had to make the first cut.

Jim and Hank approached the table and serving platter, took their positions, carving knives in hand, ready to slice the moment the sirloin was exposed. All was in readiness.

Chasen lifted the cover; on the platter were two naked midgets in diapers, syringes between their legs. As Jim and Hank reached to carve, the midgets let go with the water, yelling "Daddy!" at the same time. Their aim was very good.

Anything from here on was anticlimactic. "Annie Laurie" had stopped. Dave found the saxophonist dead to the world on the men's room floor, loaded, his lips puffed up like inner tubes.

Five

*M*UCH HAS BEEN written about the courtship and subsequent marriage of the young and beautiful Ruby Keeler and the one and only great Al Jolson. What has been written, plus what was told in the movie versions, is not the real story. The real tale is a fantastic one. As Ruby's agent and manager, I indirectly had a hand in it.

Ruby Keeler was the darling of Broadway. At a very early age she was dancing at the famous Texas Guinan's nightclub, also appearing in a Broadway musical, *Bye, Bye, Bonnie*.

Her press notices from *Bonnie* were outstanding, and in no small degree helped me to arrange a contract with Charles Dillingham for her to appear in *Sidewalks Of New York*, the musical that introduced Kate Smith to Broadway. A short run in *Sidewalks*, and another Dillingham musical, *Lucky*.

Unfortunately for Dillingham, *Lucky*, which had cost $313,000 to produce, was a flop. It was the beginning of the end of this great man's career. To keep young Miss Keeler busy, I arranged some bookings in important motion picture theaters. She was in great demand.

It was known on Broadway that Ruby and a Broadwayite named Johnny "Irish" Costello were carrying on a tacit romance. Johnny watched over Ruby like a mother hen. In the Guinan Club, woe to the ringsider who made a pass at young Ruby while she was doing her dance specialty on the cabaret floor. Two-fisted Johnny Irish would have to be reckoned with.

I didn't know Johnny's business. His constant companion was his pal Tommy O'Neil. Johnny was the quiet, nonsmoking, nondrinking type—Tommy just the opposite, talkative and prone to move in on arguments. It made no difference what subject was under discussion; pro or con, Tommy would move in uninvited.

Likable Tommy had a very annoying habit. In conversation he always repeated your last four or five words. If you were trying to explain something, it really threw you off.

Johnny and Tommy were highly regarded on Broadway. I never asked their means of livelihood, but assumed they were associated with the notorious Owney Madden, and his far-flung beer bootlegging racket. Both men were with me during my Silver Slipper days. I felt their presence there was as representatives of Madden, who had a big hunk of the operation.

As Ruby's agent, I kept Irish informed of my every move in her behalf. When I advised Ruby of a new booking, she would always inquire, "What did Johnny say?"

I received a call from Hollywood. It was Sid Grauman calling. Sid was the famous impresario of Grauman's Chinese Theater. He was planning a presentation and wanted Ruby as one of his stars. I asked $1,250 weekly, a six-week guarantee, and two round-trip fares New York to Los Angeles. Either her mother or sister would accompany her. I had been getting $500 weekly for Ruby in Eastern engagements. Grauman knew my reputation for nondickering and quickly okayed terms of $1,250.

Irish was pleased at the new salary, pleased for the Keelers. If that family had a desire in the world it was to possess money, and lots of it.

There was quite a brood of Keelers and Ruby was the big breadwinner. I was happy because studios in Hollywood were preparing musical pictures, and Grauman's would be a good showcase for Miss Keeler.

The fourth day of Ruby's engagement at Grauman's, I was at my usual table at Dinty Moore's when I was called to the telephone. It was Miss Keeler calling from Hollywood.

"Where is Johnny?" she asked excitedly.

"I don't know, Ruby," I replied, suspecting nothing. "Want me to find him and have him call you?" She was now crying. "What's the matter, Ruby, anything wrong?"

"Yes, that guy Al Jolson is out here and keeps sending me flowers and calling me to go to dinner with him. I don't want to go, I'm afraid. Get Johnny to wire me the money. I want to come home."

No use reasoning further. I knew from experience that young Miss Keeler had a mind of her own and once it was made up nothing could move her. It was her mind to come home so I went in search of Johnny Irish.

As I was leaving Moore's, a taxi drew up and out jumped Johnny. I took him to the only place for privacy we could have, Moore's men's room. There I related my phone conversation with Ruby. His only comment?

"We gotta get the kid home. Where's there a Western Union Office?"

We went to the telegraph office on West 48th Street; the money was sent to Ruby, together with a long telephone conversation. We would meet her when she arrived in New York.

Five days later Ruby was home, and in the meantime I had arranged some bookings, starting at the Metropolitan Theater, Boston, to be followed by an engagement in Philadelphia.

During the Philadelphia engagement I received a call from Jack Warner, the head of Warner Brothers. His company was planning a gala presentation at their Hollywood theater. They wanted Miss Keeler as one of their headliners. I told Warner about the Grauman's Chinese episode, pointing out that the first question I would be asked would be, "Where is Jolson?"

Warner replied, "Don't worry about Joly. He is in Florida. Took a house there. Send her out, everything will be all right."

I set Ruby's price at $1,500 with the round-trip transportation for two. Everything was agreed to.

I went looking for Johnny to tell him what had transpired. I found him and Tommy O'Neil at Moore's. Listening to my recital of the Warner phone call, he thought several moments before answering.

"You sure that guy Jolson is in Florida?"

"All I know is what Warner tells me, that Jolson will not be in Hollywood."

"You better be sure, Grady. I don't want to have any trouble."

"No trouble," echoed Tommy O'Neil.

"I know the Keelers will think twice before they turn down $1,500. Did you tell Ruby?"

"No, Johnny, not until I told you. You know she's going to ask if you know."

"Tell her I said she can do whatever she wants to do, but talk it over with her mother."

I placed a call to Ruby in Philadelphia and anticipated her first question. "Where is Jolson?"

"Ruby, I can only tell you what I told Johnny. Jolson is in Florida and not expected in California. You call your mother and talk it over with her. Irish says to do whatever you want to do." I repeated the salary twice at her request.

The decision, after a talk with her mother, was to go to Hollywood.

Warner's Hollywood, and the second day of her engagement there, I got a call at Moore's. It was from Miss Keeler in California and she was crying.

"Where's Johnny?" she whimpered.

"Cripes, Ruby, not again."

"Yes, that guy Jolson is here, not in Florida, and the same thing is happening. I want to come home. Tell Johnny . . ." We were cut off.

I had been sitting with Johnny Irish and his pal Tommy. I went back to the table and beckoned to Johnny, and we went again to the only privacy in the place. There I told Johnny about the phone call. When I finished my tale, Irish went white and threw a left into my middle. It doubled me up like a pretzel. Man, he could hit hard.

Johnny apologized and we talked.

I repeated Warner's statement re Jolson being in Florida. I was at a loss for an explanation. Irish kept pounding his left fist into his right palm. I knew he would like to be in California at that moment.

Leaving me, he went up to Moore's apartment over the restaurant and placed a call for Ruby in California, followed by our going to the Western Union office and wiring the money to Ruby.

When the fair Miss Keeler arrived at Grand Central Station,

Johnny Irish was there with a beautiful diamond engagement ring, cementing their troth.

Several more picture house engagements and Ruby was playing Loew's Washington. Again the fourth day and a phone call, "Where's Johnny?"

"My God, Ruby, not again?"

"Yes, Jolson is here in Washington. I was all wrong. I've fallen in love with him. Will you break the news to Johnny?"

When the call came in I was in the midst of dinner. I was seated alone, and on returning to my table I couldn't finish it. How could I tell the devoted Johnny Irish? This was going to be a toughie.

Irish came into Moore's all smiles. He greeted his friends and came and sat with me. Noting my mood, he asked, "Anything the matter?"

"John, this is the toughest assignment I've ever had."

"Yeah?" he replied. "What's goin'?"

"I just received a call from Ruby in Washington."

"So?"

"Jolson is down there, Johnny, and she has fallen in love with him."

This nice man lowered his head without a word and for several minutes stared at his clenched fists. The knuckles were white from pressure. That good-looking Irish face was portraying inner agony. A lapse; he looked at me, banged his fists together, and abruptly left the table without a word.

Tommy O'Neil and Larry Fay came over to me. "What's the matter with Johnny? We saw him outside. He's crying and won't talk to us."

"John just got some news about Ruby. I think you guys better go out there and be with him. He needs you mostly, Tommy. I can't help."

O'Neil and Fay left. I ordered a stiff drink and followed, but when I got outside, Fay, Tommy, and Johnny were not around.

Following Washington, Ruby was to play the Capitol Theater in New York. Irish was not around his usual haunts. Only O'Neil knew where Irish was and he wasn't talking.

I wasn't exactly getting the brush from the Moore gang, but there was a strained air about their attitude toward me. Did these men think I had a part in the Keeler-Jolson affair other than arranging Ruby's bookings? Did I know about Jolson's intentions when I first booked Ruby in California? Did I know he was in or going to be in Washington when I booked her there?

This was the Broadway mob. They knew nothing about the theatrical business, other than their interest in nightclubs and speaks as an outlet for their bootleg goods. It looked like I was in a spot. I showed up at Moore's as usual. I had nothing to hide. O'Neil and Johnny didn't appear. I heard that Johnny was taking it pretty hard.

Ruby Keeler attended an early rehearsal at the Capitol Theater, New York. Immediately after orchestra rehearsal, she and Jolson went to Greenwich, Connecticut, and were married. She finished her engagement at the Capitol Theater that week.

The Jolsons were living at the Ritz Towers, 57th and Park Avenue. I had a deal pending for Ruby and needed her okay. It was *Show Girl* for Florenz Ziegfeld, a starring role with Clayton, Jackson, and Durante as costars. Throughout this country and abroad papers were full of the Jolson-Keeler marriage.

When I arrived at the entrance to the Ritz Towers, I found Tommy O'Neil, Larry Fay, and a hoodlum known as the Slasher. Fay grabbed me as I approached. "You go upstairs and tell that dirty bastard we're gonna get him and we're waiting here until he comes downstairs."

I tried to talk them out of rough stuff. Nothing good could come of it. None of us could afford a police marker, and I think they realized it. Tommy O'Neil stood in the background. Loudmouth Fay did all the talking. He used to be Ruby's employer at the Guinan Club. I found I was getting nowhere in my peace talk, so I went upstairs to the Jolson apartment.

I'll give Jolson credit. When I told him about my encounter with the three men downstairs and their threat, he grabbed his hat, said nary a word, and left the apartment.

Tommy O'Neil told me later. "Jolson came up to us and said, 'You guys looking for me? Well, here I am. What are you going to do about it? Ruby and I are married. We fell in love. I'm sorry about Irish, but that's the way it is. Now get out of here and leave us alone.'"

When Jolson ended his talk with the trio they left, with

O'Neil in the lead. A few feet away, Fay turned and said to Jolson:

"I'm telling you, Jolson. If you ain't good to little Ruby we'll kill you."

Jolson turned on his heel and came upstairs, and not a word about the downstairs happening.

The Jolsons disappeared from the Broadway scene for a while. It was a few weeks before Ruby would be needed for *Show Girl* rehearsals. I was offered as high as $2,500 a week for the Keeler act, but booked no dates for the time being. The Jolsons were in San Francisco. It was reported that Johnny Irish called them there and said just one thing, "Jolson, don't let me ever hear anything about Ruby that isn't good." He hung up.

The Jolson marriage, to all outward appearances, was a happy one. Al was an adoring husband, as well he might be. Ruby Keeler was a beautiful young woman. There was quite a few years' difference in their ages. Asked by many the why of the marriage, I had no answer. There was Ruby, there was Jolson, it was their life.

Show Girl rehearsed five weeks. Jolson attended every rehearsal. He was devotion itself. It was a tough show for Ruby. She was the star and carried a weighty load. It was natural that after a rigorous day of rehearsal she would be a bit edgy. Possessed with a temper to begin with, there were man-and-wife differences and sulking on both sides. I would then be called in as peacemaker.

Knowing Ruby, I could only offer Al one bit of advice. "Leave her alone. These rehearsals are tough. She'll come around in her own good time," and she did.

The show opened at the Colonial Theater, Boston, after numerous rehearsals at all hours of the day and night. Miss Keeler was a tired young lady. Jolson, noted for his inexhaustible energy, demanded more attention from Ruby than he should have under the circumstances. There was a spat and I was again called in. Jolson, a softhearted guy with even more of a temper than his wife, was in tears. I suggested a ride in the country to break the tension. Jolson and I took off.

To my surprise, instead of the ride in the country, the unpredictable Jolson ordered the chauffeur, Jimmy Donnelly, to drive to the nearest Catholic church. Jolson pleaded with me to go to the altar rail and pray that everything would be all right between Ruby and himself. I proceeded to pray while Jolson lit every candle he could find. The candle stands were ablaze with light, and Jolson stuffed bill after bill into the money slot. We went through the same proceedings in three churches, but at the third Joly wanted to be really sure about the prayers so he had Jimmy Donnelly join me at the altar rail.

Show Girl got off with a bang. It was light and melodic, and the audience loved it. The air was electric. The new star, Mrs. Al Jolson, was onstage and her famous husband was seated with me second row on the aisle. Ruby didn't disappoint, she was wonderful.

Just before the finale of the first act, Ruby had her specialty. She was to sing the hit song of the show, "Liza." It was planned that she would sing a verse and the chorus, then dance two choruses, but midway in the verse Ruby forgot the lyrics.

There was an instant of silence and Jolson rose to the occasion before the stunned audience. Stepping into the aisle, he nearly knocked me out of my seat in his haste. Jolson picked up the "Liza" lyrics and sang the song, while his beautiful young wife danced on stage. It was electrifying. Jolson, with tears of emotion streaming down his face, poured his heart out in song, his Ruby danced as she had never danced in her life, she, too, almost blinded with tears. I have had moments in the theater that thrilled me in my time, but never anything like this.

Every person in the jam-packed theater rose to his feet and applauded and cheered this great moment. As Joly returned to the seat beside me he was trembling. The audience insisted, and one verse and the chorus were repeated. The audience sensed that Ruby was exhausted and reluctantly allowed her to make her exit. Anything that followed in the first act was anti-climactic: the Jolsons, husband and wife, caused a sensation.

The incident became part of the show for the next several weeks. Ziegfeld prevailed upon Jolson to repeat the "Liza" singing while Ruby danced. New York had heard of the Boston episode, but when it happened on opening night at the Ziegfeld Theater there was no holding the audience. Many encores, and again the standing ovation.

The Jolson suite at the Ritz Hotel in Boston, after the opening, was the scene of a happy gathering of friends. All displays of temper and slight differences of opinion behind them, Al and Ruby Jolson were ecstatically happy, a wonderful climax to a history-making night in the theater.

Six

*W*E HAD A few unpredictables at the studio. By an unpredictable, I mean an individual from whom you could expect the unexpected . . . without the guidance of the planned and written word, you were never sure what he would say or do.

Our number-one "unpredic" was the one and only John Barrymore. It is no secret that John was a two-fisted bottle man. I saw him, in his cups, give performances that were absolutely brilliant. On the other hand, I witnessed performances in the same condition that were pitiful. His great talent was so wasted. I had an unforgettable experience with John at the Selwyn Theater, Chicago.

En route to California from New York, I stopped off in Chicago to see some new talent lined up for my appraisal. Of the many to be reviewed there was only one worth interest—a Chicagoan, John Hodiak.

Concluding my business ahead of schedule, and with an afternoon on my hands, I requested the office to get me a seat at the Selwyn Theater where my friend Barrymore was appearing in *Dear Children*. Arriving at the theater, I was ushered to a seat, first row on the aisle. The theater was crowded with Barrymore admirers, mostly women.

As the first act progressed, I noticed that John had a few under his belt. His asides to his fellow-players could be heard in the first few rows, and racy asides they were.

In the middle of a very important scene, he spied me. Squinting his eyes to be sure, he walked to the footlights and stared down at me. Turning to his fellow-players and then to the crowded theater, and with a typical Barrymore Hamlet gesture, he pointed and dramatically shouted:

"That son of a bitch sitting there is a goddamned spy from Metro-Goldwyn-Mayer."

I crouched down in my seat, mortified. Barrymore then seated himself on the floor of the stage and let his feet dangle into the orchestra pit. It was noted that his socks did not match; one was gray, one black. He then proceeded to carry on a conversation, ignoring the actors onstage and the audience.

"Well, you Irish bastard, what the hell are you doing in this godforsaken city?"

"Just passing through, John, on my way home," I replied through cupped hands.

"And you had to come here to see if I was drunk or sober. Well, for your information, I've been drunk ever since I took this goddamned show, and it won't be for much longer."

The cast on stage, evidently used to John's unconventional conduct, sat in convenient chairs until the great one's return to the business at hand. The audience seemed to enjoy this display of the unusual, even to the profanity.

Continuing his conversation with me, he inquired about the health of some of his cronies. "How is Whitey?" (that was Bill Fields). "How are Gene Fowler, John Decker, and Hank Clive?" I replied that they were all in the pink. He rose to his full height, and again pointing his finger at me, he said, "You are a goddamned liar, you've been to Europe, you haven't seen one of my pals in weeks. How the hell would you know how they were?"

Seemingly disgusted with me, he turned to his stage coworkers and said, "Where the hell were we?" The play went on and at the curtain of the first act, he again came to the footlights and invited me backstage between acts.

In his dressing room he greeted me as though we had not already conversed across the footlights. He asked about his brother Lionel, "Doc," as he called him, and wanted to know if he was still playing Dr. Kildare. He opened a bottle of Scotch, and sent out for a bottle of bourbon for me.

He was holding up the second act, ignoring the stage manager's calls that all was ready. I was on pins and needles. He delayed the performance over twenty minutes, and thought nothing of it.

Rest assured I did not return to my seat, relieved that a most embarrassing experience was over.

I had a nerve-wracking session with Barrymore during the filming of *Romeo and Juliet*. He was on and off the bottle throughout. All but one of his scenes had been completed. The remaining scene was the lengthy Queen Mab speech. For budget reasons, it was thought expedient to wait until all had finished their roles before tackling John's solo scene.

Until we were ready for John and his big scene, to be on the safe side, we had him in a "rest home" in Culver City near the studio. Here we could try to keep him off the drinking bouts by stationing guards outside his third-floor room. All packages were inspected before delivery to him. It seemed strange that he did not protest.

Several times I went over to see John to check on his condition and each time I visited he was loaded, and I mean loaded. All the guards and attendants swore, and I believed them, that not one drop of liquor had passed through his door. How was it getting to him?

Whitey Hendry, the studio chief of police, had stationed an outside watch on eight-hour shifts. When the man on the after-midnight shift went inside for coffee, a pal of John's and a makeup man from Paramount Studio would tie bottles of Scotch to sheets that John lowered from his window. He would then haul them up to his quarters.

Whitey inspected the room and there was enough grog up there to float a drydock. No amount of persuasion would make him give it up. We hoped for the best.

Came the day for the Queen Mab speech and those familiar with *Romeo and Juliet* know its length. I called for John at the rest home and found him loaded, but I took him to the studio.

Everybody had their doubts, but he insisted to George Cukor, the director, and Irving Thalberg, the producer, that he would do the scene satisfactorily. Prompting boards were all over the set so he could read his part, but he was stiff as a goat and couldn't read, anyway.

John Barrymore stood braced against a garden wall and spoke every line and syllable of the Queen Mab speech perfectly, drunk as a lord. I have never seen the equal of it. Everybody on the set, stagehands and all, applauded. John looked at all present with a look of disdain, squinted his eyes, and uttered an obscenity, then off to his dressing room and the bottle. A man of iron constitution. Too bad such talent was so wasted, but "as ye live, so shall ye die."

Seven

*J*OHN CARROLL was a friend of mine with a God-given voice that he rarely used to help his career. He used to infuriate me by neglecting vocal lessons that I had set up for him. If he'd applied himself, he would or could have had an operatic career that would have conquered the world. He would not take his great gift seriously. Because of that he infuriated me.

John had a horse ranch over in the San Fernando Valley of California. It was a beautiful home with an almost Olympic-sized swimming pool. John is a button pusher. Push a button, a door opens; push a button, music throughout the ranch. More buttons, a wall would open disclosing a movie projection machine, a picture screen lowered from the ceiling. There were so many buttons he should have called it "Button Manor."

Carroll was giving a formal dinner. He was entertaining a high state official of the Mexican government. I was invited, and since it was a formal affair, I donned my best bib and tucker.

At the dinner I was presented to a beautiful young lady whom Carroll had befriended. The girl was unemployed and needed a place to live until she got a break. At John's suggestion she moved into his home, and with chaperone, lived there for several weeks. The lady was my dinner partner.

After the usual cocktail banter, the guests sat down for the state dinner at a beautifully decorated table. To my amazement, the formal state dinner consisted of chili con carne and a green salad.

I was so G.D. mad that I had to put on a "monkey suit" for that type of state dinner that I took my dinner partner and drove around the Valley looking for a hamburger stand.

During the drive, my lady guest told me about herself. It wasn't a pretty story and I was all sympathy. I promised the girl I would be on the lookout for something that would give her a start in pictures. Up to that time, her picture work had consisted of extras and modeling.

At MGM studios the next morning, my number-one gal, Babs, told me there was a very important script on my desk that needed immediate casting. The script was *The Asphalt Jungle.*

After reading it, I suddenly realized that my promise of help to my dinner partner of the night before could be fulfilled. I would cast her as the blonde secretary to Louis Calhern, who was to play an unscrupulous attorney in the picture.

Arthur Hornblow was the producer, and John Huston the director. I told them about my protégée. Her name was Marilyn Monroe and she had no experience. Both Hornblow and Huston hit the roof. How dare I submit an inexperienced girl for such an important role? I wound up in a verbal Donnybrook and it resulted in a complaint to L. B. Mayer by Hornblow that I insisted on Miss Monroe and would not submit another actress with experience.

Mayer sent for the insubordinate Grady. Hornblow must have really made a complaint. Mayer was in a mood of white-hot anger. I stood still for his bawling out. I was used to them by this time. No use interrupting, you had to hear Mayer out. I did. When he finished I asked him to withhold any decision about the lady in question. Hornblow and Huston left me alone with Mayer.

I made my pitch to L. B., reciting the events of the evening before. I threw in the orphan bit, no place to live, no money, and Carroll's help and the girl's great beauty. Mayer was a soft-hearted guy at times.

When I finished my narrative, I felt Mayer was in my pocket and it was now up to Monroe, who was to meet Mayer the next day.

Johnny Hyde, a William Morris Agency partner, brought Miss Monroe out to Mayer the next day. She came—Mayer saw —she conquered. Result?? If Miss Marilyn Monroe hadn't played the secretary in *Asphalt Jungle*, MGM would not have made the picture.

Miss Monroe made her debut in *Jungle*, and from that moment on her career was established as one that was sure to be important in years to come. The rest is history.

In all the stories I have read about the life of Marilyn Monroe, the unfortunate Marilyn, I have never seen a reference to the Good Samaritan, Carroll. I believed at the time, and John later confirmed it, that the only reason I was invited to the chili dinner (with the green salad) was for the purpose of meeting and helping Marilyn in her career.

And those who have jumped on the bandwagon since her death and are responsible for her career—it would take two Greyhound buses to carry them.

May She Rest In Peace

Eight

*T*HE LATE producer Charlie Feldman was at one time
founder and president of Famous Artists' Agency. I liked
Charlie. He was one agent who never wasted your time or sub-
mitted a dud for consideration. In a phone call Charlie told me
about a spot he was in: a young lady named Donna Mullinger
had won a beauty contest at City College, Los Angeles, and the
prize was a visit to a major studio and an introduction to its
casting director. MGM was selected, and if I would go through
the motions of an interview he would be grateful.

A Feldman messenger brought the young lady to my office. I
was taken by her great beauty, soft eyes, and white skin. The
young lady seemed awed by her studio visit and was quite tense.
She told me she was from Dennison, Iowa, and to ease the
tension I told her about an amusing experience I once had at
Dennison's only passable hotel. Her amusement was displayed
with a warm smile and fine teeth.

Miss Mullinger said very little during our visit, but I found
her personality commanding. A short talk, and to the astonishment of the runner from Feldman's office, I ordered a test to be
made.

It is seldom that a $1,000 test is ordered for a hopeful with absolutely no experience. But Miss Mullinger had all the requisites and with a little coaching she might come through. A scene was selected, ten days' preparation, a top crew assigned, and the test was made.

To sum up, Miss Donna Mullinger came off with flying colors in her test. My first impressions were all confirmed. To the great surprise of Famous Artists, I arranged a contract. Her rapid rise to importance was the fastest I have ever known. It couldn't have happened to a more gracious young lady . . . Oh yes, Donna Mullinger—the world knows her as Donna Reed.

And then there was the time of another "favor" visit by the messenger from Charlie Feldman's office.

Charlie had received a letter from a friend in the Midwest. The friend had given a letter of introduction to a young man desirous of getting into pictures. Would Charlie see that the young man made the rounds of casting offices? MGM and Grady were first on the list.

The messenger left his charge in my waiting room while he came to me and volunteered the information that to a man everyone at Famous Artists' Agency knew I would not be interested in the young fellow he was about to introduce.

"The guy has a Haaaaaavard, Boston accent that a butcher couldn't make a dent in. The guy tries a Mayfair English accent once in a while. That combined with the Haaaaavard nearly drove us nuts in the office. Charlie wants you to just give the guy a quick hello and I'll take him away. Charlie appreciates your help."

The Haaaaavard-Mayfair man was ushered in. Tall, well set up, and well tailored, he was typical Ivy League. Under his arm, and held so that I had to notice, were three books—*Greek Theatre History*, Shakespeare, and *Sonnets* by Stanislaus Sweeney. After the introduction I let him do the talking. What a gabby guy.

I was thinking.

I had just read *Mrs. Miniver.* It was ready for production, but we were having difficulty finding a young man to play Mrs. Miniver's son. This young man, despite his negative personality, looked the part and was young enough. Maybe? I'd soon find out. If we could eliminate some of his defects, he might make the grade. I took him to Sidney Franklin, the *Miniver* producer. He ordered a screen test.

The agency messenger nearly fainted at the news.

Several days' preparation for the test with the director and Miss Garson, and it was shot. Result? Richard Ney, Mr. Haaaaa-vard-Mayfair, was young Miniver.

I am sure that if Ney's visit to my office had taken place before I read *Miniver*, I would have forgotten all about him. His agents didn't help any. He came to me just after I had read it.

Ney wasn't blessed with the most ingratiating personality and he became very cocky. Three days into the picture, he blatantly announced that he had made up his mind he was going to marry Miss Garson. To the surprise of all and sundry, Ney and Miss Garson were honeymooning in a few weeks. Odd headlines, "Mrs. Miniver Marries Her Son."

Famous Artists tried to capitalize on their new client's important job in *Miniver* by offering him to other studios. They didn't have much success. Mr. Ney wound up as a stockbroker.

Nine

I T HAS BEEN my good fortune to have had the friendship of Dave Chasen, the great restauranteur for forty years. Dave's is the dining place of the upper brackets.

During my tenure with MGM, I dined at Chasen's practically every night, beginning with his opening. I did more business there acquiring personalities for MGM than I did at my studio office. Agents and actors knew of my Chasen habit and came to the restaurant to talk business. There are those who do not like being disturbed while they eat but I'm not one of them. In the highly competitive game of talent-seeking you have to be available twenty-four hours a day.

To insure my having a table each night at Dave's I had my own booth built. Dave put a plaque on the booth in full view of guests. It states: "You are occupying this booth through the courtesy of Billy (Square Deal) Grady. P.S. Strictly on your own."

I promised myself when I started this literary venture that I would refrain from any vengeful bites, but I must deviate for a chance to vent my spleen, to wit:

I was seated at my accustomed place one evening when a top director, Raoul Walsh, came over to my table.

"Hi, Irish," he began. "I'm glad to see you here tonight. I met a young man the other day who is trying to make the grade in pictures with little success. He's a good-looking kid, no experience beyond extra work. I don't know if he has any talent, but do me a favor, will you? Talk with him. If you like him, take him on at MGM. Pay him whatever you think he's worth. He'll be along for dinner with Mrs. W. and myself. I'll bring him over, may I?"

In a few moments Walsh was back at my table with a tall, good-looking young man. Walsh introduced him as Fitzgerald. I invited him to sit down. Walsh returned to his table. The boy Fitzgerald was personable and physically well set up. I instinctively liked him. He told me that he had been trying to get a start in pictures for several years with little success.

"Mr. Grady, I've been trying, but get nowhere."

I shocked Fitzgerald with my reply. "Fitzgerald, as of ten o'clock tomorrow morning you are under contract to MGM. Be in my office at ten tomorrow morning."

"Please don't kid me, Mr. Grady. Is this a gag between you and Mr. Walsh?"

"Look, son, not tomorrow morning, but tonight—right now— you are under contract to MGM at $300 a week. When you come to the office tomorrow we'll fix up the contract. Go back and have your dinner with Walsh. I'll see you in the morning."

He grabbed my hand and soundly shook it in a gesture of thanks.

As Fitzgerald left Chasen's with Walsh, he again grabbed my hand and added, "I hope this isn't a dream."

Promptly at ten the next morning, Fitzgerald was at my office. Babs ushered him in.

"I haven't slept all night, Mr. Grady. I still wonder—is it real?"

I brought my staff of assistants in—Webb, Ballerino, and Murphy—and presented Fitzgerald. I advised my boys that Fitzgerald was to be under contract and to be on the lookout for a small part to start him on his way. I would pass on whatever suggestion they made. In their presence, I arranged terms with Fitzgerald. The contract was to start at $300 weekly, and with yearly options graduate to $2,000 weekly over a period of seven years. As he progressed, so would the terms of his contract.

"Mr. Grady, can I tell my mother?"

"By all means, son. Here's the phone."

"She's in St. Louis, Mr. Grady. I haven't been home in a couple of years. I'd like to see her."

"Okay, Fitzgerald, tell me when you want to leave and I'll have the transportation department arrange it. It will take three or four days for your contracts to be drawn up. Be back here Friday . . . There is just one more thing—I'd like you to meet Mr. L. B. Mayer."

"Mr. Mayer, the head of MGM? My God, the things that are happening to me today!"

I tried to get Mayer on my intercom, but he was in the studio barber shop. I took Fitzgerald over there and found L. B. standing at the newsstand. I presented Fitzgerald.

Mayer sized him up, shook his hand, and said, "Glad to have you aboard, Fitz. If you're in the hands of the Irishman, you're in good hands. Good luck to you." Mayer went back to his office.

I have never seen Fitzgerald from that day to this, other than fleeting glimpses of him in fast European circles. I have never spoken to him. Today Fitzgerald's name is Rock Hudson.

I would never have mentioned this incident, but Hudson, née Fitzgerald, in an interview with the *Saturday Evening Post*'s Pete Martin, did not tell about the Walsh introduction at Chasen's. He did not tell about the meeting with my staff in my office, plus the contract arrangements. He told Martin he was at the MGM casting office for a very fast interview and some "IDIOT" took him to see L. B. Mayer, who was in the barber chair, covered with lather and hot towels. He and Mayer never saw one another, he said.

In my sixty years of show business, I have encountered but one ingrate, and thank the Lord he was from the north of Ireland.

Ten

*E*LIZABETH TAYLOR, at the age of eleven, was under contract to Universal Studios. MGM, at the time, was making a cycle of juvenile pictures. Elizabeth, we had heard, had an excellent singing voice as well as great potential as a star of the future, but Universal was not taking advantage of her talents. MGM negotiated and took over her contract.

While patiently awaiting her first vehicle, Elizabeth went to school on the MGM lot. Among her classmates were Judy Garland, Mickey Rooney, Margaret O'Brien, and others. A beautiful and sensitive child, her forte was poetry and she wrote a book about her pet chipmunk. I think it was called *Nibbles*. She had a way with animals and a great understanding of them.

Weekends I was often a spectator at the polo games at the Riviera Country Club. Miss Taylor could be seen riding with the great Snowy Baker, one of the world's best riding instructors. Elizabeth rode her mount as though she were part of it, a seat to the manner born.

National Velvet was in preparation for production at MGM. Pandro Berman was the producer and he was in a dither as to who would play Velvet, the young girl. I, as casting director, was brought into the picture and suggested our own Elizabeth

Taylor. Neither Berman nor his director, the great Clarence Brown, could see the girl in the part.

I insisted that our young contract player was very important to the studio, and that the part of Velvet fit her like a glove. I further offered the facts that she was educated in England, loved animals, and was a horsewoman of high caliber. I took Elizabeth to see them. Result? Nothing. Brown and Berman still were not interested. They insisted that Velvet had to be an English girl in both speech and manner. I had a battle on my hands.

If I believe and am not believed, I get stubborn. As far as I was concerned, Elizabeth Taylor was the only one who could play Velvet. I instructed my assistant, who was assigned to the picture, not to submit other girls.

The usual procedure when Grady was stubborn was a complaint to L. B. Mayer. Berman made no exception. My interoffice phone rang and I received a summons to Mayer's office.

Mayer and my friend, Eddie Mannix, the studio's general manager, were on hand to greet me. Both gentlemen let me have it with both barrels for being, as they put it, "your usual stubborn Irish self."

I listened. No protest, but when they had calmed down I reiterated my belief that young Miss Taylor should play the part. What the hell did we buy her contract from Universal for—to keep her on the shelf? *National Velvet* was the vehicle that would start her on her way.

Berman wasn't convinced, and as he was one of Mayer's top producers, L. B. leaned his way, his usual move. Eddie Mannix made a suggestion in the form of a question.

"Forget Elizabeth Taylor. If she were not around, where would you go to look for a young English girl?"

I explained that there was a war on. It would be impossible to import a child from Great Britain. The British government had a law prohibiting the export of a minor for profit. I reminded him how we found that out in the Freddie Bartholomew situation, when he was smuggled here for *David Copperfield.* and I mean smuggled.

Looking back at the Bartholomew case . . . Though Bartholomew was a minor, MGM's London office said nothing to the Labour Board. The boy, with his Aunt Cissie as guardian, was put aboard a Cunard Liner bound for New York. Aunt Cissie was cautioned to say nothing about the reason for the trip. To all inquiries, it was to be a holiday.

Everything was beyond suspicion to a degree. Cissie kept her silence until the boat was mid-ocean. She then opened up and boasted how things had been put over on the British Labour Ministry. A ship's reporter, hearing her statement, and knowing how strict the Labour Ministry was in such matters, felt that his employers, the Cunard Line, might be regarded as a party to the scheme unless he told what he had heard. A wireless to his home office was in order. There was hell to pay.

Upon arriving in New York, the Bartholomews were met at the pier by immigration officials and the New York British consul. Until there was a complete investigation, the boy was put in my custody. Under no circumstances was he to leave New York City, and he had to stand in readiness to return to England. MGM was in trouble.

Carter Barron, MGM's Washington representative and one of the best-liked men in official circles, was brought in. Cables were exchanged. The affair developed into an international brouhaha and could have seriously affected MGM's foreign production and distribution.

Barron, for MGM, admitted a serious wrong and offered an apology. The British ambassador allowed the matter to be thrown on the mercy of the courts. MGM was admonished for the breach, and because *David Copperfield* was an English classic and complimentary to young Bartholomew's talents, the boy was allowed to stay and make the picture.

It was a hectic three weeks.

Now, with the Bartholomew case fresh in my mind, I advised Mannix and Mayer that if I were to look for an English girl, the search would have to begin in Canada, where English families had sent their children to schools located outside the war zone. These schools were in Ottawa, Quebec, Toronto, and British Columbia. I was ordered to take off and my first stop was Toronto, where I lived in great elegance at the Royal York Hotel.

I had two very close friends in Toronto, Wall Street's Ben Smith, and the well-known Canadian industrialist, Jack Bickel.

He was a bachelor with a showplace estate at Port Credit, a suburb of Toronto. These two gentlemen had entertained me royally in the past. I now had an opportunity to reciprocate.

I had six fun-filled days with my friends. My doors at the Royal York were open day and night for conviviality. The Bickel estate was the scene of a few "whoopsiedoos." For six wonderful days, *National Velvet*, Ottawa, Quebec, and British Columbia were far from my thoughts. I was practically on the ropes. I phoned Eddie Mannix at the studio. (Please forgive me, Eddie, for lying, though I think you suspected it.)

"Eddie," I advised, "I have seen hundreds of girls up here in Canada and not one remotely resembles Velvet. I have spent several thousand dollars, and no results. What do you want me to do?"

I half-expected Mannix to send me to British Columbia, but instead I heard, "Okay, you Irish so-and-so, come on home."

Back to California and the studio. Because of my inability (???) to find an English lass, Elizabeth Taylor won the coveted role in *National Velvet*, one of MGM's most successful pictures.

The foregoing is how one star was born and if Elizabeth Taylor, or her mother, reads this, it will be their first inkling as to how it all happened.

Eleven

ON ONE OF MY frequent visits to New York on studio business, I went to see the premiere of *Pal Joey*, a musical starring Gene Kelly and Vivienne Segal. In the cast was a young man who, to my mind, typified the all-American boy; he was in the chorus and also played a bit in the second act. His name??? Van Johnson.

Johnson interested me as a prospect, but I remembered L. B. Mayer's antipathy to blonde leading men, Nelson Eddy notwithstanding. To Mayer, blonde men suggested a lack of virility and the he-man requisites. If I became interested in Johnson to the extent of offering a contract, I'd have difficulty with Mayer.

I enlisted the services of Mayer's partner, J. Robert Rubin. He agreed with me on Johnson's potential and volunteered to be of assistance in getting Mayer to agree to a contract. I sent for Johnson and he came to see me with his agent.

New York agents were a peculiar breed. They would make a contract for their client to appear in a New York play for $100 a week. For the same client, when it was a motion picture contract, he wanted $750 a week. The actor rehearsed in a New York play for weeks, and it could close after the first performance with no further liability by the management. The actor was out of work.

A motion picture contract of the long-term variety guaranteed the actor a minimum of ten out of thirteen weeks or fifty weeks consecutively. When he finished a picture assignment, it was up to the studio to find him another vehicle, but the actor continued on salary.

The contract signed for a New York play stands as written. Compensation in a contract with a studio is often adjusted upwards. As the actor progresses in importance, his salary does likewise. I have torn up and rearranged many contracts. Such adjustments were always voluntary on the part of the studio.

Because of the more liberal attitude of MGM toward prospective stars, agents came to us first; other studios got second consideration. Johnson's agent refused my offer of $300 a week for his client. I thought it rather generous in view of the fact Johnson was getting $100 or less in *Pal Joey*. The agent asked $750 a week. I had a favorite and oft-used expression when an agent was out of line. It went, "Mister, your client died last night." We could get along without Johnson.

The agent then went to Warner Brothers' New York offices and talked with "Old" Jake Wilke. His pitch? MGM had offered Van $750 a week, but Van turned it down, preferring Warner Studios where he figured he would not be lost in their list of contract players. Old Jake didn't call me for confirmation. He signed Johnson for $750 a week.

Johnson, to my mind and knowledge, had little more experience than chorus work up to that time. He was not yet ready to warrant more than a beginner's salary. I thought that I was quite liberal in my offer since I had prospectives at the studio getting much less than $300 a week.

Johnson's stay at Warner Studios was not happy. His inexperience held him back. He was released after six months with a few minor picture credits. His California agent took him to Columbia Studios where he was signed for less than the Warners stipend. Six months at Columbia, and again a release.

My "nite office" at Chasen's had two visitors. Lucille Ball and Van Johnson came into Chasen's to dine. Lucy saw me, evidently, because over my shoulder I heard Lucy's voice.

"Look, Van, there's Billy now."

"Where?"

"Over there at his table."

Van wanted to see me to thank me for my original interest

when I was in New York. Lucille knew of my "Chasen's office," and brought Van there—first, so he could convey his thanks and second, to tell me he was returning to Broadway.

"Why back to New York? You like it here, don't you?" I asked.

"Mr. Grady, I don't think the picture business is for me. I'm licked."

Lucy pleaded, "Billy, don't let him say 'goodbye.' Keep him here."

"I'm with you Lucy," I said. I turned to Johnson. "Van, I'm not going to say goodbye."

"But I have my ticket to leave tonight," he replied and showed his ticket.

"Give it to me—I'll have it cashed in," I said. "You be at the studio tomorrow morning. We'll work something out for you. Thanks, Lucy."

Johnson was at the studio bright and early the next morning. We arranged a contract starting at $350 a week. It would graduate in seven yearly options to $2500 a week. I now had a blonde leading-man prospect on my hands.

Johnson, at Warners and Columbia, had been badly managed. He was overmatched. All he got out of it was some camera experience. At MGM his spots would have to be hand-picked. It wasn't going to be easy.

Some weeks passed and Johnson had no action other than assisting in tests and some departmental training. Van, thinking of his Warner and Columbia experience, was getting discouraged. He couldn't understand my way of operating. "Never send a boy out to do a man's work." In other words, do not saddle a newcomer with too heavy a load at the outset. Be sure he does only what he can handle with merit.

The discouraged Johnson would go to my home in Beverly Hills. I was rarely there, continually being out on the prowl for new material. Van would be consoled by Mrs. G.

"Van, don't be disheartened. Bee Gee believes in you, he has faith in you, and your opportunity will come. Be patient for a little while longer."

Several more consolation visits to my house and then they ceased. Johnson had fallen in love.

The lady of Johnson's heart was a young comedienne we had brought out from New York to work in a picture. Her picture finished, she was waiting for another assignment that was much too long in coming. She too was discouraged. I had another member of my "family" down in the dumps. Misery liking company, they had much to talk about. Their togetherness advanced to the elopement stage. I heard about it and stepped in.

I was sort of father confessor to young people on the lot who had problems. I was frequently consulted, but neither Johnson nor the young lady asked my advice in this instance. I took it upon myself.

Johnson and his lady friend were as opposite as day and night. He was an introvert, she the boisterous extrovert. They came together in adversity. When it cleared up there had to be misunderstandings and tragedy.

The girl was an offbeat comedienne and a great one. Her bag of tricks should be available not only to pictures but to the stage. Though she was possessed of great talent, she would set picture assignments only now and then. Being an ambitious young artist, she had to keep going.

I sent for the young lady and pointed out that I could see nothing but difficulty coming from a hasty marriage. I told her that MGM was not going to exercise its option for her services and she would be returning to New York where she could take advantage of the numerous offers she had received. Johnson would remain in California under MGM contract. I pleaded with her to take time and think, not to rush into something that would jeopardize two promising careers.

The next day she was back. She had had a talk with her father, a wise old owl whom I knew. She also talked with Van. They would wait.

Johnson was lower than a duck's bustle, when out of the blue came a script ready for production. It was called *The War and Mrs. Hadley*. The juvenile lead in the picture was ideal for Van. The kind of a part I had hoped to start him in.

The writer and coproducer of the picture was a friend of mine, George Oppenheimer. George believed in me and my prospectives, and I went to him and pleaded Johnson's cause; Van was, I stated, "the only actor in the industry who can do justice to the part." I also suggested that Van's lack of experience was just what the part needed. I had a big thing going for me. There was a war on and Johnson had not been called. The experienced actors that Oppenheimer wanted were already in the Army or on the verge. I won a concession. Johnson would be tested for the part. He came through with flying colors. His patience had been rewarded and his joy at the news was heart-warming.

The verdict on Johnson's performance, when we previewed the picture, made me look good. It was good to be able to say "I told you so." I have a silver cigarette case from Johnson. He was very grateful for efforts in his behalf. Now he had to be kept alive with more roles. His name must always be up for consideration, so I instructed my staff. All of a sudden the studio realized they had an important juvenile star on their hands.

As Johnson grew in stature, the men in the casting office saw less and less of the young fellow who used to haunt them for engagements. For a time he had been their problem child. Now that it was over they rarely saw him.

As one grows in importance in the picture business, they also advance socially. Johnson was no exception. He was invited everywhere by the so-called elite. I might ask where the hell the elite were when the boy was struggling. He was single and eligible then, also. The only elite he knew in the bygone days were the casting office staff.

Johnson was declared 4-F by the draft board. There was a dearth of leading men because of the war, and Van's rise was fast and furious. He had good roles at both MGM and on loan-out to other studios. I weighed each loan-out carefully. Each had to be worthy of my boy.

Johnson was in such demand that he went from picture to picture and, I might add, was getting a little picky—just what you expect when you elevate a newcomer to star level. The studio and staffs were good enough at the beginning, but now our man was an authority on what was good and what he thought was not. Suffice to say he was overruled. He changed agents to the giant MCA.

In Johnson's favor I must say that he had worked on picture after picture without a holiday. MCA requested of L. B. Mayer —and it was granted—a three-week vacation for Johnson. During these three weeks he was not to be disturbed by studio phone calls or messages. To the casting office boys it was quite a change from the days when Van wouldn't go to the bathroom without a long-cord telephone lest his infrequent calls from either the studio or used car salesmen would be missed.

Jack Cummings, an MGM producer, was preparing a picture with most of the locale in downtown Los Angeles' Main Street. The first day's shooting called for the use of 500 extras as street atmosphere. Johnson was cast as the lead and would be needed in the first day's shooting. Cummings wanted confirmation from me that Johnson would be there. I told him of the studio agreement with Johnson—no phone calls. Cummings was rightly incensed.

The deadline on calling the extras was 5:00 P.M. on the Saturday before the shooting date. Cummings placed a call for Johnson at the Palm Springs Racquet Club. Johnson refused the call. I knew about the man's recent temperamental displays, so I didn't call until the last minute, though there were many things I would have liked to do.

Saturday at noon I ordered MCA to call Johnson. They refused. I hit the roof and called the Racquet Club myself. I told the club operator it was a personal call, a social call. He came to the phone. This conversation followed.

"Hello, Van?"

"Yeah—who is this?"

"Billy Grady."

"How dare you call me when I'm on my vacation?"

"Hey—wait a minute, Van. This is Billy Grady—remember me?"

"Yes, I remember you!" and he slammed down the receiver.

Oooh—What a Saturday night and Sunday I had! In my mood, I was ready for mayhem or torture. What I did not know was that the gang at the Racquet Club had "steamed" Johnson into assuming big-star status. I was the real victim. All I could see were 500 extras on Los Angeles' Main Street ready to work on Monday morning, all of them with play or pay contracts running from $17.50 to $27.50 a head, and no word from Johnson that he would be there.

As it turned out, Johnson was on the set Monday A.M., bright and early. The first day's work was the best in the picture, but, stubborn Irish Grady could not forgive or forget that miserable weekend.

I didn't speak to Van for several years, although my staff and I kept him in picture after picture. He was a workhorse and loved it.

One night I was having dinner at my usual spot at Chasen's. Suddenly there was a call to hurry to Chasen's office to see a TV show. There was Van Johnson extolling me to the skies on a late-hour talk show, and not only on this show but on others that followed. NBC wanted me to appear as Johnson's discoverer on a panel show that told the life of Johnson.

Whatever Van Johnson has achieved in show business, he has worked hard for, and I am happy for his success. He and I still correspond and visit today, all grudges forgotten.

Twelve

ONE OF MY clients during my tenure as an agent on Broadway was the Ben Hur Stables, owned and operated by Eddie Fills, a real West Sider. Eddie wasn't a "dese, dose, and dems," but he was a second cousin to that family. He really murdered the English language.

The Ben Hur outfit rented anything in the animal line to theatrical productions. Their clients ranged from the Metropolitan Opera Company to movie theaters.

Eddie Fills ate, slept, and lived Ben Hur Stables. Meet him on the street and casually ask, "Eddie, what opera is playing Wednesday at the Met?"

His reply would be short and snappy: "Lousy, only one horse."

"What's the opera Saturday, Eddie?"

His face would break into a wide smile as he replied, "Wunnerful, six horses." You had to decipher that one horse was *Aida* and six horses *Carmen*.

Fills would train any animal to fit the needs of a producer. He said he could get anything from a left-handed baboon to a giraffe that could stand on its head. You know something? I think he could. I never heard him say no.

All was not milk and honey in the renting of animals. There

were moments of embarrassment when the animals would forget their manners and "misbehave" on stage. Sidney Skolsky,
the columnist, used to say, "The animals ad-libbed."

A very embarrassing Ben Hur moment that was really disas-
trous happened during the opening night of a musical, *Rainbow.* This show was produced by one Philip Goodman. It had
a beautiful score by Vincent Youmans and starred Libby Hol-
man and Charles Ruggles. Helen Lynd and Harlan Dixon were
supporting players. This musical was produced to the tune of
$225,000, a bit high for the times.

The locale of the play was the frontier West, the opening
scene a typical mining town street: the Golden Nugget Saloon,
the Eagle Hotel, the jail, and the sheriff's office. Charlie Ruggles was playing a mule-skinner in love with Helen Lynd. In
Charlie's absence, she had been carrying on a little hanky-
panky with Harlan Dixon, bartender at the Golden Nugget.

Ruggles, the mule-skinner, had been on a trip. He returned
suddenly, leading his favorite mule. As he entered the scene
and advanced to center stage, he was shocked to see through the
open door of the Nugget his gal carrying on with the bartender.

As the mule-skinner stared, and unbeknown to him and the
other actors on stage, the mule misbehaved and really ad-
libbed. Ruggles stealthily tiptoed across stage to get a better
view of his gal and the bartender. As Ruggles walked, the mule
ad-libbed in tempo, as though rehearsed. The audience went
into gales of laughter.

To make matters worse, Ruggles, thinking the laughter was
the result of his tiptoeing, prolonged it. The mule did some
prolonging of his own. Ruggles came back to his mule, unaware of the misbehavior, wrapped his arm around the mule's
neck, and whispered in its ear, "Do you know what I know?"
The audience went wild.

When the laughter died down, the bartender, having seen the
mule-skinner, read his line, which was, "Did you see what happened?" There was no holding the audience.

Unfortunately, no stagehand had the presence of mind to do
the shovel and broom routine. The "ad lib" stayed where it was
and it was an out-of-hand audience that viewed eighteen
chorus girls dancing around it.

The curtain was lowered for the purpose of cleaning up the

mess. That done, they tried to raise the curtain but the lines became fouled. It was four feet off the floor and could neither be lowered or raised. Scurrying feet could be seen trying to rectify the fouled lines. A stagehand came on scene with a high stepladder. He tripped and fell and all the scenery came crashing to the floor. It was fully an hour before the proceedings began again.

The production of *Rainbow* was a fiasco. It never did recover from the first-act comedy of errors. The newspaper critics said nothing about the play, but they did a rave about the mule who gave the audience a good laugh night. The play didn't last out the week. The mule? That's how stars are born.

I was standing in the rear of the theater with Fills. The moment the ad lib started, he ran. When the scenery fell down, I ran. Fills and I met later at Dinty Moore's. He explained that the mule, who had rehearsed with the company, was stricken with colic that afternoon. The attendant had substituted an untutored understudy without telling Eddie.

Another ad-lib scene concerned Ed Wynn in George White's Scandals, and again on an opening night.

The scene was a restaurant, Ed Wynn playing a comedy waiter. A customer entered, Wynn ushered him to a table and tendered a menu. The customer scanned the menu for a few seconds and said, "I'm so hungry I could eat a horse."

Wynn's reply, "One horse coming right up." He ran offstage and brought in a Ben Hur Stable white mare, who stood center stage.

Wynn returned to the customer, and while he was awaiting the order, the horse misbehaved but good. Wynn, unaware of what had happened, said to the customer, "Would you like to try the special?"

All hell broke loose laugh-wise in the audience. There has never been a bigger laugh in Broadway theater history.

Bobby Connolly's production of *Sons O'Guns* needed six homing pigeons to work on cue. I brought Bobby and Eddie Fills together. The scene for the pigeons explained, Fills returned to his stable where for two weeks he trained one dozen pigeons in the desired routine. So that there would be no slipup, Eddie rehearsed twelve understudies, and had twelve others standing by, just in case. A large crate of thirty-six pigeons was off to Detroit for the opening performance of *Sons O'Guns.*

The opening was a crème de la crème charity affair sponsored by the Motor City's upper crust. They came in all their finery, amidst a torrential rain. Someone in the theater management goofed—there was no check room. The audience toted their coats and umbrellas to their seats.

In the first act of the play, Jack Donahue, the star, is behind enemy lines. He is concealed in a farmhouse attic occupied by an underground worker, Lili Damita. From his hiding place Donahue views the movements of the German army. He writes the information on a slip of paper, attaches it to a pigeon's leg, releases the bird to fly back to the American headquarters.

The afternoon of the opening, a chorus boy appeared at the theater drunk. Connolly fired him, and gave him his fare back to New York. Instead of returning to New York, the chorus boy went to a speakeasy and got loaded. At show time he returned to the theater and at the moment of the most important scene in the first act, he released all the pigeons.

Thirty-six pigeons, seeing the bright lights, flew onstage and out over the audience. They roosted on the chandelier, the box railings, and parts of the balcony. Some of the flock circled the auditorium in flight above the audience and, I might add, were very untidy as they flew overhead.

On stage, actors were reading their lines, then running for cover—birds were perched overhead. It was the only audience I've ever seen who sat with raised umbrellas watching a performance. Poor Eddie Fills.

A very funny situation, but with no ad-libbing, concerned another Ben Hur horse. The play, Ziegfeld's *Three Musketeers,* Lyric Theater, New York.

Florenz Ziegfeld had as his guests a very important and prominent Spanish duke and his duchess. The duke was in this country on state business and had been wined and dined by official Washington, plus a New York City welcome. The United States visit was to be climaxed by the *Three Musketeers* musical, New York's big hit.

Dennis King was playing the role of D'Artagnan. Reginald Owen played Cardinal Richelieu. The first act had a courtyard scene outside an inn. D'Artagnan rides in on a bay mare, dismounts, and enters the inn. In all previous performances, the horse stood center stage and faced the audience while he awaited D'Artagnan's return. For some unaccountable reason, the night the duke and his duchess were in the audience, the horse turned halfway round and his well-rounded rump faced the audience.

Reggie Owen entered the scene, followed by his secretary. The secretary said something, and Owen, the cardinal, stared at the horse's rump and without thinking read his line, "That reminds me, I must write to the duke."

The duke and his lady enjoyed the laugh that followed with the rest of the audience. Ziegfeld, the perfectionist, was furious.

Poor Eddie Fills took the rap for many happenings he was powerless to prevent. One incident, a painful one, occurred on the opening night of an Ed Wynn-starring vehicle, *Simple Simon*, at the Ziegfeld Theater.

Just before the finale of the first act, Wynn did a comedy specialty. At the finish of the routine, he ran offstage and immediately returned with a complete change of costume—comedy attire. There would be a laugh, another exit, and he'd return with another comedy costume. Wynn changed as often as the laughs continued.

The last change found Wynn center stage, dressed in a long Chinese mandarin cloak, complete with pigtail wig and skull cap. He raised his hands for quiet and announced he was "the great Ching Ling Foo, magician extraordinaire." Wynn made a few mysterious passes with his hands, reached under his coat to pull out a large white goose.

Wynn reached for the goose and let out a yell of agony. The goose had grabbed him with its iron jaws, grabbed him in the sensitive vitals, and was holding on. Wynn tried but could not pry him loose. The hysterical audience thought it part of the act and applauded wildly until two husky stagehands carried Wynn offstage to pry the goose loose.

There was never a dull moment for me as agent for the Ben Hur Stables.

In all truth there is a bit of fiction, and in all fiction a bit of truth. This tale again concerns my friend Eddie Fills, who swore it was the truth at the time he told it. I have heard it many times over the years, but nobody has told the tale to equal Eddie.

There was a "here-today-and-gone-tomorrow" picture company making short-subject pictures in a makeshift studio in Brooklyn. They operated on a very limited bankroll. One of their two-reelers was about an East Indian fortune-teller. The fortune-teller was assisted by a see-all, know-all elephant. Important people would come to the seer for advice. The seer would repeat the question to the elephant, who would shake his head yes or no in answer.

This epic short subject was almost completed, except that neither the producer nor his director had been able to get the elephant to shake his head "no." They had gotten yes all right just by throwing some peanuts to the elephant. It would raise its head to catch them and lower its head to chew them; thus came "yes." Shaking the head "no" was something else again. The company was running out of money and as yet there wasn't any "no" from Sir Elephant.

A hasty conference. A reward of $500 would be paid to anybody who could get the bull elephant to shake his no. Eddie Fills applied.

Eddie went forward and looked the elephant in the eye. He then went to the bull elephant's rear, took a heavy axe handle, and belted the animal across his vitals. The elephant let out a mighty roar but didn't shake his head. Eddie, again to the elephant's head, and whispered in his ear. The animal frantically shook his head, "No—No—No!" Success at last—the picture was finished.

The producer, curious, said to Fills, "We saw you hit the elephant across his vital spot and he just roared. What did you whisper in the elephant's ear?"

"All I whispered to the elephant was, 'Do you want me to belt you again?' "

Thirteen

*D*ID YOU EVER lie abed at night, unable to sleep, and have names and incidents from out of the past come into view fleetingly? Following are a few, and I'll introduce them with, "And then there was the time . . ."

And then there was the time I received a phone call in New York from Irving Thalberg. At the time I was the studio's eyes and ears on the East Coast. Thalberg was preparing *The Good Earth* for production. The original plan to make the picture in China had been discarded because of the lack of English-speaking Chinese. It would have to be made in California.

A site was selected in the San Fernando Valley for the erection of the Chinese village that was to be the focal point for all action in the picture. A pair of Chinese water buffalo was desperately needed and as quickly as possible. Philippine buffalo, Indian and African animals were available, but no Chinese. The studio had canvassed zoos, circuses, every spot where they might be found. The hoof and mouth disease quarantine prevented their importation. It was up to me, but HURRY.

I made inquiries. No luck. The calls from Thalberg were daily, "What about the Chinese buffalo?" He wanted action and in a hurry.

My good friend, Eddie Fills, from Ben Hur Stables, came to my assistance. He thought he knew where he could get a pair and went on the hunt.

There are some people who collect rare old coins, stamps, antiques. Fills found a man in Boonton, New Jersey, who collected Chinese water buffalo . . . honestly collected them. He had a herd of twenty-two head. The day was saved, and I called Thalberg at the studio. His reply? No thanks to me for my efforts. "Get them out here as quickly as possible. Spare no expense."

I bought a bull and a cow, the cow heavy with calf. The price $2200. I knew that my friend Fills got a hunk of that, but I figured he was entitled to it.

I summoned carpenters from Newark. It was a task to make heavy oak crates to ship these vicious animals of great strength. The first crates completed, the animals kicked them to pieces. Stronger, reinforced crates had to be built. Again the call from Thalberg, "Where are the buffalo?"

I chartered a Pennsylvania Railroad baggage car, together with an attendant for the animals. The car containing the animals was attached to a Philadelphia-bound train, there transferred to the Pennsy's crack train, the Spirit of St. Louis.

On its arrival at St. Louis the car was attached to a fast train for the trip to Kansas City, where it was to be hooked to the Santa Fe crack passenger train, the Chief.

Thalberg had to be informed twice a day as to progress. "Where are they now?" was the constant inquiry.

At Los Angeles, a waiting van and a quick trip to the studio. BUT something had happened. Production plans were delayed, after all this hurry, hurry, hurry, and shipping expense.

The Chinese water buffalo that finally appeared in that great movie, *The Good Earth*, were the grandchildren of the original pair I sent out. "Hurry—hurry—hurry!"

Fourteen

$\mathcal{E}$ NRICO CARUSO, the great Metropolitan Opera star, maintained a large apartment in New York's Knickerbocker Hotel, 42nd Street and Broadway. He liked to entertain lavishly and had many festive gatherings at this, his New York home. Caruso liked "card tricksters" and I was called upon several times to hire a card trickster for his parties. He was a very gracious host and my card-manipulating clients and myself were treated as guests.

The Great Caruso liked practical jokes. He had seen a burlesque show in which a comedy drunk was thrown out of a saloon by the seat of his pants and his coat collar. Enrico thought it a great gag, and with me imitating the comedy drunk, he tried it out on his assembled guests. Caruso had a powerful pair of arms and torso. When he gave me the heave-ho, holding me by the coat collar and the seat of my pants, he literally lifted me two feet in the air and I went through the door of the apartment. Tears from his gusty laughter were in his eyes. The gag was a great success, though the grip he had on my pants took a little flesh along with it.

One evening Lillian Russell, the great international beauty, was the guest of honor along with her new gentleman friend.

Miss Russell was beautifully gowned. A waiter, in passing a glass of wine to me, accidentally spilled a few drops on Miss Russell's gown. To me it was inconsequential, but Caruso used it as an excuse to do his famous heave-ho comedy bit. Again I was the victim. This time he overdid it and my fanny was sore from the over-grip. I didn't return to the party and took a walk down Broadway.

At the Empire Theater, as I arrived, an intermission period was in progress. A new musical had opened. I went in to catch the second act. Just as the maestro was giving the downbeat for the choral singing, a male voice made a "boo boo" and jumped the gun, so to speak. I heard a beautiful baritone chord, much like the Robert Goulet voice of today. The agent in me went into action.

It was but a moment before I was backstage, and talking with my friend Tad Gray, the stage manager. Tad pointed out the chorus man who did the one-note "boo boo." I saw a tall, good-looking young fellow with a wealth of brown hair. Further inquiry from Tad gave me the news that it was the chorus boy's first show. Other than church choir solo work, it was his first public appearance. I arranged for Tad to send him to my office the next day.

I will call my man "Tom Slade," and for obvious reasons—the following tale will explain.

A closeup of my man Slade told me he had a voice that showed good training. He was tall and good-looking, and his personality showed star material. Singing juveniles were few and far between.

I arranged auditions with prospective musical producers, preferably those who were contemplating revues. The hearings were all successful and the offers started to come in. The best was from Ziegfeld for one of his productions. I wound up with a contract for my man at $500 a week, a money goal he had not dreamed of achieving in so short a time. From $35 to $500 in the short space of three weeks. To my surprise I got a bit of an argument from my singer. He protested my 15 percent for services rendered. Money seems to do things to people. I made him sign a contract, the only contract I ever had with an actor or actress as an agent.

His success in the Ziegfeld show was outstanding, and he drew good notices and attention from nightclub owners. That part of the business I wouldn't go for. I wanted to create a matinee idol image, not a saloon singer.

My man was married, but this fact did not deter him from an interest in romantic interludes. On one of his extramarital excursions he met a cute chorus girl. Large, luminous eyes, doll-like stature, and pouty red lips. At times she looked as if someone had just removed a trombone from her mouth.

There must have been some Irish in my singer's forebears. He developed into quite a man with the romantic phrase. Not content with love letters, he went to love verses. Everyday, Marcia of the pouty lips would receive reams of passionate poetry. My man poured out his soul.

Now our doll-like pretty one had been around and knew the value of the written word with signature. She saved all of her Tommy Boy's missives, bound them neatly in blue ribbon, and put them away for reading in her old age. Oh, yeah?

Finishing the Ziegfeld production, I arranged for my singer to do a new revue and to be costarred at $1,350 a week. Quite a jump again from the Ziegfeld $500. Again a beef over my 15 percent fee, but I took the precaution of having my commission paid me each week by his newly acquired attorney, also a friend of mine. My contract was still in force. Any of Tommy's occasional beefs just rolled off my back.

Another success for my man in the new revue. My objective of him being a matinee idol was in full swing. The affair with Marcia Pouty Lips was still on. The daily missives arrived as usual. Seems he never ran out of subject matter.

Several weeks of the new revue, and I had a Hollywood film star come to me for representation. In a very short time I had arranged a contract for her with Lee Shubert. The day the contract was signed, I took my Hollywood lady client backstage to meet my singing star. He was a fast worker and she fell for his charm like a ton of bricks. It wasn't long before she got an invitation to share a bottle of wine at his apartment after the matinee. Three people can be a crowd at given moments. I took my leave.

M'Lady from Hollywood and her singing friend went to his

apartment after the matinee and put on their own production, BUT forgot to lock the door. Marcia Pouty Lips walked in and OOOOOOH what she saw!

Marcia's shocked sensibilities and pride prompted her to go commercial. Her scarred soul must be compensated.

Ten days after the apartment matinee with the unlocked door, I received a phone call at the Friars' Club. The call was from a friend of mine who was the head of a newspaper syndicate. He gave me the news that Marcia had brought the blue-ribbon-bound love missives to his office and offered them for sale. Inasmuch as my singing star was a celebrity and a national figure, what with records and his Broadway successes, the ribbon-bound "pash" poetry would be sought-after reading. The girl asked $10,000. My friend's editorial staff read the missives and advised purchase for their Sunday supplement section. They offered $5,000 and compromised with $7,500.

The reason for my friend's phone call? He was of the opinion that it would make my man look rather foolish in the public eye if the didoes were published. If my friend's syndicate didn't publish, a rival one would. To save my man embarrassment, he would turn them over to me for the purchase price. Otherwise he would publish.

"The letters will make tasty reading, Billy. It's pretty sloppy stuff, but dames will go for it."

"His looking foolish isn't worth $7,500 to me personally. I didn't write them."

"The only reason I'm calling is I know what you did for the man and I'd hate to see him look ridiculous in the public eye. Your man also has a juicy divorce case coming up. These letters won't help his case any. I recommend you get your man to buy the letters back. Keep my name out of it. It's all your idea."

I was grateful to my friend for his consideration and asked him to withhold any publishing decision until I talked with my star.

With the divorce case only two months off, it wasn't difficult to convince my man he should buy the letters. Now comes the BUT. He didn't have the money. He was broke. Furthermore he was overdrawn on his salary. He was really in trouble.

His lawyer had no funds of his, he had been paid up to date for his recordings. Only one thing to do—go to the management and get what he could as a further advance on his salary.

Two days of pleas to the management and they advanced him
$5,000. I loaned him the balance of $2,500 on a sixty-day note.
The letters were turned over to my star, who threw a wingding
of a party at his apartment. It was a wine, women, and song
turn-out. There were readings of a few of the choice missives
and all were destroyed in the gas log fireplace. So far so good.

My sixty-day note became due, and there was no attention
paid to meeting it. I asked for a payment just as a token, but it
was not forthcoming, and there was resentment that I would
deign to ask.

Sixty days . . . seventy days . . . ninety days . . . and still no
action. I got mad. My man avoided me on the street and in
public places. He would not return phone calls and was too
busy to see me at the theater. I went into action. I needed money
for a new venture I was in.

I arranged to serve papers on my man, a lawsuit to recover.
With a process server, I arrived at the stage entrance of my
star's theater and sent my name to his dressing room, but as
usual he was too busy to see me. His very prissy valet, who
relayed the "too busy" message, was holding a beautifully
wrapped flat package.

"Mr. Slade is so sorry he is unable to see you at the moment,
but he told me to tell you that inasmuch as it is approaching the
Christmastime, he hasn't forgotten you. He said to wish you a
Merry Christmas." The prissy one handed me the package and
glided off.

The ornate cover removed, I found my gift to be a solid gold
cigarette case. A beautiful thing. The inside cover was inscribed:

To all I am, or ever hope to be, I
owe to Billy Grady. Merry Christmas.
Tom

I felt like a stinker. The guy did owe me $2,500, it was overdue
and I needed it, but though he was in trouble, domestically and
financially, he still thought enough of me to make me a beautiful and expensive gift. A bit ashamed, I turned to the process
server, took the subpoena, and tore it up, throwing the pieces
in the gutter. The process man dismissed, I went my way.

It was just after the first of the year that the shock came. My man suddenly sailed for Europe. He was on the high seas only three days when I got a bill from the jeweler for the cigarette case. It was for $265.

That episode happened quite some years ago. Recently, I had occasion to drive over to Brooklyn. In a small basement rathskeller, I was shocked to find my man, my former star and matinee idol, a singing waiter. Mercifully I saw him before he saw me. I excused myself and left my friends. Some time later I told them the reason.

Now the why as to "Tom Slade." My singing star came into hard times. He married again, and has several grown children. I knew the gal he married. A swell gal, and what she didn't know about her husband's early peccadillos won't hurt. A friend of mine mysteriously delivered some of my 15 percent of my former client's earnings. It was in appreciation of one of the songs he sang in that dingy rathskeller. *Tempus fugit.*

Fifteen

*W*RITING THIS book, I sit back and think of outstanding incidents that at the time seemed minor but upon reflection emerge as very interesting.

During the "Thin Man" series with Bill Powell and Myrna Loy, we were continually looking at outside pictures for stand-out types that would lend themselves to the "Thin Man" stories. In one particular picture I saw a beautiful girl, and I mean beautiful.

The gal was about five-foot seven; she was svelte, with a wealth of chestnut hair and brown eyes, and I judged her to be about twenty-two years old. She was really stacked, as the saying goes. In the picture, all the girl did was walk into an office scene, place some papers on a desk, and exit. Though there were four important players in the scene, all eyes were on her as she did her bit. I delegated one of my staff to ascertain the gal's identity and invite her to the studio.

She was a recent graduate from college and was interested in a picture career. The beauty I had seen on the screen was more so in the office. She had personality, was very definite. The gal had possibilities; time would tell.

At the time the girl came to the office, MGM had a stock

company of 253 players. The list included everyone from top stars down to young prospectives. It cost the studio nearly a million on the red side to carry the load, and orders from New York were no more contractees. This seemed shortsighted to me. Better to drop a few that would not produce results and not overlook a personality with a future. I'd try a new tack with this gal. I hoped she would cooperate.

I asked the young lady if she, without a contract, would devote her services exclusively to MGM. My staff would find opportunities for her in the many features and short subjects we were making. As she gained experience her roles and compensation would progress. I would personally supervise her career. She had everything to gain and nothing to lose. She agreed.

After six months of doing progressive parts in shorts and features, she was an accepted lady of talent. Her work had been noticed by other studios and offers were made, but she remained loyal to MGM, as per our arrangement. Her salary was now $750 weekly, with a three-week guarantee. All original thoughts of her possibilities were confirmed.

Just before Christmastime I had heard that the young lady was going to gift my staff, as well as myself. I sent for her and explained that we were very appreciative of her thoughtfulness but it was a rule of the office—gifts in appreciation of our services were taboo. I hoped she would accept the ruling with good grace. She was disappointed, but understood. Her very creditable performances were thanks enough for the casting staff. Her career was now well launched.

Since my early days of selling carnations on the streets of my hometown, Lynn, Massachusetts, I had been a boutonniere man. Up to recent years I was always adorned with a white carnation in my lapel. I felt undressed without it.

Our appreciative young lady was aware of my habit. Being a smart young lady, she went to a florist and left a standing order: for one year, a white carnation was to be delivered to my desk each morning. The white posy started my day.

There were times at the studio when I had serious differences of opinion with L. B. Mayer. If he had an argument with Nick Schenck, the president, or one of his executive staff, and lost, he would take it out on the next person he met. I seemed to be that next person quite often.

During the filming of *Captains Courageous* we had a beaut. He had been misinformed about something and wouldn't listen to reason. I was right and he was wrong. The argument wound up with me telling him what to do with his new contract, my job, and his studio. Two quickly summoned studio police ushered me to the sidewalk outside the gate.

Two days later, I was executive in charge of all talent at RKO Studios. Each morning, as usual, my white carnation was on my RKO desk. The lady of the carnation visited me at my new office and asked if she was still obligated to MGM. I advised her that she was now on her own, but said I would still be available to her for advice at any time.

I didn't have to be hit over the head to realize the frequent visits to my RKO office for advice carried a little more import. I was the object of a very deep affection. Flattered??? Who wouldn't be, but the kind of a married man I tried to be prompted a heart-to-heart talk with the young lady.

The talk resulted in tears and a parting, but could she still come to me for advice? Naturally the answer was yes. A paternal kiss and she was gone. The carnations still came to the desk each morning.

It was several months before I saw her again, but I had heard rumors. Her visit confirmed them. She had fallen in love and wanted me to know about it. This beautiful girl, just past twenty-two, with the world and fame at her feet, had listened to the protestations of love and planned a whole new life. The "schmuck" was three times her age. I knew him and was astonished and disappointed.

He was a beautician, or makeup man, and the kind of individual who would still look like a baggy-pants burlesque comic if you put a $400 suit on him. He had short stubby teeth here and there, thick-lensed glasses, and was very sparse in the hair department. He had the personality of a bucket of pig's entrails. He was no conversationalist, and no matter where the girl went with him she had to make apologies for him. He was a grandfather with grown children older than she.

His only credit—he was an expert at his trade. We in the

industry knew him as an eccentric. His line to the gal? He was going to make her another Elizabeth Arden or Helena Rubenstein in the cosmetic business. If Revlon were in business at the time he would have thrown them in.

To sum up, the gal fell for the guy's line and her acting career was over. She was sunk and no amount of reasoning on my part could convince her or change her plans.

"Ruth, there isn't a man alive who can understand a woman's thinking processes when it comes to falling in love. You possess everything that embodies beauty in a woman. To be brutally frank, I think you are throwing your life away."

I heard her tearful answer, "I can't help help it, I am so in love with him."

"So you're in love with him. You've been in love before and got over it."

"This is different," she offered as defense.

"I'll say it's different. Here you are marrying a dull, and I repeat, dull, old man. He hasn't one attractive feature other than his qualifications as a beautician. He lacks personality and most of all he lacks the vitality that you, a young girl, must have in your life. You are in love with a phlegmatic hunk of nothing, no salt, no vinegar, no pepper, and most important, no PAPRIKA. I think I know you. You must have paprika in your life."

"I'm sorry you think that way about him. For your information, I am through with paprika, this man has what I want in life. I am content."

A moment passed and tears welled up in her eyes. I put my arms around her.

"I'm sorry to be so harsh, but you came to me for advice. I have spoken my piece, but remember, NO PAPRIKA." There was an embrace, a kiss, and she was gone.

The foregoing transpired on Thursday. She eloped on Friday and was married Saturday. As usual my carnation was on my desk Monday morning BUT IT WAS COVERED WITH PAPRIKA.

I never saw the girl again. I wish I had. I will always be curious. Was there a deficiency or an abundance of paprika?

Sixteen

I HAVE BEEN told that I am a slave to habit. Looking back, I'll admit that it is so. If, in my world travels, I found a good hotel or restaurant, I'd be back the next time around. In these places I got to be a regular, known and favored.

I am not a sightseer. I just like to watch people. Give me a table at a sidewalk café, a favorite bar, and I am content, just observing.

I have an idiosyncrasy. My favorite melodies are "When Day Is Done" and Gounod's "Ave Maria." When I am on my third or fourth belt before dinner, I like "When Day Is Done." During an after-dinner drink, "Maria." "Maria," if played and sung well, kind o' gives me the weeps and I don't have to have a snootful to get the watery eyes. Sounds foolish, but it's me and I can do nothing about it.

My favorite hangout in Rome was Georges, an excellent restaurant on a street behind the Excelsior Hotel. Good food, great service, and my favorite bartenders, who anticipated my visits and managed to dig up a bottle of Old Forester. The bottle was secreted and its contents poured only for the "Irishman" by my friend Mario, barkeep extraordinaire.

Lunch and dinner, day in and day out, was not unusual for me in Georges. I went through three managements. The bar faces you as you step in off the street. There was an alcove and outside dining area. I am told it was the scene of the Pope's first garden. Very scenic and restful.

A fixture at Georges was Papa, an old Italian gentleman. In all my years of patronage, I never knew his square moniker, nor did I hear him speak one word of English. Papa came to your table on invitation and sang Italian love songs, accompanying himself on a guitar. He sang and played with that heart and soul only an Italian can put into his music. Papa was short, round and, I'd say, in his seventies. He played the guitar like a youth, and his voice still held up.

Once I became a regular at Georges, Papa needed no invitation from me to sing and play my favorites. He timed his numbers perfectly. I'd get "When Day Is Done" while I was on my fourth belt of Old F. "Ave Maria" would fall in its natural place while I was at the bar after dinner.

During my last visit to Rome and Georges, I was at the bar and Mario was telling me about his newly born bambino. Only an Italian could go into such raptures in telling about his new son. It was a joy to listen. As I was sipping my third Old F., Papa approached and went into "When Day Is Done." He was in better-than-usual voice.

He finished, and there was the usual *"grazie."* Just as he was retiring to the extreme end of the bar, a lady entered. Papa seemed vexed, the lady seemed to be an intruder. She greeted Mario, turned with a hello to Papa, who gave a slight nod and turned his head. Seeing this, the newcomer humped her shoulders as much as to say, "The hell with him."

The lady was blonde, a bit on the chubby side, well dressed in ensemble and stole. I remarked her nice white teeth. She greeted Mario and ordered Rhine wine and seltzer. I was a bit on the friendly side and said, "Wine, Signorina?"

"That is my good-girl drink."

"What is your bad-girl drink?" The obvious answer to her remark.

"I drink Scotch"; I asked Mario to pour for her.

The chubby blonde ordered a double and polished it off like a canary dipping its beak in a puddle of water. Mario poured another double, and then introduced me.

Her first name was Greta; an Italian name followed that I did not catch. Greta was German; she had married and divorced a Roman, and was now a hostess on an airline plying between Rome and the Far East. An interesting gal. Her tales about passengers and her experiences as a hostess fascinated me. In the midst of a tale about King Farouk, I got hunger pangs and invited her to dine with me. She accepted with alacrity.

Bear in mind that Greta was belting the Scotch as though it was going out of style—and with no visible effect whatever. What a constitution! This damsel not only had a hollow leg, she had a cavernous fuselage, as she proved at dinner.

Throughout dinner Greta continued her tales about air passengers, all the while belting the Scotch and a bottle of Chianti. With half of what she had aboard, I'd be in the mood to throw rocks at the Mona Lisa painting hung in the grotto.

As usual with all people who are only fairly interesting, there came a lull in the conversation. Greta was no exception. With the wine aboard she started to repeat herself. I wanted out and suggested an Irish coffee at the bar. It being near the door I could make a quick exit.

The lady had never experienced Irish coffee. She liked them and had two. As we stood there, Papa, not wanting to lose out on his usual lira, sang "Ave Maria." It seemed to be more schmaltzy than usual. I did my weeps, and he retired.

I thought I could speed my leave-taking by telling my female companion that I had a very important phone call coming from New York, and before receiving same I would like to take my usual stroll. Not to be outdone, a stroll before retiring was Greta's habit also. I was stuck.

As we passed Dony's, the famous sidewalk café next to the Excelsior, she glanced across the street and spotted Farouk seated at the entrance of the Café de Paris.

"Ah, there is Papa Farouk. Let's go and say hello."

I had met Old Blubber in Paris and was curious. Would he remember me? I doubted it. As we approached, he invited Greta to have a drink, ignoring me. As I walked away I heard her order a double Scotch. A call from Greta and I turned. Farouk gestured and I returned to receive an apology. He thought she was alone. I wished she was. At the table I ordered brandy and listened. She was on intimate terms with the old boy. Some minutes passed and I excused myself, but Greta gave His Highness an *a rivederci* and joined me.

As we walked down the hill she explained she had to have permission from Old Fatso to publish some material in a book she was writing with another hostess. He was concerned in the writing. The book was finished, and would I like to read it? It was at her apartment a short distance away. Sure, I'd like to read it. From what I had heard, it could be a bit racy and mebbe picture material.

My walking companion volunteered that I would not like her apartment. "I am a very poor girl, but it is the best I can afford. You will see."

My curiosity was aroused. She was well dressed, the stole was good quality fur. She wore a small diamond ring, plus an expensive Swiss wrist watch. She was leading up to the usual: a friend of Farouk and well known at Georges which, after all, was not a drive-in. I had a yen to see her layout.

Turning a corner, she pointed. "That is where I live." We came to a type of high wooden gate peculiar to Italian tenements, passageway into a courtyard, washlines crossing from window to window. Refuse in every corner. She was right—I wouldn't like her place.

Up three flights of stone steps to an iron door. A long metal key opened it. As we entered, she pulled a string and a single-bulb drop light illuminated the john in the hall. To the left was an empty room. Through it we came to a six-by-six kitchen adjoining a bedroom furnished with a bed and dresser. Just in case, I looked out the window. We were on the side of a hill; though it was five stories in front, it was only a one-story jump in the rear. I said, "just in case."

A bit weary from the walk and the schnapps, I sat on the edge of the bed. It was like sitting on a manhole cover that was covered with a thin blanket. Greta, in the meantime, had excused herself and I heard running water. Through a crack between door and wall, I could see her preparing for a bath in a tin washtub set in the middle of the floor. Now I really wanted out. Not that the Puritan was rising up in me, but I was a bit on the leery side.

I yelled to the lady of the bath that I must get back to my hotel for the phone call and headed for the door without awaiting her reply. The big iron door was locked and barred. As I returned to the bedroom she emerged from the kitchen attired in a very sheer nightgown. On a clear night I could have seen Naples through it.

Here began the wrestling routine and I'm not in the mood. I like surroundings, not manhole covers for resting places. She thought I was nuts. Maybe I was, but I insisted the phone call was too important. With a slur she said, "Okay, I see you to a cab."

Attired in a skirt and coat over the nightie, bare feet in a pair of shoes, she opened the door. She must have kept her clothes in the small icebox. There wasn't a closet in the place.

As we proceeded down the stone stairs, I thanked her for a pleasant evening and slipped a U.S. bill into her hand, which she gratefully accepted with an apology for not being able to find the book. It proved to have been the come-on.

In the street several cabs passed. She would have none of them. We walked to the Spanish Steps a few blocks away. Arriving there, she went to one of forty taxis parked in a jumble, opened the door of one, goosed me in with an *"a rivederci,"* and the driver was off like a bat out of hell.

The speeding taxi had proceeded about twenty yards when the driver, holding the wheel with his left hand, turned, holding a flashlight in his right. It shone on his face as he started singing at the top of his lungs, "Ave Maria." It was Papa.

With never a look at where the hell he was driving, he kept on singing. BOOM, a high note and he hit a pushcart. Another high note, and BOOM, he hit and scraped the Roman wall. I held on for dear life.

Papa was Greta's outside hustler. He had tipped her off that I was a live one and the evening's activities resulted. I have had wild rides in my time, but that ride back to the Excelsior with Papa singing "Ave Maria" at the top of his voice was the ride of all rides. He never let up.

Arriving at the hotel, I ordered the doorman to pay him off. I had to get to my room. And it wasn't for a phone call.

Sacrilegious as it may seem, every time I now hear "Ave Maria" I see a dame taking a bath in a tin bathtub through a crack in the wall. Gounod, old boy, you didn't write in vain.

Seventeen

*B*EN SMITH, better known as Wall Street Ben, and I were close friends. We kept in contact, either by phone or in person, throughout the world. He had telephonitis. I have sat with the man in his New York office while he placed as many as a dozen phone calls and talked to me at the same time. Not one would be a domestic call—they went to all points of the world.

I was in Paris at the Ritz and received a call from Smith inquiring as to my plans. I never have a schedule in Europe, or anywhere else for that matter. I like to live "ad lib." I advised Smith, who was in New York, that I thought I would hang around Paris for a few days. He said, "Okay, I'll call you tomorrow." He did, but from the next room at the Ritz.

One time he called me from New York, asked where I was going to have dinner. I answered that I had accepted an invitation to a very formal charity affair to be held that night in the main dining room of the Ritz Hotel. It was to be a very elegant affair attended by the elite of Paris. I was to be the guest of some French people I had met in the Philippines.

Smith knew of my "When Day Is Done" and "Ave Maria" habit. The moment I joined my hosts at their assigned, prominent table, the orchestra leader approached and played "When

Day Is Done." To me it was a bit embarrassing, but the Ritz orchestra had done it before when I dined there.

This violinist was really murdering the tune, and I turned. It was not the regular leader. I winced at some of his chords, as did my hosts.

When the musician had finished his musical crime, he asked, "Was eet not beautiful, Monsieur?"

I turned on the guy, sore as hell. "I have a drunken uncle in Ireland who could play it better with a pick and shovel."

BOOM! The violinist belted me over the head with his instrument, and it flew into a thousand bits all over the place. The man ran out of the room. I was too stunned to follow.

The regular leader now made his appearance. It seems that my friend Smith, a privileged character at the Ritz, had arranged through a Montmartre contact to have the comedy violinist do the "When Day Is Done" job on me. I felt the top of my head for a lump. There was none. The comic had placed his hand there first and hit his hand with the instrument—a special breakaway.

Never a dull moment.

Eighteen

*A*T MGM we had people we called "chintzie." A "chintz" is someone who is very close with a buck. The stingiest man I have ever known was Wally Beery. I handled the charity drives at the studio for many years and know movie people to be the most charitable in the world, always ready to give of their time and money for worthy causes. From Beery, I couldn't get the rinse water from one of his old sweat shirts. This guy was really a "chintz."

Beery received a salary of $7,500 a week, fifty-two weeks in the year. I approached him for contributions to the Community Chest, Red Cross, or other worthy charities. His answer: "I buy government bonds, these bonds are supposed to take care of the needy." Where the hell he got that reasoning I'll never know.

In contrast to Beery, I'll cite Lew Ayres. This young man was paid $1,500 a week for forty weeks out of the fifty-two, and time after time I received his whole salary check in response to a charity request. Not only did he turn his salary check over to the Red Cross during during the war, but he conducted first-aid classes far into the night after a long day in the "Dr. Kildare" series. This man Ayres is a helluva man in my book.

We had occasion to cheer a Beery mishap at the studio that cost him a hunk.

He was driving down Washington Boulevard in Culver City one eve, and picked up a girl. They drove up into the Hollywood Hills for a look at the scenery and some stuff and nonsense.

The stuff and nonsense and the scenery behind them, the very liberal Mr. Beery gave the gal an autographed picture he just happened to have with him, took her back to the spot where he picked her up, then proceeded home to rest up.

Removing his clothing for retirement, old Wally Goodheart discovered that the pickup dame had picked his pocket and her take was $3,500. Wow, did we cheer when we heard it. We knew of his penchant for displaying large bankrolls to dames.

We wanted to blow the siren at the studio that night; we couldn't because it was out of order, but we did give three lusty cheers for that gal.

Nineteen

THE STORY of Gina Malo—née Jennie Flynn—will be recorded in Broadway theater history as one of the best promotion stunts of the era.

Bobby Connolly's production of *Sons O'Guns*, for which we had so much difficulty getting financing, was one of New York's big musical hits. It starred Jack Donahue and Lili Damita, of Sam Goldwyn film fame. I was her agent.

Though the temperamental Lili had a run-of-the-show contract, she tired of the routine sameness and delivered an ultimatum. "More money or else." The "or else" being she would leave the show if the raise was not forthcoming. No amount of persuasion on my part could get La Belle France to change her mind. The ultimatum stood at "or else." Connolly was not a man to have an "or else" thrown at him. When I told him about his star's decision, he used an expression of mine in answer, "So she died last night."

There had to be an immediate replacement, but whom?

Two years before I had, as agent, booked an Albertina Rasch Ballet of nineteen beautiful girls to appear at Les Ambassadeurs' Restaurant Cabaret in Paris. This was the most important nightclub in all Europe. Accompanying the ballet was a group of twenty-two statuesque showgirls, the pick of America.

Les Ambassadeurs was the gathering place of the world's elite. An oddity: 60 percent of all the gals I sent over, including the ballet, remained in Paris. Some to further theatrical pursuits, others to make marriages to important world personages, mostly from South America.

My group of beauties was booked to sail on the French Line S.S. *Paris*. I went to the pier to see them off. There was a twelve-hour delay in sailing because of mechanical trouble, and all hands had a get-acquainted "run of the boat."

To help pass the time of delay in the sailing, impromptu entertainment by the pros aboard was in order—as audience, the passengers and crew. One Rasch girl named Jennie Flynn, of the Cincinnati brick-laying Flynns, was the star and charmer of all assembled.

Jennie was a bouncy, personable, good-looking youngster, her flashing black eyes coupled with a wonderful smile. She was a natural mimic, and after listening to the Paris boat staff, she became a pretty convincing French lady. A smattering of high school French helped considerably. Jennie Flynn was the darling of the voyage.

The season at Les Ambassadeurs was a particularly successful one for all concerned. At its end, some did the marriage routine. Others stayed on in Paris for work, among them Jennie Flynn.

As Connolly and I mulled over our Damita dilemma, Jennie Flynn's name flashed through my mind. I knew that her life in Paris had been a busy one doing French plays and movies. At the moment Connolly and I were wondering about a replacement, I knew that Jennie was starring in a French version of an American musical, *Follow Thru*. I told Connolly what I knew about Jennie Flynn.

Bobby asked late returnees from Paris if they had seen *Follow Thru*, and whether they liked the star, Jennie Flynn. Not one dissenting opinion. All were loud in their praises of her. Connolly did not say what he had in mind for La Flynn, but the information garnered was all he needed.

A call was placed to Paris. We wanted to talk to Connolly's partner, Arthur Swanstrom, who was vacationing in Paris.

Through his hotel, we traced him to a little bistro on the Left Bank.

Connolly and I took turns explaining to Swanstrom Damita's "or else" and the extreme, quick need for a replacement. We asked him if he could locate Jennie Flynn, talk with her, and call us back. Swanstrom let us talk about $50 worth of phone conversation before he let out with a laugh. Lo and behold, Jennie Flynn was his dinner companion at that very moment. Will wonders never cease!

Swanstrom was enthusiastic about La Flynn as replacement for Damita, but there were complications—the gal who played the Damita role must be a bona fide French girl. The name Jennie Flynn was a far cry from suggesting that. It would have to be changed.

While Connolly and I sat in my office awaiting the location of Swanstrom in Paris, we did a bit of thinking and made plans. If they came off they would be sensational.

Back at his hotel, Swanstrom called Bobby and me. I talked with Jennie. Would she like to come to New York and replace Damita? She agreed, since *Follow Thru*, her French production, had just closed and she was footloose and fancy free. I further asked Jennie whether she would place herself in our hands for anything we felt might promote her, even to changing her name. Jennie was a real trouper; she agreed to go through with anything we might suggest.

Number one: a new name. On the portable bar in my office was a gin bottle. To the word "gin," Connolly added an "a." We had a first name, Gina. Swanstrom, in Paris, was smoking Melo cigarettes. Another added "a" and we had a second name, Malo. Damita's replacement would be the French star "Gina Malo." So far, so good.

Our plans were outlined further. Gina Malo, as a French star, from that moment on could not speak one word of English. She would have to disappear from her usual Paris haunts until she sailed for the States. Swanstrom was advised to outfit Gina Malo, née La Flynn, in the latest Paris fashion, the sky the limit. Upon completion of the wardrobe, take the first available boat to the United States. Above all, no English from Malo.

Connolly and I released to the press the news that the great French star, Gina Malo, was leaving her beloved Paris to come to New York and replace Damita. Columnists and reporters wanted to know, "Who the hell is Malo?" They had contacted their Paris office and nobody there had ever heard of her. The same question was repeated, "Who is she?"

The mystery of it all gave us wonderful advance publicity. People were talking. Our plans were bearing fruit.

The great Gina Malo arrived on the S.S. *Bremen*. Every available French-speaking newsman was at the pier to meet the mysterious importation. The regular steamship reporters went out on the pilot boat and boarded the *Bremen* down the harbor. There were many international celebs aboard, but the press was interested only in the mysterious French star, Gina Malo.

Connolly and I were proud of our Jennie. She did not utter a word of English the whole voyage. The press came, they saw, and she conquered. They were loud in their praises of this wonderful girl, but to a man they all said, "She is wonderful, but she'll never learn English in time to open in the play *Sons O'Guns*."

A large suite at New York's Savoy Plaza Hotel was engaged for Mlle Malo. Here she held court for more newsmen and celebs at a cocktail party. Again she captivated all present.

The reception was at its height when the guest of honor took my arm and whispered in my ear, "Please, for the love of the good Lord, let's hide somewhere and talk good old United States. I'm going out of my mind as that French dame."

A large bedroom closet was our hiding place. Jennie Flynn and her agent friend sat on the floor and "cut up a touch." The masquerade was taking its toll. There were a few doubters, but even they could not be sure. Most of the assembled guests were admirers due to the magnificent job our Jennie was doing.

In the closet a few new stories she hadn't heard, and in turn she, an excellent storyteller herself, relayed a few I hadn't heard before. The closet session eased the tension, and she joined the assembled guests again as Gina Malo.

Bobby's and my plans continued. She must keep up with the no English routine. She could only be seen in public with Connolly, Swanstrom, or myself.

We had a close call. One of Jennie Flynn's old admirers saw us in Dinty Moore's. The admirer was sure and then again he wasn't. Gina Malo nearly flipped. She liked the guy and had a helluva time convincing him in broken English, but convince him she did to a degree. The young man apologized for his familiar approach, but he left our table shaking his head. He was still not fully convinced.

My French, as interpreter, was something to hear, but the young man didn't know French from Hindustani. I was on safe ground and got away with it.

I took Gina to meet Mr. Broadway himself, George M. Cohan. George was appearing in a play and we went to his dressing room for our visit. As usual, his pal and constant companion was with him—Steve Reardon, a retired New York police captain. Steve had an Irish brogue that was like lilting music. I loved to hear him talk. After a few moments of conversation Steve said, "You're charming enough to be an Irish colleen. Could you have any Irish blood in you?"

The Jennie Flynn nearly came out of Gina Malo in reply to Steve's question. Gina answered with something that sounded like "maybe" and Steve was pleased, though he took me by the arm to the corridor outside George M.'s dressing room.

"Grady, you and Connolly must be daft. This child will never make it. You're unfair to expect this child to speak English enough to open in so short a time." To this George M. concurred.

I advised them both that Gina was constantly being tutored in English and that her English-speaking French director would arrive the following day to direct her in *Sons O'Guns*. George M. had his doubts and repeated that he thought we were being unfair to the girl.

Well, we got away with it, and I figured that if we could fool the astute George M. we were a success. He was completely enmeshed in her charm, though he pleaded for the delay in her debut so she'd have a better chance.

"If she's a flop, and she might be, you and Connolly will be a laughing stock, and deservedly so. Please think it over."

Well, to make a long story longer, Gina Malo, née Jennie Flynn, of the Cincinnati brick-laying Flynns opened in *Sons O'Guns*. To put it mildly, she was wonderful and acclaimed. The critics and public were loud in their praises of the little "French charmer" who overcame great obstacles to open as a replacement for Damita.

When news that Damita was leaving the cast got around,

future ticket holdings were canceled and business dropped down to $26,000 weekly. With the notices on Gina Malo, business was upped to $38,000, and poor Jennie continued her French masquerade. She did meet some of her old friends but swore them to secrecy, and I must say they respected the request and were loyal to her.

There was one major difficulty. Jennie used to phone her parents in Cincinnati. The hotel operator heard the flow of excellent English from the French star. I put the operator on the payroll.

Some weeks passed, the deception still working. Business dropped a bit, and to improve it, we broke the story of Jennie Flynn and Gina Malo. The story of the masquerade made the front page and again business was on the rise.

I'm kind o' proud of the Jennie Flynn achievement. Events like it make the wonderful world of show business the glamour business that it is.

Jennie Flynn, of the Cincinnati brick-laying Flynns, kept the Gina Malo name. She married a very prominent English playwright-actor and moved to London, where she starred in pictures and the theater. Hers is a very happy life. Though I haven't heard from or seen her in years I still say, "Long live Jennie Flynn of the Cincinnati brick-laying Flynns."

Twenty

*A*ND THEN there was the time . . .

C. D. Dillingham had a Fred Stone show ready for its out-of-town tryout. Buffalo had been selected and special cars attached to a New York Central westbound train for the trip. Every conceivable inch of space on the entire train was occupied. I had a drawing room in the regular section.

Arthur Houghton, company manager for Dillingham, came to me in Grand Central Station while we were waiting to depart. He had a friend whose name I did not catch, and it was most important for that friend to be in Buffalo the next morning. Inasmuch as I had a sole-occupant drawing room, could his friend share the room with me for the trip west?

Arthur was a good friend of mine and I agreed to share the room; after giving him the number of my space, I proceeded to board the train for a good night's sleep.

About an hour after departure, and I well-blanketed, my sleep was aroused by the creaking of the drawing room door. In the dimly lighted room I watched Houghton's friend disrobe.

Meticulously he draped his trousers and coat on the hanger.

His shirt and tie were carefully folded on the side couch. Not one word passed between us, nor was there any sign of recognition.

I was about to turn over and go back to sleep when I saw my room sharer remove his undershirt. Draped around his neck were several strands of pearls. What the hell was I in for? Was this guy a female impersonator or a jewel thief? I quickly snapped on the lights.

Standing there bejeweled was Jules Glaenzer, vice president of Cartier's, the famous jewelers, on his way to Buffalo to display the pearls to a wealthy dowager.

All right, what would you think if you were roused from a sound sleep and saw a naked stranger bedecked in strands of pearls standing near you in a dimly lighted room?

The incident could have been serious, but it was good for laughs.

The Queen didn't have a very good "Knight"—Painting by artist John Decker

Ben Blue—still going strong

A funny, inventive man

W. C. and the "Bobsey twins"

Gene Fowler, David Chasen, W. C. Fields, Wall Street Ben Smith

The first one and only Mr. Broadway—Mr. Yankee Doodle Dandy

Billy Grady, Jimmie Stewart, Sam Levene, and Sidney Skolsky (columnist)

A "happy times" group

Jimmie and Gloria Stewart, David and Maude Chasen

The Jimmie Stewarts

To Bill
Our friend —
Slats
and
Sadie

Mr. and Mrs. Al Jolson

Al Jolson

Marilyn Monroe

Elizabeth Taylor

Van Johnson

Donna Reed

Lillian Russell

Wallace Beery

John Barrymore

Red Skelton, Rags Ragland, and George Murphy "hamming it up"

Will Rogers and Walter Winchell

Dan Dailey

A boy who left the swamps for the first time to audition for *The Yearling*

Judy Garland

Maurice Chevalier

Kathryn Grayson and John Carroll

Howard Keel

Billy Grady was presented with a silver tray by the MGM roster of players

Bill Powell and other guests

Jimmie Stewart, Hank Fonda, Billy Grady, Bill Powell, Spencer Tracy, and Mickey Rooney

Eleanor Powell, Spencer Tracy, Billy Grady, Ruth Hussey, and Jimmie Stewart

Hank Fonda, Rags Ragland, Jimmie Stewart, and the author

Long live the "King"

Ruth Hussey and the "boss"

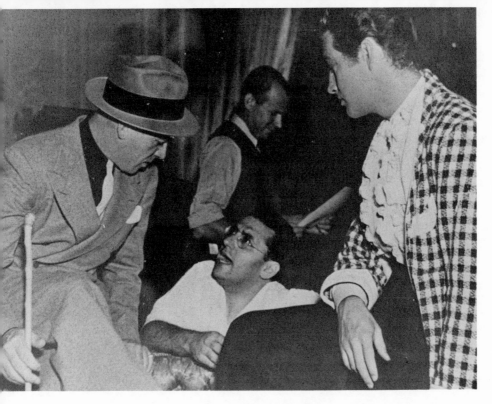

The author, George Cukor, and Robert Taylor discussing a scene in *Camille* with Greta Garbo. Eddie Waller, unit manager, in background

Billy Grady and Luise Rainer

Billy Grady and Mervyn Leroy

Spencer Tracy, Eddie Mannix, Clark Gable, Carole Lombard, and Billy Grady

Billy Grady, Louise Tracy, and Spencer Tracy

Billy Grady and Gloria Grahame

The late Sam Wood, Billy Grady, and the "King"

Robert Taylor and Billy Grady

Norma Shearer, her husband, Irving Thalberg, and Billy Grady on their way to San Francisco to see the Marx Brothers' vaudeville show

Billy Grady and Ingrid Bergman

Frank Sinatra and Billy Grady

John Carroll

Greer Garson

David Chasen

Rock Hudson

Eddie Mannix, Rags Ragland, and Billy Grady

Charles Ruggles

Senator George Murphy and Lassie

Joan Crawford

Greta Garbo

Myrna Loy

Jean Harlow

Walter Pidgeon

Rosalind Russell and Brian Aherne

Donna Reed and Mickey Rooney

Robert Taylor and his "boss"

Lew Ayres

High in my regard—Cary Grant

Twenty-One

*D*URING the Roaring Twenties and the Prohibition era, one of the more successful nightclub-cabaret operations in Manhattan was the Silver Slipper, located under the Chelsea All-Night Bank at 48th Street and Broadway. I was part of the management and it will always be an unforgettable experience for me.

A well-liked group of bootleggers and racket boys, whose domain lay between 34th and 59th streets, were nightly patrons of various Broadway cabarets. Proceeds from their illicit operations kept rolling in and they were very free spenders.

Suddenly it dawned on one of them, Hawkeye Horowitz, that the money the group was spending nightly would be enough to open their own spot. A meeting was held and plans put into operation.

The group consisted of the aforementioned Hawkeye. Then came Bill Duffy. Bill was a recent parolee from Dannemora Prison. He had finished a rap for manslaughter. His sidelines were managing fighters and bootlegging . . . Next came Frankie Marlowe, a Boston Italian, track bookie and fight manager. Frank, some years later, was reported to have been ambushed and slain in an Italian restaurant. Seems he ran out on a wager

... A client of Frank's, Johnny Wilson, ex-middleweight champion, had a small interest. A mysterious but well-known Broadway character with the euphonious name of Pete the Goat was also in the combine. Pete's line was the checkroom concession in various night spots. It was Pete's deposit of $20,000 for the Silver Slipper's checkroom privilege that got the venture off the ground ... Two very well-liked guys, representing the Owney Madden interests, were next—Johnny "Irish" Costello and his pal, Tommy O'Neil. Johnny and Tommy were called the Twins —they were always together. Johnny Irish was also Ruby Keeler's constant escort. It was rumored that they were engaged.

Owney Madden, who operated several breweries and was one of the most powerful men in the East, underwrote the Slipper operation. A quiet, unassuming man, Owney was seldom seen. Though his operations were agin the law, he was well liked on both sides of the fence.

Hawkeye found the location for the Slipper and supervised all the preparations. He wanted a headline-star attraction to open the Slipper. He approached my star-team, Van and Schenck, stars of the Ziegfeld Follies and vaudeville headliners. Gus Van told Hawkeye I did all the Van and Schenck business.

After several meetings, Gus Van and Joe Schenck consented to appear nightly and were given 50 percent of the profits. I was to be the headman, representing both sides, for which I was given a percentage.

The group mentioned above was not in great favor with the police licensing bureau. There had to be a front man to obtain a license to operate. Joe Schenck was elected, the license granted. We were off and running on New Year's Eve.

The opening was hectic. At 9:30 in the evening carpenters were still laying the dance floor. Draperies were being fireproofed, with Fire Department supervision. Tables and chairs were being installed with patrons standing four deep waiting to be seated.

Notice of the Silver Slipper opening had been sent to the heads of all bootlegging combinations from Chicago to the East Coast. Their response was typical of gangs who work together.

The tab was $25 a head for the opening. Capone sent an emissary with cash for 200 tickets ... The Cleveland mob bought 150 . . . Atlantic City and Philadelphia came through with an order for 150 . . . New Jersey, Boston, Brooklyn, and Long Island factions 50 each. Over $15,000 in the till before the opening. The Madden breweries would favor all contributors when it came to supplying beer.

As the last nail was being driven into the dance floor, Hawkeye called me aside and introduced a white-haired, pink-cheeked old gentleman named Bill Brady. Brady was there to collect the "ice," as the payoff to New York higher-ups was called. The payoff amounted to $500 every two weeks, this in return for information and warnings as to when a raid would take place. The raids would be token and all we had to do was to move "wet goods" through a wall to a room in another building. The raiders would report to their superiors that the Slipper was clean . . . Brady's info applied only to New York's Prohibition forces, not Internal Revenue men, who were known as feds. Fed men could not be reached. We took our chances on that score.

The Slipper sold champagne to patrons at $35 a serving. The wine was served in water pitchers. Each pitcher also contained a slice of pineapple, a slice of orange, and a lemon peel. Any waiter who did not return these slices was discharged. They were made of celluloid and hard to get.

Naturally patrons were told the champagne was imported. It was . . . from Vermont and New Hampshire. It consisted of New Hampshire hard cider with a spoonful of Vermont maple syrup. If sweet wine was ordered, two spoons of the syrup; dry wine, one spoon. Three glasses of the stuff and you'd throw rocks at your mother, but the customers went for it. One Wall Street broker had taxicabs at the door, and with Western Union messengers, wine was delivered to all his friends around town.

Our imported champagne cost the house about 66¢ a pitcher, exclusive of the fruit slices. At $35 a copy, wouldn't you say it was a tidy profit? The Scotch we served was the real McCoy, delivered off a boat at Montauk Point, Long Island, a week before. It had been cut before delivery, but it was Scotch whiskey. Oh, the heads that must have needed major remedies the next morning!

So help me, when we counted up the first night's revenue, which included gang contributions, it was just $200 short of

$34,000. Think of it! One night's receipts in a joint seating 250 people. Some ball parks today would like to equal it.

For me, being the headman was a grind. I kept up my agency business throughout the day, left at 7:00 P.M. to bathe and change into the monkey suit, and then went to the Slipper. I was averaging four hours' sleep a night and my long hours awake were beginning to take their toll in health.

Van and Schenck, after the seventeenth week, took a hiatus and accepted some vaudeville dates. Ruby Keeler and a line of girls were now the attraction, and business continued to be the best in town.

We had an ex-heavyweight fighter as a doorman. His name —Sailor Grande. The Sailor rushed up to me one Friday night. I was alone in the place, the partners had gone to Madison Square Garden to see one of Marlowe's fighters. The Sailor told me that the Palais Royale, one of Broadway's plusher dance clubs, was being raided. The Palais was a showplace and Paul Whiteman and his orchestra was the attraction. It was a federal raid and I got a sneaking idea that the Slipper would be next.

I went to my office in the Palace Theater Building and called Van and Schenck in Washington. I advised them of the Palais raid and my thoughts about the Slipper being next. We should get OUT. The boys agreed and told me to make the best deal I could.

The fights at the Garden were over, and Hawkeye, Duffy, and the Goat drove up with Frankie Marlowe. He was driving a beautiful new Lincoln coupe, just delivered that day. I called a meeting downstairs.

Seated around a big table, I told them of our desire to get out of the Slipper. Nineteen weeks and I was dead on my feet. Van and Schenck had ten weeks to go on their present vaudeville tour, and were not too anxious to participate further in the Slipper operation, though their 50 percent was still a deal.

Billy Brady came in for his biweekly ice and I left the table so the boys could talk matters over. When I returned, Duffy asked me what I wanted for our end. Remembering Van and Schenck's advice, "Get what you can," I said to Bill, "ten thousand and Frankie Marlowe's Lincoln coupe at the door."

Instantly, hands went into pockets and bundles of money were on the table. Duffy, on my right, was fastest on the draw.

I chose his roll. He counted out $6,000, Hawkeye and Pete con-
tributed the balance. Marlowe produced the ownership tab for
the car. A trip to my office in the Palace a block away to sign
papers for the transfer of the car, and a bill of sale for the
Slipper. Inasmuch as no papers were signed when we made the
deal, it was a handshake all around. I had to have the bill of sale
to get Joe Schenck's name off the license.

On the way back to the Slipper, I deposited the $10,000 in the
all-night Chelsea Bank. We gathered around a table downstairs
to celebrate the deal over a bottle of surefire champagne.

As we started on the second bottle, five men came down the
stairs and announced, "We are federal officers. No one move.
This is a raid." I nearly became ill.

Pete the Goat, to my left, pulled a knife, switched open the
blade, and stuck the point through my coat, pricking the skin.
My right hand, on Duffy's side, went to my coat pocket. I had
reached for my rosary, which I always carried. Pete the Goat's
knife, in my side, was hurting.

Duffy grabbed my hand and pulled it to the table. The rosary
had been caught in the crook of a finger.

"Take that shiv away, Pete. This lucky Mick is on the level."
Pete had shifty eyes that haunted you. I will never, to my dying
day, forget that look. I am sure he believed that I was in on the
whole thing, with the feds.

"Thanks, Bill," I said. "It was just shanty Irish luck. I talked
with my doctor today and he warned me that unless I got some
rest I was a dead pigeon. I'll go upstairs to the bank and get the
ten thousand and here, Frankie, here are the papers on the
car."

"Wait a minute. What was the deal we made with you when
you and Gus and Joe came in with us?" asked Duffy.

"Fifty percent of the operation," I replied.

"That still goes. We made a deal. That still goes. Pete wouldn't
trust his mother. Forget him. Let's have another drink."

The federal men came to the table. Hawkeye accepted the
papers. In court several days later it was ordered that the Slipper be padlocked for three months. It reopened, but it was never
again the success it had been.

Did ya ever hear that expression: "Honor among thieves"?

Twenty-Two

*T*HE Roaring Twenties were days of almost unbelievable happenings. The power of money and how it corrupted, even in high places, is almost beyond belief. If some of those happenings were incorporated in a motion picture, it would be said that they were the product of a warped mind.

I recall the unbelievable.

A phone message was delivered to me one night as I entered the Silver Slipper. A Mr. Max Greenberg had called—would I please return the call. When I reached Mr. Greenberg I was invited (????) to come to his office in the Fitzgerald Building on Broadway and 42nd Street. I was to be there the following Saturday at midnight.

I had heard of Greenberg as a sort of overlord of the New York rackets, and a bootlegger on a giant scale. The territory he controlled was everything east of Chicago. Al Capone and his mob had Chicago and everything west, with an inroad in Cleveland.

My only interest was the Silver Slipper, and being curious about the invite by Greenberg, I asked Bill Duffy and Hawkeye, my Slipper partners, about it. Both men echoed: "Invitation, my eye, that's an order. We got it too. We'll be there." The three of us represented the Silver Slipper.

Greenberg was a well-tailored, heavyset man, soft-spoken with a relaxed approach. His searching dark eyes fascinated me. In a luxuriously appointed office overlooking Broadway was a jam-packed representation of cabaret owners operating in the Broadway district. We awaited Greenberg's convenience and the reason for our presence. It wasn't long in coming.

Some of Greenberg's hoodlum henchmen had been collared by the law for major crimes. The majority were two- and three-time losers, and were in for long stretches. The usual prison for felony prisoners was either Dannemora, called the Rock by inmates, and Sing Sing, the well-known prison on the Hudson. Dannemora was, and still is, a maximum security prison for the dangerous and habitual criminal. Sing Sing for death row and the less dangerous.

There was also Comstock Prison Farm. This was for short-termers and favored prisoners. Greenberg's men, all hardened felons, were at Comstock. How they got into Comstock, being the type they were, is beyond me. Someone got to someone.

The reason for the meeting??? Greenberg wanted to give his boys at Comstock a Christmas present. It was to be in the form of entertainment by New York cabaret stars. We of the night-club set had to supply it. Greenberg smiled throughout his speech. One would think he was pleading for a charity benefit for an orphanage. The big man had spoken, the big man knew his orders would be carried out.

The penalty for not cooperating? Quite by accident your storehouse of liquor would be stumbled upon by unknowns, and the contents taken away. A fight might break out in your club on a very busy Saturday night. The police would be called, customers would run out without paying their checks. There would be wholesale damage to your club furnishings. Under the circumstances, if you wanted to stay in business, it was best to cooperate. Besides, Duffy and Hawkeye were personal friends of Greenberg's, and many of the boys to be entertained were their bosom pals. Small world.

Representing the Silver Slipper, I furnished the orchestra and our stars, Van and Schenck. Our place of assembly on the appointed night was Grand Central Station, Sunday at 1:00 A.M. On Track 19, a special train of eighteen sleeping cars, plus two well-stocked dining cars, was waiting to take us to Comstock.

There was a baggage car for band equipment and some acrobatic apparatus. I went forward to check its delivery.

Immediately behind the engine were four drawing-room sleeping cars. The curtains were drawn and husky Greenberg hoodlums were guarding each door. Mysterious??? It was to me, and no amount of questioning brought an answer. There was much speculation, but any guess was far from the surprise we were to get upon arrival at Comstock in the morning.

A night of card games and dice, plus viands of the highest quality served in the two diners. It was a journey with a holiday atmosphere.

We arrived at Comstock at 8:00 A.M. On the station platform was a welcoming committee of well-dressed prison inmates, evidently trusties. They were immaculate in flannel shirts, trousers of gray material, recently barbered hair, and close shaves. Lilac shave lotion was very evident.

Big Max and his immediate staff were first to get the embraced greetings of the prisoners present. They were Greenberg's men. Their pals, and there were many among the travelers, were next to be greeted. The four sleeping cars with the drawn curtains showed no signs of life. The guards had not made an appearance.

We boarded the buses for the trip up the hill to the prison without our curiosity being satisfied. As our bus turned, we all looked back. The gray flannel men were making a beeline for the four drawing-room cars, and disappeared inside.

It seems Mr. Greenberg thought of everything. Those drawing room cars were occupied by eighteen members of a notorious New York brothel. Each was to be paid $150 for her weekend labors. Their madam received a bonus for services rendered.

While the prison show was in progress there was a constant stream of favored prisoners going down the hill to the Pullman cars. At the prison we were served a late buffet supper in the dining hall. I thought eight o'clock rather unusual, but there was a reason. Some of the boys hadn't been serviced at the railroad station.

So ends the tale of an unusual happening, one of the hardly believable happenings of the period. Is it surprising that these years were called the Roaring Twenties? Money could and did

corrupt a lot of people. There was a behind-closed-doors investigation of the Comstock affair and many heads rolled and got
the heave-ho. The Department of Prisons kept it very hush-
hush. If it ever got into the newspapers there would have been
a major scandal that would have given the administration a
black eye. You think mobs and hoodlums do not have influence? Ho Ho Ho and a Ho Ho!

Twenty-Three

*I*N MY humble opinion, one of the great restaurants of our time is Dinty Moore's on West 46th Street, New York City. This restaurant has been in existence more than fifty years. I can remember its start.

Jim Moore was a fish and vegetable huckster on the West Side. His store was a horse and wagon, his route Eighth to Eleventh avenues, 38th Street to 59th. Jim and his wife Mary conceived the idea of a corned beef and cabbage restaurant-bar, and found a location, a brownstone house on 46th Street just off Broadway. The George McManus cartoon "Bringing Up Father" was later to give the place national fame.

With a bartender-partner named Murphy, Dinty Moore's opened for business. Jim supervised the food and Murphy took care of the bar. From the very beginning, the partners fought like two cats. Murph was a disappointed actor and liked having actors around the bar even if they were freeloaders. Jim despised them, and thought that Murphy was giving too many free drinks to his friends. There was a knock-'em-drag-'em-out battle, and the partnership came to an end. Moore dug up money enough to buy Murphy out. He was on his own.

At first it was a tough struggle for Jim. The restaurant was a small place with a low overhead, but customers just didn't seem to come in. There were a few of us who were regulars, but not enough to insure payments and take care of Mary and the four kids. Jim started thinking.

I doubt that Jim Moore was ever in a theater. He had read in the papers about this and that star, but never met one. There was one star that everybody talked about, Mr. Broadway himself, George M. Cohan. "Jeez," thought Jim, "if I could only get that guy in for a customer!"

Jim tried ways and means of all kinds to lure Cohan, but he didn't show up. It became an obsession with him. Lots of beer-drinking actors, but no Cohan.

One of the hangers-on at Moore's bar was an important dramatic actor named Barry. Moore's was his second home. Managers, agents, and writers contacted him there. Barry, unfortunately, was loudmouthed when in his cups, which was often. Moore warned him time and again, "Quiet, actor, or out you go."

One day Barry really got out of hand. Moore threw him out bodily and threatened to punch him in the nose if he ever entered the place again. This was the ultimate in disgrace for the very important Barry—to be thrown out of Moore's. "I am a great man in the theatuh," he said. He had to get back in Jim's good graces—but how?

A brain flash. George M. Cohan. Barry knew about Jim's hopes that Cohan would become a patron. Barry was appearing in a play at the Cohan Theater on West 43rd Street, so he paid George a visit.

"Hiya, George, old boy," was Barry's greeting.

"It's about time you showed up," said George. "Where you hanging out these days?"

Barry proceeded to tell George about the gang's new hangout, a restaurant and bar run by a good Irishman named Jim Moore. (By the way, Moore was not Irish, but in all the years I knew him he neither denied nor affirmed the fact.)

It so happened that Cohan was a good corned beef and cabbage man, as well as a top Irisher. Barry was told to come to the theater after the performance. He and Cohan would then go to Moore's.

In high glee, Barry was at the Cohan Theater promptly at

11:45. He and George went to Moore's. Twelve midnight, Barry proudly walked into Moore's, followed by the great George M. Cohan. Moore took one look at Barry.

"Hey, actor—I threw you outa here this afternoon and I meant what I said. Now get out, stay out and take that son of a bitch with you." He pointed to Cohan.

Jim had waited for Cohan for years. When he showed up, he threw him out. The incident did the rounds on Broadway and Moore's gained importance; the restaurant was on its way to success. Jim and George became great friends, but Moore, stubborn as a mule, would never allow Barry in the place again.

Dinty Moore's became the favorite restaurant for the Broadway crowd, as well as others. The food was the best. Jim Moore's supervision bordered on the fanatical. Complain once about the food and you were never welcome in there again. For years he never allowed catsup on the table—it spoiled his food. He never served water. "What d'ya think I got beer for? If you want water, eat home," and he meant it.

During Prohibition, Jim sold openly. He was raided and arrested many times. When there was a raid, Jim would be closed long enough to appear in court. Jim would pay his fine, return, and open up again. Oftentimes the very judge who fined him would be in that night for his schnapps.

Moore never, in all his career, sold any inferior liquor. Other bars and speakeasies around New York were selling rotgut and getting top prices behind locked doors. Jim's doors were always open, except when he was in court.

The rule at Moore's was cash, and I mean cash. Nobody had an account. The waiters paid for the food as they took it from the kitchen. They paid the cashier, a midget named "Bluey" Rice. Bluey stood on a beer keg in order to reach the register. Little Bluey liked to tipple, and was always sneaking drinks. When Jim caught him he'd take him by the seat of the pants and slide him along the bar much as you would a beer glass. Bluey would be through for the night, but back the next day. He was a good-luck charm to Jim.

Jim had a few "hates." One in particular he called "Women-men." He'd insult them loud and lustily, then throw them out. One day a woman-man came in for dinner. He sat near the bar and front door. Across the table sat a little fox terrier. Jim got one look. "Get oudda here, but quick. I'll feed the dog, but you —OUT!" Moore went to the icebox, cut up a hunk of steak, ground it, cooked it, and the dog had his dinner, while his woman-man owner stood on the sidewalk and watched.

Jim had a son, Willie, and three daughters. Willie, at a very young age, preferred dancing for silver cups in night clubs that held contests. He would rather do that than help Jim in the restaurant. Willie was the apple of his mother's eye, and because of that he got away with murder. It caused a rift in the Moore family that was to last until Jim's death.

Jim's ally was his daughter Anna. They were pals. They were opposed by Mrs. Moore, and the other daughters, Cora and Mary. Willie was neutral. Anna ran Moore's subsequently just as her father did. Same menu and the same wonderful food, the same atmosphere.

Motion pictures were making inroads into the theater business, the use of actors was diminishing. Many of us on the street —Broadway—were short of cash.

A pal of mine, Bobby Connolly, had a play, *Sons O'Guns*, that needed financing for production. He needed an angel and came to me for help in finding one. I had heard of a salvage dealer in Newark, New Jersey, who was interested in the theater as an investment. I contacted him. The interest was still there and he wanted to read the script. I sent it to him.

While our angel was reading the *Sons O'Guns* script, I did a little research. The salvage dealer had the money, but he was dame crazy. He figured being connected with a musical play might help him with the ladies.

Anticipating a meeting with our angel, Bobby and I hired three beautiful showgirls to grace our luncheon table when we met with the man from Newark.

Now Bobby and I really had the shorts. We'd have to have lunch where we could sign the tab, but where? I tried Jim Moore. To hear him, you'd think I'd asked for his left leg. He all but threw me out. I made a pitiful pitch, you know: "Pal, my chance to make a killing. Do it for a guy who loves you," etc. After quite some pleading, Jim relented, but only on the condition I have the money back the next day.

Our angel, the salvage man, showed up at Moore's for the luncheon meeting. He was the original Mister Five-by-Five.

Five feet wide and five feet tall. He wore a pongee suit, a yellow tie, and a Panama hat turned brim-up in front. As I shook hands with him I found he had a case of halitosis that would be noticed at forty paces.

When we were sitting at the table, the girls kept trying to edge away from the guy. As they edged, either Bobby or I would push them back. The guy had very busy hands under the table.

Our man liked the script and inquired how much we thought it would take to produce. Connolly supplied the information—$125,000. To our amazement Mister Five-By-Five said, "Why don't you take $150,000 and be sure?"

Our man no sooner had the $150,000 amount out of his mouth when Connolly excused himself, went to a wall telephone, and called a second-hand automobile dealer on 53rd Street. He ordered the Isotta Frachini car he had seen in the window on the way to the luncheon.

I called Earl Benham, the town's top tailor, when Bobby returned to the table. I ordered five suits. Benham was told to send his tailor to my office for measurements. I was much too busy to go the four blocks to see him.

With preluncheon drinks and snacks, we were into Moore for over $50. Nothing but the best for Connolly and myself, and we were feeling no pain. Mister Five-By-Five was in his glory— surrounded by beautiful girls and important theatrical people, of whom he would soon be one. The next table was occupied by the famous Hearst columnist, Damon Runyon.

I was the last at the table to order my lunch. Moore's was famous for its corned beef hash, a little peasanty, perhaps, but that was what I wanted and I so ordered, stressing no onions. I didn't know what the afternoon would bring forth, and anyway I didn't like onions.

Jim Moore, up to this moment, had not made an appearance. Out of the blue, he came down from his upstairs apartment and inspected our prelunch tab. He was furious. Going to the kitchen to see what we had ordered for lunch, he noted my hash in the pan and without the onions. He roared at the chef:

"Where's the onions in the corned beef hash?"

Pete, the Greek chef, answered, "Grady no like onions in his hash."

"He don't, huh?" growled Moore and hurried to our table.

"Hey, Grady, what are you trying to do—put my place on the bum?" and he gave me a belt on the back of the head that nearly threw me off the chair.

"What's the matter, Jim?"

"Where's the onions in that corned beef hash?" he yelled menacingly.

"I don't like onions, Jim."

"You don't, huh? Well, get the hell out of here and go over to the Automat where you belong." He threw us all out bodily.

The salvage man was so insulted and humiliated, and in front of the beautiful girls and Broadway celebs no less, that he called a cab and left us flat on the sidewalk. Neither Connolly nor I ever saw him again.

Runyon had a very funny column in the paper the next day. Again Moore's was the talk of New York. I was barred for over a year.

If you were one of Jim Moore's privileged, you were allowed to eat in his open kitchen. It looked out over the rest of the restaurant. We, the privileged, were Florenz Ziegfeld, Stanley Sharpe, his general manager, Charlie Dillingham, Sam Harris, Billy Rose, Irving Berlin, Lee Shubert, W. C. Fields, and Will Rogers. There were others, but we were the regulars. When a celebrity came in from Hollywood he was allowed, but Jim frowned on women.

Larry Fay, the operator of the famous Texas Guinan Club, used to sit at the long table once in a while. Larry's club was world-famous and a "must visit" for visitors to New York. I can remember when the present duke of Windsor was missing from a weekend party out on Long Island. The State Department had men looking for him, but he was holed up with his entire ménage at the Guinan Club.

Fay had an annoying habit when he sat at our table. He would sample everybody's food, picking it up in his long bony fingers. While tasting, he would laugh at our annoyance. At first it was amusing, but then maddening, and you would bawl Fay out.

Walter Winchell was in his prime at this time with his "Border to Border and Coast to Coast" broadcasts. He came to Moore's on Sunday nights at eight. He was a must for everybody's listening. I was no exception. Up on the second floor Willie Moore would turn the radio on full blast so it could be heard throughout the restaurant.

Fay dropped in one Sunday night. I was alone, and feasting on my favorite Moore dish, filet of flounder. As Fay and I gabbed, he reached into my plate, in his usual annoying manner, and sampled my fish. I jabbed at his hand with a knife and a warning. He did it again, and I jabbed with the knife, and again missed. Fay was having a helluva good time—I was furious. He made a third grab at my plate and I yelled loud enough to be heard all over the restaurant, "Fay—if you do that once more, I'll have you killed."

Fay reached once more, grabbed some fish, and ran for the door with me at his heels. "I told you, Fay, if you did that again I'd have you killed." He was out the door and gone. I went back to my unfinished dinner.

At the moment of eight o'clock, Willie Moore turned on the radio and to the consternation of everybody in the place we heard Winchell's opening line: "Flash—Flash—Larry Fay just killed by a gunman outside his nightclub!"

I felt sick in the stomach. All eyes were on me because it was only fifteen minutes before that I was heard to yell: "Once more, Fay, and I'll have you killed!"

Twenty-Four

AT ONE TIME, years ago, I was Red Skelton's agent. It was for a very short period of time. He was working with his wife as a two-act and was brought to me by a client, Jim Harkins. Harkins and his wife had just returned from a tour of the Keith Southern Circuit.

In Atlanta, Georgia, they went to see a dance marathon. This was supposedly a spectacle in which young couples dance continuously for three hours and rest one. The couple that was on its feet at a specified time, and feigned exhaustion better than the others, was declared winner and got just enough money to get them out of town. Phony nurses in white, phony doctors in uniform, and rented ambulances were always in attendance to administer to the participants. The whole thing was as phony as a three-dollar bill.

Red and his wife were the best actors, and naturally Red clowned all through the thing, a grueling ordeal. The Atlanta caper over, the Skeltons were invited to New York by the Harkins couple to meet their agent—me.

I liked the skinny redhead when I met him. Ready smile, deep dimples, a man of perpetual motion and running conversation. While I talked with Red, trying to get some information about his act, he was three blocks of gab ahead of me, anticipating what I was going to say and ready with a gag when I finished. I became exhausted just listening.

I gathered that the Skeltons were a comedy talking act. Edna would ask a leading question and Red would be off. There was no stopping him. Whatever clothes they owned were on their backs. It was both street and stage wardrobe. Red's bright red hair was covered with a flat Buster Keaton hat. He was continually throwing it in the air or striking at imaginary objects to accentuate a gag.

I felt that the talent the Skeltons possessed should be given to the world, and to that end I procured an engagement where they could display their specialty at Proctor's 125th Street Theater, on the East Side of New York City close to the New York Central Railroad at Second Avenue.

The 125th Street Theater was a place where women sat in the first few rows and nursed their young. A very illustrious audience. If the act onstage interested them, the mother would nurse the child. If there was no interest the kid would be taken off his feeding and allowed to bellow. The kids bellowed all through the Skelton act. Red talked so fast they couldn't understand a word he said.

The theater manager wrote a report, "If this act is funny, will somebody tell me what the hell he says?"

Four days and $50 later, the Skeltons were out of work.

MGM was looking for new young comics. I prevailed on them to give Red a test. Again Red talked so fast and moved so fast that neither the director nor the camera could follow him. I called MGM for a report on how they liked the test. They said it was a waste of money and Red was again out of work.

The only excuse I could give the young comic—I said MGM didn't like his hat. The Skeltons disappeared from the New York scene, back to more friendly people in the Midwest.

In rehashing the early days recently, Skelton reminded me of an episode in New York, and insisted it would bear repeating.

At 47th Street and Broadway, Times Square, there was an electric clock. It was a very large clock with a dial about eight feet across, and it could be seen for blocks. Come up out of the subway and the first thing you sought with your eyes was the clock. Emerge from a building, theater, cab, or streetcar, from long habit your eyes sought the time from the landmark.

My office was in the Palace Theater Building, diagonally across the street. This was the vaudeville actors' center where they came looking for bookings, known as "time." The actors would say they were on the Keith time, the Loew time, Orpheum time, and so forth.

This Times Square landmark—the clock—broke down and was removed from the building front, leaving a gaping hole four floors above the street. The Broadwayites missed their timepiece convenience. It seemed as if an old friend was missing. I came to the rescue.

To the tune of 75¢, I bought a second-hand alarm clock in a pawnshop on Eighth Avenue. I then hired the janitor of the clock building to hang the alarm clock in the big opening. Accompanying the little alarm clock was a large six-foot square sign and it read: "For time, see Billy Grady, 903 Palace Theater Building."

I hired the janitor of the building for $10 a week to wind the clock and set the alarm to ring at twelve noon and twelve midnight each day.

The first day the tinkle got a minimum of attention. Then word got around. The second day crowds gathered, and as the tinkle came there was a thunderous cheer from the curious onlookers; the fourth day and a traffic jam. The police gave me a citation for creating the condition and I was ordered to remove the little clock "forthwith."

The janitor heard of the citation and would not remove the clock unless I gave him an additional $50 ... $60.75 for publicity that was well worth the expenditure.

Now that I have told the story, Red is happy.

Twenty-Five

*A*ND then there was the time I saw the most beloved and famous American star of our time booed off the stage at the very height of his popularity. Only four people knew about the incident. I was one of them, and quite by accident.

It is said in the world of show business that "baggy-pants" low comedians want to be Shakespearean actors, acrobats want to be dashing leading men holding the beautiful heroine in their arms as they fade away into the sunset. A hoofer, so-called, wants to play Romeo to some beautiful Juliet. He will even go to the slow poison finish.

My good friend, Will Rogers, had a secret yen to be a black-face comedian. This he confided to Bill Fields and myself at Dinty Moore's one night, where we used to meet regularly for a bottle of Frontenac ale. Bill and I had no inkling as to how far Rogers had gone with his yen.

Will was starring in the Ziegfeld Follies. In the show with him were Moran and Mack, a blackface act known as the Two Black Crows. Rogers took Charlie Mack into his confidence; Mack in turn volunteered to coach Will in a blackface routine.

Rogers lived at the Astor Hotel on Times Square when working in a New York production. From the hotel he would go to his dressing room in the New Amsterdam Theater and lock himself in his room. Standing before mirrors, Will practiced a slouching walk and rehearsed dialogue, complete with wig and second-hand wardrobe bought at Guttenberg's second-hand store. He borrowed a battered silk hat from Charlie Mack.

When Rogers considered he was ready, he brought Winnie Sheehan, a close friend and a William Fox associate, into his confidence. Fox controlled a circuit of vaudeville theaters in the New York City district. Sheehan was asked by Will to arrange a theater where he could try out his act for one matinee performance under the name of Shufflin' Sam. Sheehan was sworn to secrecy.

Will's top secret venture was to debut at the Fox City Theater on East 14th Street. No one around the theater knew Will's identity, not even the manager. All they knew was that Shufflin' Sam was a tryout for the big boss, Sheehan.

Rogers dressed and blacked up in his New Amsterdam Theater dressing room. A waiting cab took him to the stage door of the Fox City Theater. The doorman, unaware of his identity, assigned Will to a tiny dressing room on the fourth floor, there to await the call for his stage appearance.

I had written an act that was playing the City Theater, and for no good reason chose the day of the Rogers debut to see my act, unaware of the added attraction I was to witness.

A troupe of hoop-rollers finished their specialty and the stage card was changed to one reading "Shufflin' Sam."

I saw a loose-legged, blackfaced man shuffle onstage. He went center, stopped, and stared, with mouth agape, at the audience. To me it seemed that the man had either forgotten his lines or was stagestruck. Nothing happened.

The East Side audience went into the action for which they were famous. Catcalls, boos, and Bronx cheers, coupled with staccato hand-clapping. The laughter was of the derisive variety. Our comedian Sam was licked. He made a shuffling exit. Throughout the debacle I had a hunch, and then it dawned on me. Shufflin' Sam was the beloved Will Rogers.

I hurried through a box to the stage door but Will had left in the waiting cab. The doorman, still unaware of Sam's identity, told me that "the poor man had tears streaming down his face as he left."

Will told Charlie Mack about the flop, but did not mention it to Bill Fields or myself when we met as usual at Moore's. I said nothing, since I figured Will wanted the whole thing buried.

Several years later, on a trip to California, I visited Will at his beautiful showplace ranch high in the Santa Monica hills. Bill was proudly showing me around and in the tack room I got up the courage to tell Will what I knew. When I finished, he walked to the window overlooking his polo field and said, "I'll be dad-gummed."

Will repeated the story of the ill-fated day and we laughed heartily. I don't think Will ever forgot my keeping the secret. Dear Will—up there with the right people—forgive me for today.

Twenty-Six

*H*OW OFTEN have you heard people saying, "If I had done this..." or "If I had done that..." "If... and it would have been different." I cannot explain the fascination of the word "if," but I can illustrate how important it was in some folks' lives.

Mimi Lilligren, newly graduated from a university in Washington State, came to Hollywood bent on a theatrical career. She came to my office at the studio for an interview.

I found Miss Lilligren to be a very striking miss of twenty-two years, with no illusions about the requirements for success in her chosen field. She was interesting and compelling, though inexperienced except for some amateur theatricals in Seattle. I was so impressed by this very vital young lady that I gave her a studio contract.

All of my staff were attracted to this determined, serious young lady. At the beginning she decorated sets with her poise and good grooming. It was extra work, to be sure, but it helped her in gaining stage presence.

Next came one-line bits, and because of her lack of experience we were ever-careful not to give the young lady more than she could handle. Following the bits came small parts, then graduation into a featured role in a "Dr. Kildare" picture, a role from which she emerged an "arrived" young actress.

The foregoing reads as though this was an isolated case and Miss Lilligren's arrival took a very short time. All young people got the same start, but unfortunately not the fulfillment. In the process of development Miss Lilligren had a new name. Mayer didn't like Mimi, thought it unsuited to the girl's personality. I didn't agree, but a rose by any other name smells just as sweet, so to please the great man, I changed Mimi Lilligren to Jo Ann Sayers. Don't ask where I got it, I just got it. It was as Jo Ann that Mimi graduated to featured roles at the studio.

Even when one has arrived in the circle of importance there are disappointments and reversals. Jo Ann Sayers was no exception.

MGM had many unreleased pictures in the vaults. Orders came from New York to cut production and release contract players who were not at the moment concerned in productions for the immediate future. Jo Ann, née Mimi, fell into that category. Reluctantly I did not exercise her next option and she was a free agent.

Other studios were in the same position as MGM, and Jo Ann was among the unemployed for quite a spell. With her savings, she determined to try the New York stage. I gave her letters of introduction to New York producers that would at least get her entrée for an interview and a hearing.

Several weeks of making the rounds of New York with no success; Miss Sayers, funds getting low, had thoughts of returning to Seattle.

I was on one of my periodic trips to New York and called Jo Ann. It was a rather discouraged young lady I took to dinner at Dinty Moore's. During dinner she told me she was leaving for Seattle the next day. I prevailed on her to wait a week, promising that when I returned to the studio I would try to find a film role. A few moments of mentally counting what was left of her funds and the reply. She would wait a week.

On my way west, I had occasion to stop off in Chicago and checked into the Blackstone Hotel on Michigan Boulevard; I had my meetings and on their completion planned some shopping at Marshall Field's department store.

To get to Marshall Field from the Blackstone you turn right on leaving the hotel. For some unaccountable reason I turned left to Michigan Boulevard, which was very much out of my way.

I had progressed two blocks on the boulevard when I ran into a friend of mine named Joe Fields, a playwright. Joe had just finished a play, a musical called *My Sister Eileen*, and was on his way to New York to cast it. Shirley Booth was already signed up as the star.

Joe told me there was one part that was giving him trouble. He described the role and inwardly I jumped for joy. It was ideal for Jo Ann Sayers. My description of Jo Ann and her fitness for the part exacted a promise from Joe that he would call her the moment he arrived in New York. We parted.

My shopping completed, I called Jo Ann in New York to tell her about the Joe Fields meeting and warned her to be prepared for a call from him.

Well, to get into the element of the word "If." Jo Ann Sayers got the part of the gal in *My Sister Eileen* and received excellent press notices. I returned to New York, saw her in the play, and was proud of her.

The show enjoyed a long run and Miss Sayers enjoyed an out-of-theater popularity. At a social function she met a young man from Wall Street named Anthony Bliss, a member of an upper-strata New York family. There was a courtship and a very elite wedding.

The marriage of Seattle's Mimi Lilligren and Mr. Bliss has been a very happy one resulting in a wonderful family and a social position of note.

I wonder what would have been the future of Jo Ann Sayers "if" I had turned right instead of left the day I left the Blackstone. It is a foregone conclusion that I would not have met Joe Fields to tell him about the lonesome, despondent little girl in New York who just wanted a chance to prove herself.

What about the word "if"?

Don't go away, I have a couple more ifs that might have changed the lives of some folks.

I Married An Angel, a musical play from New York, opened

an engagement at Los Angeles' Biltmore Theater. It starred a well-known actor, Dennis King.

For a few years I was associated with the William Morris Agency in New York. Among our roster of clients was the afore-mentioned King. One of the roles we contracted for him was the costarring role in Florenz Ziegfeld's *Three Musketeers*.

I had a season ticket for all Biltmore attractions, situated in the second row on the aisle. Opening night of *Angel* King spied me in the audience, and as MGM's casting director I began to receive a little too much attention from him onstage. At times Mr. King went overboard to the discomfiture of several support-ing players who were also trying to arouse the interest of studio representatives in the audience.

In one scene a young man named Dan Dailey was playing a small part as an office boy. King gave Dailey a very difficult time and confused him. I felt sorry for the youngster. At the play's finish I went backstage planning deliberately to ignore King.

To reach the dressing room area in the basement there is a winding staircase leading to the stars' rooms. Quite a distance down the hall are the large rooms where chorus and small-part players dress in a group. King, anticipating my visiting him, was keeping other visitors out of his room.

I arrived at the first landing of the staircase and yelled out, "Is there a young man down there named Dan Dailey?"

At the very end of the hall Dailey, in T-shirt and shorts, emerged from a crowded room and meekly answered, "I'm Dai-ley."

"Glad to meet you, Mr. Dailey, and may I compliment you on your performance this evening? Come here, please, and take this card. Come to see me at the studio. I'll arrange to have you under contract at Metro-Goldwyn-Mayer."

Dailey stood there, his mouth agape, staring at my card. He managed to whisper, "Thank you, sir," and with a whoop, ran down the hall to his dressing room companions.

King's door, opened slightly when I yelled for Dailey, then closed quietly. I did not visit him.

The rest is history. Dan Dailey's career is one of importance and long standing. To be sure there were other men in the theater who might have recognized Dailey's talents but I do not think his rise to stardom would have been as rapid *if* Mr. King had not been a bit on the unprofessional side that night at the Biltmore.

Just thought of another if that I will be forever grateful I was part of, and grateful too for a tooth that needed filling.

The dental office at the MGM studio is at the East Gate entrance. I was on my way to keep my appointment. As I approached the office I heard sobbing. Turning, I met Kathryn Grayson, a young and beautiful recent addition to our studio ranks. We all knew this young prima donna with the cute upturned nose that enhanced her lovely freshness.

Kathryn, very young and inexperienced, got it into her pretty head by way of bad advice from individuals who should have known better, that her appearance would be greatly enhanced and improved if she had her cute, upturned nose operated on by a plastic surgeon. She was on her way to meet the doctor with fear in her heart. She would have had more fear had she known the doctor. I knew him to be a quack.

I forgot all about my dental appointment, took the sobbing little girl by the arm, and had a heart-to-heart talk, a talk that was later to be echoed by L. B. Mayer. Result? No operation for Miss Grayson.

Now for if. If I had not been at the East Gate and heard the sobbing Miss Grayson, I'll bet all the peat moss in Ireland that beautiful Kathryn Grayson's lovely face would have been scarred for life by that operation, with no telling what effect it would have on her God-given voice.

That if is something, isn't it? Just look back and recount the ifs that have affected your life.

Just one more if and I'm through.

I had a golf date with Jimmy Stewart at the Bel Air Country Club. We were to tee off at 1:30. As I was leaving my studio office, a call came through from Paris. My friend Ben Smith was calling. In the midst of our conversation, we were cut off. The overseas operator said it would take a little time to reestablish the connection.

While awaiting the call, my number-one gal, Babs, asked me to see a young man who had tried earlier to see me. The man was on his way to Lockheed Aircraft for an employment interview. Babs brought in Howard Keel, the well-known singing star of today.

In the talk that followed, Keel said that he had been having a tough time getting engagements since returning from London, where he had played the lead in *Oklahoma!*—an engagement he had gotten by a fluke.

Understudying the lead in *Carousel* in New York, as well as playing the last few performances of *Oklahoma!* before it closed, he was asked to go to London and play *Oklahoma!* there because the contemplated lead had been taken ill. In London during the engagement he also played in a B-picture called *A Small Voice*. I had just seen the picture the week before.

Back in the United States, engagements were few and far between. Keel was on the point of taking any kind of employment that would provide sustaining money for him and his family. On his way to Lockheed he took a chance that I might be able to see him.

Well, the result? A test for the role in *Annie Get Your Gun* and he came off with flying colors, plus a long-term contract at MGM. Howard is an actor very much in demand today. More power to him, and just between us, don't take the guy lightly in a golf match.

What about the if?

If I hadn't been cut off from my Paris call, I'd have been on the tee with Jimmy Stewart at the appointed time and missed Keel's visit at the office, and one of the warplanes of the period would probably have had its nuts and bolts installed by a baritone who sang *Oklahoma!* while he worked.

Twenty-Seven

*A*ND then there was the time I was visited by a Mr. and Mrs. Taylor from a mid-Pennsylvania city. Mr. Taylor was a banker. They had a problem.

Their son, contrary to their wishes, wanted to be an actor. He was in college preparing for a banking career that held no interest for him. Could I be of help?

The son, Don, was a well-set-up six-foot, two-inch twenty-one-year-old; good-looking, with a very inviting smile and personality. The boy impressed me with his manner and good breeding. He didn't want to hurt his parents, but throughout his college life a business career had not interested him. He wanted to be an actor.

I asked Mr. and Mrs. Taylor to leave me alone with the boy for a few moments. I found him to be very intense and determined to embark on an acting career, whether on the stage or in motion pictures. He had a jut to his chin that stressed he meant what he said. I was impressed and sent for his parents.

"Mr. and Mrs. Taylor," I began, "your son Don is determined to try his hand at this business of acting. I must tell you in all honesty I think he can make a go of it. I realize this is a disappointment to you, but this boy's heart will not be in the banking business—it never will be until he has had a fling at my business. If I were in the same position as a parent, I would let him have his way. It is insurance for the future. If he, as a dutiful son, does his parents' bidding against his will, and does not make a go of it, he will always blame you for what might have been."

Mr. and Mrs. Taylor had a talk privately. Their impression of things theatrical was not a very high one. Cheap gossip magazines and irresponsible headlines in newspapers had led them to believe that people in the show world were rather unsavory. My presentation changed their minds; they gave their son permission and their blessing, and took their leave.

Don Taylor was contracted as an actor at MGM. I watched his career like a parent. His progress, carefully guided, showed great promise.

During the war Taylor was drafted. The Air Force was doing its musical *Winged Victory*, and George Cukor and Moss Hart were the headmen in the production. I contacted them and prevailed upon them to cast young Taylor in a prominent role, Pinky, the Italian barber's son.

He was great in the part and returned to us at the studio as a full-fledged actor and picture personality. I felt very proud.

Through the efforts of the casting office, Taylor was soon in the feature-player class. One of my men came to me with a problem. He had a small but an all-important role in a picture. Its bearing on the outcome of the story depended on the role being cast perfectly. The perfect casting would be Don Taylor.

I sent for Taylor and told him our problem. Would he help us in our difficulty and play the role? He read the script, and like a lot of actors, counted the number of lines instead of considering the importance of the part to the picture. He refused to play the part. I was astonished and tried to point out its value to him. He still refused. I then did something that I had never done before or since. I put it on a personal basis. "Do it for me as a favor." I was again refused.

I felt hurt, not so much by his refusal to play the part, but because his memory had failed him and friendship was held so cheaply. When you are sincere and sentimental, you get hurt that way.

Twenty-Eight

I HAVE OFTEN remarked the lure and fascination of motion pictures. The extent of this lure was exemplified during a tour of the South some years ago while I was seeking a boy to play Jody in MGM's production of *The Yearling.*

In our production planning, it was decided that an unknown youngster should play the all-important juvenile role.

If there is one thing that exasperates a columnist in the trade papers or newspapers in general, it is an announcement by a studio publicity department that the producer of a particular picture has decided to cast someone unheard-of in an important role. The role is described, and immediately thousands of amateur talent scouts are on the prowl.

The producer and the studio are deluged with letters, snapshots, and expensive photographs. Each correspondent insists his or her choice is the one, and the only one, to play the part.

When interest is at its height, comes another studio announcement quoting the producer. "He has decided to cast a studio contract player or a well-known Hollywood name instead of the unknown."

Instantly the disappointed and disgruntled self-appointed talent scouts send letters of protest. Newspaper people are resentful of the fact that they have been used in a publicity hoax. I certainly agree with them.

Does this hoax harm the box-office receipts of the picture when it finally hits theater screens? No. All the protesters go to see the picture and compare their choice with that of the producer. I think it's cheap publicity and warrants no place in the industry.

In MGM's planning for *The Yearling*, it was decided that an unknown boy should play the part of Jody. I extracted a promise from L. B. Mayer that if I went on the search, a boy of my selection would be cast in the part. He agreed.

The youngster had to be from the South, Southern in speech and manner. It was of the utmost importance that the boy selected be the perfect type. As the part of Jody went, so went the picture.

It was decided that two publicity men would precede me into selected Southern cities to spread the word. A composite picture of the producer's idea of how Jody should look would be prominently placed in all local newspapers. Attached to the picture would be a description of the boy. Blonde—eleven or twelve years of age—about five-foot one or five-foot two—not to weigh over seventy pounds. A caption would introduce the picture of the boy. It read in essence:

SHIRLEY TEMPLE AND JACKIE COOPER AMASSED MILLIONS OF DOLLARS IN THEIR MOTION PICTURE CAREERS . . . PERHAPS THE SAME GOOD FORTUNE IS IN STORE FOR A BOY WHO CAN FIT THE DESCRIPTION OF JODY . . . IF YOU KNOW OF SUCH A BOY HAVE HIM MEET MGM'S BILLY GRADY AT . . . ON . . .

Had I realized the furore this advertisement would create, I would have planned differently. I set out alone. I should have had the Marines with me.

My first stand—Atlanta, Georgia; the Grady Hotel. (Sorry, no relation.) The newspapers said that applicants were to meet me at 9:00 A.M., the day of my arrival.

Due to foul weather, I had a miserable flight from California. I was twenty-three hours in transit and it was a tired individual that put his weary bones to bed at 5:30 A.M. for a very short rest.

It seemed as if I had hardly closed my eyes when the phone began ringing. One look at the clock. It was 7:30. The hotel management was calling. The voice on the phone was pleading but had overtones of command.

"Mr. Grady, something will have to be done about this mob in the lobby. They are clamoring and waiting to see you. Our hotel guests can neither get in or out of the hotel. We suggest you come down here immediately."

Ten minutes to shower and dress, and a few moments later I was fighting my way out of the elevator into the lobby. It was a bedlam. A solid mass of humanity, mostly adults with screaming kids in tow. The outpouring began arriving at the Grady Hotel as early as 6:30 that morning.

As I fought my way through the crowd, paper airplanes were skimming through the air. One old gal was holding a handkerchief to her eye. She had been hit and was yelling blue murder. There were kids up on the mezzanine shooting wet wads of paper by means of elastic-band slingshots into the crowd below.

To add to the confusion, it seemed that every kid in the lobby had to go to the men's room. Even that was jammed. Kids who couldn't hold out were using convenient and remote corners. The coffee shop was another mob scene. Guests wanting breakfast, kids wanting water. I could see that I was in for a helluva day, and here I was alone.

The hotel management had called for extra police; it was a necessity. The adults were appropriating all the stationery and postcards supposed to be for the convenience of guests. The youngsters thought the candy displayed at the newsstand was a gesture of hospitality by the hotel. It was gone in a very short time, to the dismay of the clerk. Everything from ashtrays to decorative flower containers were taken as souvenirs. Yes, quite a day!

Four of Atlanta's finest were trying to get some semblance of order inside the hotel, while outside the crowds were still coming, creating a traffic jam. Ancient vintage automobiles were racing their motors, the drivers with their hands glued to the horn. What a din. They were parked anywhere and everywhere. Riderless horses, horses hitched to all varieties of rigs, hitched to anything that would take a rope. Bicycles parked on the sidewalks made passage almost impossible. The police were in an uproar and everything was blamed on me.

In my wildest anticipation, I told the police, I hadn't dreamed of such a turnout. I could do nothing more than get on with the interviews and try and reduce the crowd in numbers. I started to operate.

The difficult job was to separate the kids from the adults. There were parents, uncles, aunts, cousins, and neighborhood friends. None of the adults with the kids wanted to leave their charges with me while they, the adults, waited outside. After some police work, enough of the elders were out of the room so I could operate.

The kids were herded into the ballroom, three deep along the walls. Groups of twenty-five would pass before my table. Those that were near the type I wanted I asked to step off the line. Rejects were directed through a door into the street.

The first group of boys behind me, and there was a rush of parents from the street, all in protest.

"Why did you refuse my Everett? He read the book and knows all about it. You ain't fair." Everett was as big as a blacksmith.

"You're crazy! My boy is just like the pitcher in the paper. You crazy or somethin'?"

"I tol' my old lady you were a fake. Lookit here at this boy. If he ain't Jody I dunno what is. He wuz born in Ocala and knew that family the lady wrote about."

Nothing that I could say would pacify them. I was a fake and a phony and let it go at that. The police again took a hand and in the confusion four girls got into the room and were trying to attract my attention with a concert on musical saws. It seems every other kid had a harmonica and none of them knew anything but "Old Black Joe." Between the harmonicas and concerts around the room on banjos, I was going nuts. With all the confusion, I had to go the bathroom and none was available.

I saw kids until I was blue in the face. There were kids who could double for Wallace Beery, and imitations of Jimmy Cagney and George Raft were common occurrences. Anything to attract my attention.

At 5:30 P.M., with over 600 kids behind me, I was feeling punch-drunk; I called a halt but the parents, uncles, aunts, cousins, and neighbors still hung around. They had brought picnic lunches. The place looked like a city dump.

I had selected twenty-five boys for a preliminary reading of a scene from the picture. I knew most of them would be a waste of time but I had to make a showing, both for the press and the disgruntled parents. After an explanation of why, some were turned down; I thought that the press articles in the paper would pacify the losers.

I had engaged a camera crew from New York to photograph those I selected to make tests. Because of union jurisdictional rules, all camera work east of the Mississippi had to be done by an Eastern crew. This outfit from New York was a dilly. Photographing the Hudson River on a sunny day they could do, but a little boy in a ballroom they couldn't. I'd have been better off with four caribou and a Brownie. How I wished, but in vain, for a regular Hollywood crew.

My first selection in Atlanta proved the most promising. His name was Gene Eckman, a perfect type, and the son of a local telegrapher. I could have stopped right there, but I was committed to eight other cities. In all I tested in five.

I had not eaten since early morning, and it was a tired and hungry mess of bones that bathed and had supper in my rooms, but there was no rest for the weary. The phone rang incessantly. The calls coming from the disappointed; I was called everything from "stupid Irish" to "Yankee phony." There were a few that questioned my parentage.

My next stop was Birmingham, Alabama, but before leaving for there I was profuse in my thanks to the management of the Grady Hotel in Atlanta. I made apologies for the confusion I had caused. They were very gracious.

Only one prospect from a large but orderly crowd in Birmingham. I could just as well have passed it up. I tested three to make a showing of sincerity . . . Jacksonville followed. Again a dud. Large crowds turned out but they were curious rather than serious. I had one uncomfortable session that bothered me.

An elderly lady, with a whimpering boy of five and a little girl somewhat younger in tow, insisted that I hear them recite. With restraint and patience I tried to explain to the old lady that I would not be interested in anyone but an eleven-year-old boy. She would have none of my explanation, and to avoid the rising commotion I consented to listen to the kids.

She led me to a remote corner of the hotel lobby. There, in a telephone booth that she had surrounded with potted palms appropriated from the writing room, stood the little boy.

I listened to him recite a nursery rhyme. My heart went out to the kid—he was bawling throughout and the old lady had to prompt him. As pleasant as I could be under the circumstances, I repeated my explanation of what I was looking for. She would have none of it. I had to call the hotel management to remedy the difficulty. Jacksonville was a wasted stop.

Ocala, Florida. This was the residence of Marjorie Kinnan Rawlings. I thought she might know of a boy in the vicinity who could play Jody. Miss Rawlings, a very outspoken lady, told me I was wasting my time. If there was a Jody anyplace around there she would know about him. I saw about fifty uninteresting youngsters and called it a day. I welcomed this shortened interview period since it let me get to bed for some much-needed sleep.

Retiring early, I was awakened by small voices coming from the next room. The voices were reciting some familiar words, now and then being prompted by an adult female voice.

On investigation I found it was the old lady from Jacksonville. She had followed me to Ocala with the children, and having found some discarded *Yearling* scenes that I had used for tests, she was teaching them to the youngsters. She had told the management she was my assistant and that it was her job to rehearse prospects for me. She insisted she had to have the room next to mine.

This was something serious and I had hotel management call the local authorities. I later found out that she had been en route from Knoxville, Tennessee, to Miami with her daughter's children when she read in the papers about my talent search. She had gotten off the train at Jacksonville, with the foregoing results. The mother came down from Knoxville and took the children home.

Tampa, Florida, and another mob scene, but an orderly one. There was the usual all manner of transportation à la Atlanta, to the utter confusion of the police and the hotel management. I was so organized here that there was little confusion inside the hotel. My publicity men were with me and were of great assistance. The usual passing in review in groups of twenty-five. Only twenty out of about six hundred got a second look and just three were to be tested.

In the fourth group I noted a shy, bewildered boy. Rusty hair, a mass of freckles with a reddish hue. His big brown eyes roved the ballroom; everything seemed so strange to him. He was barefoot and attired in a suit several sizes too large for him. I beckoned to the boy to step out of the line and come to my table, but he paid me no heed and remained in line with the others.

A lady standing by took the frightened boy by the hand and brought him to me. He stood trembling, with his face deep in the folds of the lady's dress. He was like a frightened baby with its mother.

The lady was the boy's schoolteacher. The lad was from the swamp country, and believe it or not, this was his first glimpse of the world outside his swamp home. Incredible, what with Tampa, a metropolis, less than fifteen miles away.

The boy was one of eleven brothers and sisters. His father had died of snake bite and the family supported themselves by trapping and fishing. The clothes the boy wore were his elder brother's, shoes were nonexistent in the swamps.

This child was a wonderful type for my purpose and I had to know more about him. The confusion of the ballroom was hardly the place, so I called "lunch" and took the boy and his teacher to my rooms upstairs.

I will never forget the terror on the boy's face as the elevator rose to the fourth floor. He clung to his teacher, burying his face in the folds of her dress again, and didn't dare to venture one look at the passing walls of the elevator well. He was trembling from head to foot with fright.

Miss Bostwick explained the boy's fearfulness. He had never seen an automobile until that day. Horses were an unknown quantity to him—he thought they were wild beasts. The boy's life was small boats for fishing and trapping, together with his brothers and sisters. He was about an average third grader in school, though he was eleven and a half years of age, but the best hunter and fisherman in the swamps.

Miss Bostwick was a church worker and a volunteer teacher in the swamp schools. She taught in a makeshift building that held twenty children of all ages. She read the Tampa papers and had seen the picture of Jody, and as a consequence—the boy's first trip to the city.

I could not get the boy to converse. He kept making pitiful pleas to Miss Bostwick to take him home. I ordered lunch, and while awaiting service I tried to buy the boy's confidence. I tendered him a half-dollar. He looked at it curiously, turned it over in his hand and gave it to his teacher. I offered a dollar bill; he looked at it, crumbled it in his hand, made a small pellet, and tossed it into the air. As he caught it he smiled, displaying a beautiful set of white, even teeth.

Lunch was served and the boy watched every move of the white-coated waiter in wonder. Silver table utensils gained his undivided attention. While eating this strange food, he could master a spoon but not the knife and fork. I had seen the same situation in Africa and Asia, but this was America, civilized and modern. It was beyond me.

Reluctantly I bade goodbye to the boy and his patient teacher but not before dipping into the "swindle sheet" and giving the lady money for clothes for the whole family, as well as for remembrances of the first trip into civilization. For me an unforgettable experience.

I returned to the ballroom and an impatient, restless crowd of waiting prospects. By 5:15 I had selected four boys for tests. None held much promise.

The tests over, I called a halt to the proceedings and dismissed the camera crew. I was about to go upstairs when I was approached by the hotel manager. "Please, won't you see just one more group? It will mean so much to you and the hotel." I was about to plead weariness but remembered the cooperation I had received from the hotel. I consented to see this new group. "Bring them in," I said resignedly.

Through a door came a giant of a man, followed by a motley group of comparable giants, each dressed in a Buster Brown costume, complete with bobby socks and yellow wigs. I doubled up with laughter.

The group was the Cincinnati baseball club, in Tampa for its spring training. Their manager, Bill McKechnie, a good friend of mine, arranged this gag. I'm a pushover for gags and this was a topper. The lead giant was Jewel Ens, their farm manager and Bill's aide, and I know he realized how ridiculous he looked. A wonderful laugh to close my stay in Tampa.

A few milk-train stops and I was at the Columbus Hotel, Miami. A complete waste of time. Everybody talked like a New Yorker. I beat a hasty retreat to the airport for the trip to the next stand, Tallahassee, the state capital.

I paid a short visit to friends in Palm Beach and as a consequence, missed my connection for the capital city. I had to charter a flight for the short trip. For a pilot I had a former crop-duster who evidently had been disbarred. It seems we were never over 400 feet off the ground, and on sighting the slightest hill or hummock he would ZOOM into the wild blue yonder while I strained against the seat belt. Without the belt I would have spent the flight on the ceiling. Yelling at the maniac did no good against the noise from the prop. OOOH, how I prayed.

He missed the first pass at the air strip and ZOOOOMED up again, a quick turn, missed an outlying hangar, and landed like a ton of bricks. Before the egg crate came to a stop, I kicked the door open and was on my way to make a complaint. I never heard any more from it, and I hope I never encounter the likes of this aerial wildman again.

The ride to the city through the beautiful countryside was restful to my otherwise shattered nerves. Here was the gentle South in all its native splendor. Friendly roadsiders waved a welcoming hello. They didn't know me, it was just their friendliness that prompted it. I was going to like Tallahassee . . . Oh, yeah?

I was not prepared for the sight that greeted me as I entered the city and approached the small hotel. All I could see was a milling mob storming it. Some trying to get in, others trying to get out.

Kids of all ages were climbing the outside fire escapes. There were kids shinning up the water spouts, reaching into windows, appropriating whatever was in reach and tossing their loot to accomplices below. Women, in all manner of disarray, were yelling at the miscreants to cease and desist. There were hotel people on the roof flailing at the kids from above, while a police officer was brandishing a switch from below. Were these my little darlin's waiting to see the moving picture man? What was I in for?

As my driver edged his way to the hotel entrance, kids swarmed all over his car for a better vantage point. The driver jumped out of his car and started belting the kids. One kid got it a little on the rough side and soon there was a fight between the driver and the kid's father. I beat a hasty retreat.

I was halted at the hotel entrance by a policeman. I had quite a time convincing him I was a guest with a reservation. A bellboy came to my rescue. The lobby was a shambles—yelling, rushing kids were everywhere. The lady custodian of the newsstand was standing before it with her arms outstretched across the merchandise. The expression on her face was a reminder of "They shall not pass."

When I approached the desk to register, the weazened clerk looked at me with a leer. As I wrote my name on the register, he let out a WHOOP and yelled for help. A little man with pince-nez glasses came running, looked at me, then at the register, then drew himself up to his full five feet, two inches and yelled, "So—you're the one!"

I realized that this was either the owner or the manager. The little man grabbed me by the arm with a grip of iron and kept up a continuous line of complaints.

"I want to show you what a wreck your hoodlums have made of this hotel. Just look here," and he pointed.

It was the hotel poolroom, one table. The green cloth was ripped and torn in many places. Pool sticks everywhere. Ivory balls were rolling all over the floor with the building's vibration. The wire score markers, torn from their anchor, lay a twisted mass in the corner. Cuspidors were overturned and there were two broken windows. My little angels did this?

I was being pulled toward the lobby again and the tirade continued.

"I want you to see our toilets. Unusable and not a plumber or maintenance man available in the city. Your company will pay dearly for this. You take your bags and get out of this hotel, and get out quick!"

Just at this moment a middle-aged lady guest appeared. In her left hand she carried a squawking parrot in a large cage, in her right arm was curled a snarling Siamese cat. The old gal was toothless and in this condition was complaining that kids had reached into her room window and stolen her dentures, plus a hair switch, stretched on the sill to dry. She was having trouble in her toothless condition trying to describe the "thwitch." Several repeats and it was clear. Mr. Five-two was trying to pacify her but was interrupted by two plumbers, both calling to do the repair work on the men's room. Each insisted he was the one that was going to get the job. It was nearly a contest of wrenches and blowtorches.

In the midst of the two arguments—the toothless woman *vs.* the manager and the two plumbers—I made a hasty retreat, but where to go?

Through the milling crowd on the porch I was collared by my driver. He wanted to be paid; though I had hired him by the hour, he wanted no part of all this.

As we were talking, a boy on the porch roof dropped a bag full of water on a man below. Some splashed on the driver. He was livid, and the man that was squarely hit called the kid on the roof everything he could think of. They have some peculiar swear words down South that apply to bad boys.

Again I was alone. My camera crew was hidden somewhere; my publicity men, their job done, I had sent home. Where was I to go with this unruly crowd? I was late getting into the city and they had been waiting since early morning, their nerves on edge. Again I was a phony and a fake in their eyes.

In the midst of my dilemma a man sidled up to me. For a consideration he would arrange for me to use the Elks Club. For a consideration, I'd use a slaughterhouse. I dispatched him to the Elks.

While the stranger was off arranging the Elks, a cleric, accompanied by a hatchet-faced girl of sixteen or seventeen, began telling me what a great voice she had. "Her voice should be given to the world," said he.

"Go ahead and give it. I'm not interested, I'm here looking for boys."

Two burly men came up, each with a boy in tow. "Take a look, Mister. I've gotta get back to work. Look at my boy," said the first.

The second burly started an argument. He had been there earlier than the first, his boy should get first consideration. Harsh names called and some fancy-dan pushing. I beat a retreat toward the Elks messenger who was approaching. I could have the Elks for $25. I gave him three twenty-dollar bills.

Like the Pied Piper of Hamelin, I led the mob, with a kid blowing some toots on a battered bugle as a musical escort. As I walked, carrying my heavy bags, there were mothers and fathers running at my side trying to draw my attention toward their offspring, their lives in constant danger from the taxi driver, who was sidling his car along the route yelling for his money, with me yelling back to meet me at the Elks. Peaceful Tallahassee, me eye.

The Elks Club was rather small, and it was practically filled with curious onlookers who had run on ahead. I had difficulty forcing my way in. I sent the man who had arranged for the hall to get me some policemen. He returned with three off-duty men dressed in overalls, each with a boy in tow. I hired them at $10 each to restore order, if possible. My crew was hidden in a garage up the street. They feared for their equipment. For all the good they were to me I didn't care if it was wrecked, but under the circumstances they were necessary evils.

"Will someone stop that kid with the bugle?"

A quick explanation to the police of my plan of operation. They arranged groups of twenty-five, but the hall was cleared of the adults first. These exiled grown-ups went to places in the windows, yelling encouragement to the kids they left inside. You couldn't hear yourself think.

As the first line approached, the cleric and the little battle-axe broke in again amid protests from the onlookers in the windows. The police were in a spot. They didn't want to give the heave-ho to a man of God, but, after all, the people in the windows were their friends. I stepped in. The parishioners were on one side, the nonbelievers on the other. Me—in the middle, and that G.D. kid with the bugle.

There was only one thing—to listen to the dame sing. From out of nowhere came a woman with a portable organ. She opened it up and started to pump, the girl started to sing. She should have been arrested. With hands folded across her flat chest, she sang. It sounded like a knife being drawn across a plate of glass. The cleric, the dame at the organ, and the girl must all have been demented.

When the prima donna finished, the man of the cloth wanted to discuss her with me. I bade him wait until I had finished with my boys. He retired to a corner of the hall.

The first group of boys produced nothing, and that included one of the police sons. The cop started to protest, but upon getting nowhere with me demanded his $10. I gave it to him and he left.

In the second group was a pair of twins. Slender, blonde, and accompanied by a nervous beagle dog on a rope, they both looked like Jody. This was too good to be true—if only they had even a semblance of talent. Child labor laws limit the time a child can work in front of a camera. With twins I would not be hampered by the law—first one and then the other. What a timesaver—money, too.

I pulled the boys out of line and proceeded to find out about them, but I had not progressed far when the cleric yelled and came running.

"You mean to say you're interested in these bastards?"

"What's that you say?"

"You heard me right. These bastards. They don't know who their father is and their mother is in the city jail right now for lascivious conduct. We of Tallahassee cannot allow those bastards to represent our city."

"Listen, Mister, whoever you are . . ."

"I'm a man of God."

"Makes no difference to me, Mister. These two boys I might be interested in, and you and your goddamned bigotry will get out of here before I throw you out, and as big as you are I can do it. Get out!"

The bigot turned to the police for help, but got nowhere since two of their sons were in the next group I was to see and they didn't want to jeopardize their chances. The adults in the windows and room were divided in their allegiance. The camera crew, the cowards, anticipating trouble, started to dismantle their cameras.

While the argument over the twins waxed hot and heavy, I sneaked into an anteroom for a talk. I would have given anything to take them if they were encouraging in the slightest, but unfortunately they had nothing. One had a speech impediment, the other was sub par in intellect. It was a blow. I dismissed them with another hunk of the expense account and returned to the next group.

Would my troubles never cease! In the middle of this group came a union man. If I were to use the camera in Tallahassee, I would have to add as many local men as I had on my crew. No additions—no tests in Tallahassee.

After a discussion, we compromised. I would add two locals.

The two locals that he had in tow couldn't operate a ten-cent mouse trap, and as things turned out I was right. I proceeded with my inspection of applicants.

First, the boys fathered by the police. The police should have been jailed for bringing them into the world in the first place. I recognized one of them as the kid on the hotel porch roof throwing the bags of water; the other, by his looks and shifty eyes, had to wind up in the gas chamber. To their fathers I showed great interest. I had a plan to save trouble. Now came the kid with the bugle. How I would have loved to blast him over the head with it. Everybody called him Moon. It wasn't hard trying to know why. The biggest head I have ever seen on a kid and a mouth big enough to blow forty bugles at the same time.

I had selected four boys for tests, plus the three police kids. Manny, the cameraman, advised he had only enough film for the four natural tests. There would be no film for the extras, the police kids. Food for thought, with a bright idea. I instructed the cameraman to photograph the police kids with no film in the camera. Nobody would be any the wiser. Oh, yeah? There was one of the local union men standing nearby. I wasn't sure whether he heard my no-film instructions. Time would tell.

We were ready for the first test. One of the locals on-camera was instructed to throw the switch for the current. There was a five-minute wait and then, BOOM and another BOOM with smoke. The thick-head had thrown the main switch and the overload blew the fuse, and no spares available. The hall was in darkness and that G.D. kid blowing taps on the bugle.

A wait and I am tapped on the shoulder by an important-looking man. One of the policemen presented him as the city manager or someone just as important. Big mouth on the camera had spread the word I had run out of film and all tests would be without film. One of the cops got word to the man before me. He was very direct and deliberate in what he said.

"Grady, this was a peaceful community yesterday. Today it's an armed camp. People who have been friends and neighbors for years are out there fighting as bitter enemies, all because of you and your G.D. publicity scheme. Now I'm giving you orders, and you better heed them. Pack up and get the hell out of

Tallahassee, or I'll throw you all in jail. You have one hour."

"Now wait a minute. This is not a publicity stunt. I am here on a legitimate search for a boy. I had hoped your city could produce one. It would be good for your city of Tallahassee."

"Yes, and you're going to photograph the local boys with no film in the camera. What do you think we are, G.D. fools?"

The man walked away, but in a moment he was back with Mr. Pince-Nez from the hotel, plus an attorney. Pince-Nez had a bill for $413.

"What about this? The hotel wants payment for the pooltable, the plumbing, and the articles stolen from the lady's room, plus articles stolen from the newsstand. There is a hole in the porch roof caused by boys running over it. This is your responsibility, Grady. Nothing will be taken from this building until payment is made."

"He ain't paid us yet," said the cops, and the local union cameramen nodded their head in agreement. And me with less than $60 in my pocket and I have to get to Jacksonville.

The camera crew, taking advantage of the argument at the other end of the hall, packed in a hurry, got out a side door with their camera equipment, loaded it into the panel truck, and sped away, BUT the stupes went the wrong way and were nailed as they made the return trip past the Elks hall.

My only recourse was to enlist the aid of the local theater exhibitor. I asked him to call his district office in Jacksonville and let me talk to the manager, whom I had met while on the hunt in that city. I was allowed to use the Elks Club phone but had to pay for the call before talking. Everything that I said about the city on entering it I took back by the time I was ready to leave.

To sum up! Tallahassee gave me nothing but a headache. I paid off by personal check and proceeded to Jacksonville with a motorcycle escort to the city line. I came to town at peace with the world. I was lucky I didn't leave town on a rail.

New Orleans. I have never seen so many people around a hotel. The Roosevelt had them everywhere, inside and out. They were mostly adults. A suggestion of Mardi Gras without the costumes. The police were called long before I arrived.

Even the cops applauded when I was introduced by the assistant manager. They were applauding in relief.

I quickly went into action with the great assistance of the police and hotel staff. Lines of fifty were inspected. There was every type but a Jody. They were tall, short, fat, skinny, dark-complected, and one albino.

At the end of the first line there was a husky olive-skinned kid with a bright yellow wig on. I passed it off as a gag and called for the next group. There was the same kid with a red wig. Again my thoughts of a gag. When he came the third time I blew my top and yanked him out of line.

"This is serious business, son. What's the idea of the wig?"

The kid started to blubber. "I didn't wanna do it. My mother made me."

"Where is your mother?"

"Out there," and he pointed to the door.

I stomped out with the kid, and there was his mother with a shoe box filled with wigs. Every time a line went in, she clamped a wig on the kid's head and pushed him into line. I soon had a cop give her the heave-ho.

Halfway through my inspection, the assistant manager came in with four Al Capone types. They had a skinny ten-year-old girl in tow. The manager asked that I hear her sing.

Another voice to be given to the world, I thought, but I was soon to learn otherwise.

I was informed that the four sinister-looking men were members of a high state official's bodyguard. The child was the daughter of their boss. One look at the kid and she'd frighten the FBI. At ten she looked like an old hag. I didn't know who the boss was but I was taking no chances. I had met Huey Long once. If these hoodlums worked for his office, better hear the monster sing.

Before I could say Poindexter Abernathy, she was into her first number with accompaniment by a fat-fingered bodyguard a hundred feet away on a piano that must have played for Sherman as he marched to the sea. Between the flat notes on the piano and the shrill bellowing of the kid, it was an ordeal. Know what she sang? Sophie Tucker's "One Of These Days," guttural notes and all. I could have shoveled hot mud in the singer's face all day long and never tired.

Finishing the first song, she went, with no waiting, into "St. Louis Woman," hip movements and all. Her escorts never looked at her, they watched me for my reaction. Thank the good Lord they couldn't read my mind. Finishing "St. Louis Woman," she went into a dance. Her movements, and mind you, she was ten years of age, her movements would have had a smoker raided.

At the finish of the dance the quartette with the child left as abruptly as they entered, the leader saying, "Seymour will talk to you." Seymour was Seymour Weiss, the owner of the hotel, and a factor in Louisiana politics.

I found two good prospects in New Orleans among 700 boys. It took me well into the night but I finished, and by midnight I was on my way back to California.

Back at the studio we developed the twenty-odd tests, only four of which were of compelling interest, Gene Eckman from Alabama in the lead. To be on the safe side, I brought the four boys to the studio for more extensive tests and in a week the decision was made—Gene Eckman would be Jody.

A contract for Gene demonstrated how the family's whole life can be changed from the usual to the unusual. Gene was to receive $500 a week, plus $100 for his father, who had to give up his telegraphic job to act as Gene's guardian.

Inasmuch as the boy's job in The Yearling dealt with his love of animals and their love for him, he spent every daytime hour that he was not in school feeding and romping with the several young deer that were to be his constant companions in the picture. His way with the four-footed animals was something to see. There was a mutual love.

"The best laid plans of mice and men . . ."

While young Eckman was being trained in the Jody part, as well as working with the animals, a crew was dispatched to the Florida location of the picture to plant the corn crop that was to be a principal background. If you will remember, Jody's folks lived in a makeshift "pore white trash" cabin, and their principal foodstuffs came from their own labors on their plot of land.

The studio farming group in Ocala, Florida, advised the studio that the corn had enough growth to start the picture. That was the signal to send 126 people to the location. There were actors, mechanics, camera crews, makeup and wardrobe people, plus livestock and rolling stock. It was the beginning of *The Yearling*, MGM's big picture for the year.

Four weeks of shooting and everything came to a halt. The growth of the corn did not match up with the story. The corn had been planted by California time standards rather than Florida standards. Therefore a meeting of studio heads to discuss this colossal error in judgment.

The picture was postponed for a year, and back to California came the 126 people, plus livestock. Over $1 million spent to date and not one foot of film that could be salvaged.

A year passes. The corn, this time, had been planted by Florida standards and word came that everything was in readiness. Again the 126 people prepared for the trek to Florida, but this time there were new stars and a new director. During the preparations, we had sent for Gene Eckman.

Glory be to Frankie and Johnny. When young Eckman reported we found that he had grown a foot and gained fifteen pounds. He was no longer Jody, we had to get a new one. This picture was jinxed.

I was in Europe when the Eckman news broke and could not be of help. Clarence Brown, the new director, took over. He would find a Jody. Brown visited his home town of Knoxville, Tennessee, and paid a courtesy call on his former schoolteacher and schoolhouse. There he met and signed the boy who was eventually to play Jody—Claude Jarman.

The rest is history. *The Yearling* was one of MGM's best and a money-maker from the beginning; but for the corn error there would have been an additional million dollars in the bank.

Twenty-Nine

1916. W. C. Fields was a star in Florenz Ziegfeld's Follies, the crowning achievement in any actor's career. It came quite by accident and was preceded by one of the most heartbreaking experiences any actor could be confronted with.

Charles Dillingham, one of Broadway's most respected and best-liked producers, was preparing Irving Berlin's revue *Watch Your Step* for production. Eight weeks before the planned break-in opening at Syracuse, New York, Dillingham decided the show needed a comedy specialty. He had seen a comedy juggler named Fields in a Berlin Music Hall, and it was this act that would fill the needed comedy spot.

Fields's representative was the powerful H. B. Marinelli, who operated worldwide. Marinelli's office was contacted and Dillingham was informed that Fields was just finishing a tour of Australian and New Zealand music halls. Cables were exchanged and a contract finalized, with a promise from Fields that he would be in Syracuse in time for the opening of *Watch Your Step*. He was in seventh heaven. No more second-rate hotels, back-breaking travels, and indigestible foreign food. He had lived for this opportunity to prove himself.

The very first trans-Pacific boat available was a freighter

that would dock in Vancouver, British Columbia. A fast connection for an overland train would get him to Syracuse in time. Fields, for the first time in his life, called on the Man upstairs to help him.

The boat trip was an ordeal. Rough seas, inside cabin, and unpalatable food when his stomach was in condition to receive it. To make matters worse, the booze supply gave out, but constant thoughts of home kept his spirits up.

Vancouver and the baggage-transfer man got lost. Fields pleaded with the train conductor to delay departure. For an hour the rail terminal was aware of a crazy American running between the baggage room and the train conductor yelling choice, unheard-of phrases. Fields vowed he would kill the baggageman, but upon his arrival, with his great size noted, Fields thought better of the threats. Because of the late arrival, only an upper berth was available for the trip East. The train stopped at way stations for meals; it had no diner and no drinks were served anywhere along the line. A helluva situation for Fields, but the thought of what was in store for him kept his spirits as high as before.

He arrived in Syracuse the afternoon of the dress rehearsal of *Watch Your Step*. His specialty was to be spotted just before the finale of the first act. Dillingham had great hopes for Fields's specialty from Australia, to spot him in that important position.

The dress rehearsal took place before an important invited audience. Society friends of Dillingham's, plus the all-important ticket brokers from Broadway. Fields's reception by this exceptional audience exceeded his wildest dreams. They couldn't get enough of his comedy and applauded into the beautiful first act finale, disrupting the running order of the show. Fields was in his glory, Dillingham was in trouble. A hasty conference with his production staff and it was decided to spot the Fields specialty in the second act, so that it would not interfere with the beautiful finale.

Opening night, spotted in the second half of the show, it was a repetition of the night before. The show was stopped cold, applause lasting several minutes. Another hasty conference and the momentous decision: Fields would have to be dispensed with for the good of the production.

Exhausted after his long journey, but elated at his success, Fields retired early but was awakened at 2:30 in the morning by a phone call from Dillingham, and a request that Fields come to the Dillingham suite in the hotel.

Mystified, he hurriedly dressed and made his appearance. Upon hearing the decision to let him out, he cried for the first time in many years, unashamed. All his hopes dashed, it would be back to the grind he had been so happy to leave behind. But he reckoned without Dillingham. Dillingham and Flo Ziegfeld, together with Abe Erlanger, operated the New Amsterdam Theater in New York. Atop the theater was the Ziegfeld Roof, where Ziggy was preparing a revue called *The Midnight Frolic* for his plush after-theater nightclub. Dillingham phoned Ziegfeld and told him about the Fields episode, insisting that Bill be used in the new *Midnight Frolic* show. That was the beginning of the great Fields association with Ziegfeld and his introduction to and acclaim by Broadway audiences.

Thirty

*T*ED HEALEY? I hope some of you remember him. A very funny man, cut down just at the time in his career when he was really about to come into his own as a comedian. A lovable, unpredictable guy who didn't have a hate in the world. It was someone who didn't even know him who belted him over the head with a bottle outside a Sunset Strip nightclub. To have that kind of death was appalling to us who knew and loved the guy.

Healey's whole life, onstage and off, was one of impulse. He made his start in small-time vaudeville with a girl partner, graduating into Broadway musicals with a motley gang of stooges. He never did the same routine twice in succession—that is, line for line. He would start out and something would happen. A sneeze from the audience, a noise backstage, or a movement in the orchestra. These happenings would send him off into something new. Again, on impulse, he did whatever came into his humor-filled head. Impulse was also present in his private life. To illustrate:

Healey wasn't the most attractive guy in the world, and he was bald to boot. His baldness he attempted to cover up by continually wearing a hat. I think he wore it to bed. The wear-

ing of a "grass mat" he disdained as being effeminate. When on
the prowl around the nightclubs he liked to have a very pretty
girl companion dressed in the latest fashions, which he provided. The gal had charge accounts all over town and made
good use of them. Mink coats, stoles, evening gowns, shoes, and
hats. Her taste pleased Healey.

I remember one beautiful brunette that Teddy had set up in
a beautiful duplex in Westwood. That was his hideaway when
not at the studio.

MGM was doing a musical. Healey had a very important role.
There was a mechanical device that was a vital part of a
comedy routine in the picture. The device went haywire one
morning, and until it was fixed, Healey was on the loose.

The morning of Healey's early dismissal he met his pal, Rags
Ragland, another comic, and incidentally a two-bottle man.
Rags could easily dispose of two quarts of bourbon in a day and
not show any effects. Ragland and Healey went to an alley
saloon and did a bit of "lifting" with their lunch.

Finishing lunch, Healey, feeling no pain, went to Westwood
and M'Lady's duplex. Upon entering, Healey detected the odor
of stale cigars, and he was a chain cigarette man. On the living
room table was an ashtray containing two cigar butts. Impulse.

The very possessive Healey went into the lady's boudoir,
gathered all her finery in his arms. It included the mink coat,
stole, evening gowns, and lingerie. He made a second trip for
the hats and shoes. With his arms full of finery, he went into
the kitchen, placed everything on the four burners of the gas
stove, and turned them on full tilt. Everything was in flames,
including the duplex apartment.

Fire apparatus arrived to extinguish the blaze. The wardrobe
was all gone and the house saved, though there was considerable damage. My man Healey was arrested for arson, and we
have him in a picture.

Fortunately for MGM, the industry at that time had a position
of considerable influence in the community. A little pull here
and a word there, a promise hither and yon, and our man's
arson charges were reduced to a misdemeanor. A fine plus the
bill for damage in the duplex were ordered paid. Healey
resumed his services in our picture.

The gal? Oh, yeah. I almost forgot. She was out with an auto salesman, getting a demonstration in a car she was going to surprise Healey with on his birthday. The salesman was her brother, who smoked good Havana cigars.

I had to make a trip to New York with a stopover in Chicago. It was January and I wanted to be prepared for the miserable weather at that time of year. I had shopped around for a camel's hair coat and saw one to my liking at a gent's shop in Westwood. After lunch at the studio commissary, I was driving through the East Gate when I was hailed by Ted Healey, inbetween pictures and visiting the studio from force of habit. He greeted me with:

"What's with you, Irish?"

"I have to go East, so I'm going over to Westwood to buy a heavy coat I saw there this morning."

"What are you, a wise guy or somethin'? Why didn't you tell the great Healey you wanted to buy a coat? I got a joint in Beverly Hills, the best in camel's hair coats and at a nice price."

"Teddy boy, I saw just what I want in Westwood. That's it. Next time I'll come to you."

"I still say you oughta come to my joint. I'm goin' to go with you to see you don't get robbed." With that he opened the car door and was with me on the way to Westwood.

Arriving at my destination, I entered the store, followed by Healey, who looked with disdain at anything and everything. A clerk handed me my morning selection of a camel's hair. I was very pleased with myself. Healey fingering the material, turned to the clerk, and asked, "How much for this rag bag?"

The clerk looked at the embarrassed Grady, who looked at the nasty Mr. Healey.

"Hey Mister," repeated Healey to the clerk, "how much for that rag bag?"

The clerk hesitatingly replied, "It's $250."

Healey literally grabbed the coat from off my back, threw it on the rack, grabbed me by the arms, and led me out of the store, yelling over his shoulder, "You're a lot of thieves." I tried to pantomime to the clerk that my companion was a little "nuts" and that I would be back when I got rid of him.

Outside, Healey really laced into me for even considering

$250 for the coat I had selected. His man in Beverly Hills had the same coat but cheaper. I prevailed on him to go to one other store in Westwood just to compare. The second store had exactly the same coat but the price was $225. I could save $25 and wanted the coat. It was almost the same routine.

"You're a lot of thieves," and again I was dragged from the store. The second clerk thought we were both crazy.

To get rid of Healey and his shenanigans, I consented to go to his store in Beverly Hills, but with just one more stop. There was a men's shop in the Beverly Wilshire Hotel. I wanted to see what they had. To my surprise the same coat as Westwood, but $200 was the price. I had shaved the price by $50. I didn't think that price could be beaten, but to save embarrassment from Healey I told the clerk I would return.

Healey's joint was on the next block. A little Jewish man met us at the door. He was the kind of little man who sang his conversation and did a sort of dance movement as he spoke.

"Hello, Teddy boy, glad to see my friend again," he sang, and did a half-waltz while rubbing his hands.

"This is a friend of mine; very, very important. He wants a coat. Shake hands with Mr. Grady."

"Mr. Gravy, I'm glad to see you," he sang. "You must be a nice man to be with Teddy boy. I got just the coat you want," and he turned to the rack.

"Hey, Papa, wait a minute. I'll pick out the coat. You keep singing."

Ted finally selected a camel's hair coat. It was the duplicate of the first I had seen, only this coat had a half-lining of chamois. It just fit, looked rich and warm. I was all for it.

Before I could express my satisfaction, Healey grabbed it and went to the rear of the store, yelling over his shoulder to try on other coats Papa was ordered to show me. I tried on several. They were not what I wanted. I yelled to Healey to return with the first coat. It was a moment or two before he returned and held the coat for me to put on.

I looked at my new array in a full-length mirror and asked Papa the price. To my surprise it was $150. Gad, I had saved $100 over the Westwood coat. Healey jumped with:

"Hey, Papa, this is a Healey customer. What about the discount?"

"Always for Teddy boy's friends. Take the coat for $125, Mr. Gravy, and wear it in good health." The saving was now $125.

There was no stopping Healey. He looked at the shoulder of the coat, and pointed out several small holes to Papa.

"What's this? You got moths in the joint? Look, there, into this coat."

Papa looked, and was dismayed to find what looked to be moth holes.

"I'm sorry, Teddy boy. It shouldn't happen to you a thing like this. You're going to New York, Mr. Gravy. They got good weavers there, have the coat fixed. You can have the coat for $100."

Well, Healey was a help, after all, and sharp-eyed too. I got a beautiful overcoat that I wore for years, and it cost me $150 less than I intended to pay just because of a few little moth holes.

It wasn't until I returned from my trip to New York that I learned the truth of things. When Healey took the coat to the rear of the store, he took a nail file and pricked the few little holes and told Papa they were moth holes.

I was a little ashamed, but Papa was compensated beautifully by furnishing all the sports clothes for a Pasternack picture at my recommendation, and I might add, no little help from Healey, who was also in the picture.

The Healey caper to end all Healey capers nearly ended in a major tragedy. It's a long story and worth repeating.

Gilhooley's on Eighth Avenue in the 50's was Healey's hangout, as well as the hangout for the sporting element of the theatrical district. Being close to Madison Square Garden, Gilhooley's, Dinty Moore's, and Billy La Hiff's Tavern on West 48th were the meeting places for the gang.

On a Saturday night, Healey was at Gilhooley's bar. He was listening to, but not participating in a conversation. Standing next to Ted, but not one of the group, was a little guy who kept tugging at Healey's coat sleeve to attract his attention.

"Hey, Mister, wanna buy a yawl?" the little man said.

Several tugs and "Wanna buy a yawl?" a few more times and Healey is annoyed. He turned on the little man.

"Hey, Shorty, I don't know what you're selling, but I don't wanna buy a yawl."

"It's a nice yawl, Mister," persisted the little guy. "You'll like it."

"Here, Shorty, here's five bucks. Gimme one and don't annoy me."

"Five bucks won't buy my yawl. It cost thirty-five hundred. I'll sell it for eight hundred."

Now if the little guy had said $8 or $80 Healey wouldn't have been interested, but $800, that was something else again. He was all ears. He turned his back on his companions and concentrated on the, up to now, annoying little man.

"What's this thing for $800?" inquired Healey.

"It's a boat, Mister. Look, I'll show you pictures." From out of his wallet the little guy drew several snapshots of a trim little craft. He showed them to Healey. "I got it moored up at 74th Street and the Hudson River. You ought to see it close up."

Healey took a close look at the snaps, one by one, and in astonishment he said, "Hey, Shorty, a yawl is a 'yatchett.'"

"You mean yacht," corrected the short one. "A yawl has two masts, one big one center and a shorter one aft. I live aboard my boat. I've been a tunnel sandhog in the new Hudson River job and I wanna go back to Idaho. I gotta sell the *Viking*. It's a great buy, if you like to sail."

Our friend Healey's knowledge of watercraft was confined to trips on the New Jersey ferry, plus one drunken outing with his pal Dave Chasen in a Central Park rowboat.

It was Shorty's suggestion they take a taxi to view the *Viking* close up. No sooner said than done. In twenty minutes they were dockside, and looking at a trim small craft moored and bounding in the river current. In the taxi on the way to Shorty's yawl there was an exchange of identities. Shorty was Wilbur Higgins of Boise, Idaho, ex-sandhog, and he was homesick. Higgins had never heard of Healey, the Earl Carroll Vanities, or anything theatrical. All he wanted was to dump the *Viking*.

Aboard the *Viking*, Healey's eyes popped and he rubbed his hands in anticipation. There was a small cabin with a galley. The cabin could comfortably take care of ten midgets. Four adults would kind o' crowd the place. On the walls of the cabin were antiques: a cutlass, a blunderbuss, and a three-cornered musical-comedy admiral's hat. The little craft was immaculate and showed good care. Shorty was a pretty handy man with the bathtub gin routine and as they drank copious slugs of the stuff, Shorty showed Healey around the boat.

The sails were hoisted and lowered. The steering apparatus was explained, together with an auxiliary engine. The engine would give Healey trouble. He was so nonmechanical he had difficulty driving thumbtacks. The motor situation would be taken care of. He would hire a second-in-command who would also act as an engineer. Next thing, who to get as an engineer? Deep in thought, he had an inspiration.

One midnight the previous winter, Healey had had difficulty starting his car. The garage car-washer came to his assistance. The washer took one look inside the hood, kicked a tire, sat in the seat, turned the switch, and the great Healey was ready to roll. Nils Bjorkin, the washer, would be his second-in-command and engineer. Reasoned Healey, "All them Swedes are good sailors."

Little did Healey know that Bjorkin was born in the Bronx and had never left Manhattan. His only contact with water was passing over the Harlem River as a passenger on the elevated subway train. Another thing Healey did not know: the night the automobile didn't start, Healey'd had the wrong ignition key in the slot.

Healey spent the night aboard the *Viking*. He and Shorty Higgins celebrated with snorts of gin-ginger ale, and it was decided the final act of payment would transpire Monday A.M. at eleven o'clock at Healey's bank.

Shorty was at the bank at the stroke of eleven. Healey was nearly an hour and a half late. When he did show up, Shorty didn't recognize him. Healey had been to Brooks Brothers, the famous gentlemen's clothiers. Inasmuch as he was a "yachett" owner he should be suitably dressed to conform, and he was rigged out in a commodore's regalia that would do great credit to a Gilbert and Sullivan operetta. He wore enough gold braid to win over a tribe of savages, or scare them to death.

Shorty smiled, but said nothing. The payment of the $800, plus $60 for the antique cutlass, blunderbuss, and three-cornered hat, and Healey, self-styled Commodore Healey, if you will, was now sole owner of the "yachett" *Viking*.

The next order of things—the hiring of Bjorkin. Healey would pay him by the trip; he took him to Louie Guttenberg's, the second-hand clothes specialists, and bought the Swede an outfit that would outdazzle Captain Bligh, Captain Kidd, and Long John Silver. Bjorkin wore everything but a parrot on his shoulder.

Healey became a recluse. Not one word to his pals, with the exception of Dave Chasen, did he say about the *Viking.* Aboard the boat every night, surrounded by every yachting magazine he could find on the newsstands. So intense was Healey's reading, his pal Chasen expected any minute to be invited on a world cruise. He knew Healey.

The good commodore's week of intense magazine study behind him, a weekend cruise was proposed. There would be a few "grummets," as Healey called his girl friends, together with a few pals. Chasen would be the guest chef in charge of the galley.

Chasen reminded the commodore that Earl Carroll had committed his Vanities stars to a charity benefit at Asbury Park, New Jersey, on Sunday evening. "Fine," said the skipper, "we'll sail down."

With that statement, Healey visited the New York Auto Club for road maps of New Jersey. Here was an innovation. Road maps for an ocean voyage. This should prove interesting.

Three young ladies from the Vanities chorus; Big Jim Carroll, Earl's 240-pound brother and an ex-motorman from the Pittsburgh trolleys; Chasen; two doctor friends; and Bjorkin and Healey were the passenger list. When all were aboard the little *Viking,* her deck was within eight inches of the waterline. They might have to throw Big Jim overboard if things got tough.

It was a laughing skipper that ordered Bjorkin to start the motor. Twenty minutes later Bjorkin reported that due to lack of use the engine would be difficult to start. He suggested they use sails for movement until he got the thing started.

The current of the Hudson River is treacherous, so treacherous that ocean liners have difficulty docking. Commodore Healey, with his magazine knowledge and rowboat experience in the park, would handle the situation.

All hands, directed by Commodore Healey, hoisted sail. A

sudden gust of wind and they were off. BOOM, helmsman Carroll, the 240-pound ex-motorman, lost control of the whirling steering wheel. A crash into a beautiful sloop anchored nearby. It was nightclub star Harry Richman's prize possession. There was no attempt to ascertain the damage—all was confusion aboard the *Viking*.

Midstream the *Viking* raced toward the opposite, New Jersey shore. Somewhere in the yachting magazines Healey had read the word "tack." He yelled through his cupped hands, "Tack, tack." Nobody knew what the hell he was talking about. Bjorkin looked at all the seats, may be some joker had planted a tack for a gag. Just as they were about to crash into a pier, the wind changed and they were again on their way downstream. A miracle. The Lord was with the *Viking*. In water that would cause the intrepid Lord Nelson or Admiral Dewey to worry, the Healey craft slipped out of danger.

The yawl pitched and rolled. Bjorkin had to give up on the engine. He was lying in the cockpit, green-gilled. Boy, was he seasick. The three girls, also sick, were in the cabin, being soothed by the very uncomfortable doctors. There was nothing aboard to help the guests overcome their *mal de mer*. Dave Chasen, in the galley, didn't know lard from butter . . . seasickness had gotten him too. Big Jim Carroll was yelling his head off. "Go ashore, go ashore, call a cab, I'm dying." He was delirious.

Healey was atop the cabin, fully attired in commodore's regalia, plus blunderbuss and cutlass, shouting orders, to which nobody paid heed. He had been sampling the viands brought aboard by Chasen. He was not feeling any pain as he tightly grasped the mast and brandished the cutlass, giving out with orders much in the style of the infamous Captain Bligh. All were too sick to pay him heed.

In the annals of seamanship, the voyage of the *Viking* should be recorded in the historian's book of New York Harbor, notorious for its unpredictable currents and winds. This unmanned craft, with nine amateur sailors aboard, wound up becalmed off Bedloe's Island, the base of the Statue of Liberty and the entrance to New York Harbor. Wonders will never cease.

The fog was a pea-souper. They couldn't see across the deck. Commodore Healey noted the calm and lack of movement and ordered the anchor thrown overboard. Not a soul stirred. They couldn't lift a pint of moose milk in their condition. The good skipper had to do it himself, not knowing they were in the middle of the deep-sea channel and the anchor would not grab. He also lowered the sails. As the sails landed on deck they looked like a circus tent that had been blown down.

All night Saturday, all day Sunday, and Sunday evening, adrift in the fog. The bedraggled, seasick *Viking* passengers were panic-stricken. Not a soul was on his feet, including the doctors. Captain Bligh Healey didn't care whether he was asea or on land, he was crocked.

Monday morning. Jim Carroll was all for getting into the dinghy and abandoning ship and rowing ashore. But where is the shore?

Earl Carroll, when his actors and brother did not appear at Asbury Park, called the New York newspapers. The newspaper management, knowing Carroll's penchant for sensational arranged publicity, gave it cursory attention. News of the affair was relegated to a short item on an inside page. Carroll called the police, but they too, knowing Carroll and his publicity bids, were not very impressed. They bided their time.

Aboard the *Viking* there was a panic meeting in the cabin. The arguments were because of physical discomforts. Healey was blamed for their predicament. Jim Carroll was the loudest accuser. He wanted to go ashore, as did the others. Healey had an answer to all the protests. He gave the boat to Jim Carroll. It was his to do with as he pleased. Healey promptly went to sleep atop the cabin, enmeshed in the tangled sails but not before his girl friend weakly belted him for things in general.

Poor little Dave Chasen, as sick as he was, kept bemoaning the waste of the wonderful food he had prepared for the trip.

Two in the afternoon, Monday, Jim Carroll, now the skipper of the *Viking,* pulled up the rowboat tender. All who wanted to chance it could go with him. Bjorkin was the first over the side. Healey was awakened in the ensuing argument and protest, and forgot he was no longer the owner of the *Viking.* He started giving orders again, all directed toward Bjorkin, threatening him with the cutlass and the order "women and children first." Bjorkin reluctantly came back aboard the *Viking.* The three girls and the doctors piled into the tender. Jim Carroll was last, and with his bulk had the bow of the little boat six feet in the air. It took some time to distribute the weight so that it would be safe.

The two doctors took the oars but in which direction should they go? The ex-motorman Carroll, wise and sage, solved the dilemma. He spat in the palm of his left hand, he pounded his palm with his right, and the saliva went that way. That's the way the doctors started rowing.

Fifty yards from the *Viking* the rowboat scraped bottom. They had been marooned fifty yards off the shore of Bay Ridge, Brooklyn, out of sight because of the thick fog. Two of the girls knelt in the sand and prayed. Healey's gal yelled things off-shore for Healey's ears that should have created a hot wind and blown them to sea. It was an odd scene of thanksgiving. Two girls praying, drowned out by the curses of the third.

Jim Carroll rushed to the nearest telephone to advise his brother, who in turn called the Coast Guard. News of the survivors was still inside-page news. But when neither Healey nor Chasen appeared for the evening performance of the Vanities, it went front-page. But there were still those who thought the whole thing was a publicity stunt.

Aboard the *Viking*, Healey, Chasen, and Bjorkin were now panicky from the two days and nights of fog drifting. Healey, the ex-commander, now commander again because of Carroll abandoning ship, had a crying jag. He figured all was lost, and thought they might drift to a foreign port. In that case he would need currency. The commander started to sell his valuables. Dave Chasen was not interested. Bjorkin, optimistic, bought Healey's ring, wrist watch, stickpin, and the commander's braided coat for $45, this amount not to include the $25 Healey promised for the weekend of services as second-in-command. He also sold the *Viking* to Bjorkin for a delayed payment of $100.

Dave Chasen put all his belongings in a glass bottle. When it looked like all was lost he would throw it overboard, containing a note to his family in Port Chester.

Suddenly the fog cleared on Monday evening: Staten Island ferry passengers saw the *Viking*. The three shipwrecked victims waved shirts and arms aloft. The ferry passengers waved back. They had read the papers about the supposed publicity stunt.

Well, to sum up: the Coast Guard got a towline aboard the

Viking in the middle of Ambrose Channel and towed the craft to Sheepshead Bay. Bjorkin did not want to leave *his* boat, as per purchase. Healey insisted the sale of the boat and other objects were conditional. If they survived, everything was off. Bjorkin would have none of it. The battle was on.

Jim Carroll showed up with an attorney. They had hastily drawn up papers for the possession of the *Viking*. There was a bitter argument between the Swede, Carroll, and the attorney. Chasen stood to one side and listened.

All of a sudden he missed Healey and went aboard the *Viking* to investigate. He found Mr. Healey chopping a hole in the bottom of the boat with a fire axe. Just as Dave saw what was taking place, Healey yelled, "All ashore that's going ashore." Carroll, the Swede, and the attorney saw the *Viking* sink in fifty feet of water.

Never a dull moment with Healey and his impulses.

Thirty-One

Y EARS AGO, when the selection of an entrant for the Atlantic City Beauty Contest was a very important event in the respective states, the governor of Texas requested L. B. Mayer to send me down as a judge. I had turned down several of these contest judgings and tried to back out, but L. B. told me he had a political reason for my accepting and to go to Texas.

The Texas display of beauty was to be held at the Casa Manana, the spot made famous by the great Billy Rose, located on the highway between Fort Worth and Dallas.

Bill Coleman, MGM's Texas public relations man with an office at Dallas, met my arriving plane at the Fort Worth airport. With him was a very pretty and personable newspaper woman named Kathryn Howard. Coleman had made reservations for me at the Fort Worth Hotel, and upon arrival there he briefed me on the happenings to come.

There seemed to be a movement afoot by a local element to railroad Miss Dallas into wearing the beauty crown. I suspected something because two messages were handed me on arrival at the hotel. They read:

MISS DALLAS IS IT

THAT CROWN WILL LOOK GOOD ON MISS D

In the hotel suite we ordered lunch, preceded by a cocktail. The waiter serving the drinks had a card fastened to the lapel of his coat by a paper clip. It read: "Welcome, Pard—you're going to like Miss Dallas."

I asked the waiter if he knew Miss Dallas, and he replied, "No, I don't. Some guy in the elevator gave me four bits to wear this paper."

Lunch was served and under each plate was a rundown on the Dallas dame. She had to be some dish. I hated her already.

My two partner judges on the selection committee arrived. One was a local, and he was scared to death. He had been buttonholed and badgered wherever he went and the intimation was that if Miss D. didn't win he, the local, was a dead duck. I sympathized with him.

The second judge was a little guy from New York named Lou Wolfson. He was there also as a representative of the William Morris Theatrical Agency. The agency was to represent the winner in all theatrical endeavors. Wolfson had a deep tan on his arrival at Fort Worth. Three threatening notes and he had a death pallor.

I remarked that I had a hunch the Dallas dame would be an old bag. Wolfson and the local dashed to the windows to see how high a jump it was to the street. Miss Howard was enjoying the discomfiture of the two men, but poor Coleman kept repeating, "I gotta live here when this is all over."

The luncheon check had "Miss Dallas" written all over it. I pointed the names out to the waiter. "Another four bits?"

"No," he grumbled, "a buck, Mister."

I asked the waiter if any of his coworkers had ever seen Miss Dallas and he replied, "Cripes no, Mister, and I hope they never do. Those guys downstairs are driving us loco."

I talked with my two companions on the judging staff, the local and Lou Wolfson. I told them I wouldn't care if Miss Dallas was the governor's wife; if she didn't warrant the title of Miss Texas she wasn't going to get it.

In great confusion the local judge stood up, grabbed his hat, and made for the door like a jet. He stopped and the man held a plane ticket aloft crying out to Coleman, "Hey, Mr. Coleman, phone my wife, will yuh? I ain't got time. Tell her I'll phone her tonight from Juarez. This man's crazy," pointing at me. He was gone. That left me with Wolfson, who was himself looking over plane schedules he found in the room.

I thought a preliminary look at the scene of action was in order. Coleman had a car downstairs and we took off for the Casa Manana.

Arriving at the stage door we had to identify ourselves to the doorman. When Coleman advised who we were, the attendant bowed and scraped, slapped me on the back, and said, real clubby like, "I just know you're goin' to be right nice to Miss Dallas!" Him, too?

The workmen erecting the staircase midstage stopped their work and one of them pointed to a spot and said, "That's where she's goin' to stand." Just then I heard a yelp from the stage door. Two dogs came bouncing in. Each had a crude oilcloth sign attached to their sides. One sign read: "Hooray, Miss Dallas"; the other, "A yelp for Miss Dallas." It promised to be quite a night.

As we drove the highway on the return trip to the hotel, we were followed by two cars. The first car had "Miss Dallas" signs all over it. The driver recognized Coleman as he pulled alongside to pass and yelled, "Hi there, pardner. Goin' to be all right, ain't it?" He hesitated when he said, "Ain't it?"

Coleman didn't seem to be driving like a calm man should, and as for Wolfson, I looked and he was on the floor out of sight. Miss Howard, bless her—was having the time of her life.

The second car pulled alongside. There were no Miss Dallas markings, BUT two guys in the back seat were fondling double-barreled shotguns. WOW! Coleman nearly ran off the road, and Wolfson was kissing a mezuzah.

Back at the hotel, messages about the Dallas dame, notes pasted to the door about this Dallas dame, and in the room was a case of Scotch, compliments of Miss Dallas and a friend. Any friend of mine knows I'm a bourbon man from way back. Miss Howard got the Scotch.

My little friend Lou Wolfson wasn't feeling too chipper. I reasoned a couple of belts would help. Instead they nearly killed him. He was not a drinking man. Coleman drank to steady his nerves. Boy, he was uneasy. His only thought was the fact that he had to remain in Dallas while I went back in California. That is, if I lived through the night. The more he drank, the more protective and more concerned for my safety. He seemed to be continually pushing me away from the windows. Snipers, perhaps? And we were on the twelfth floor.

The time came for the journey to the scene of battle and the lion's den. I, Daniel, arrived with my companions purposely late, and besides, I had a helluva time half-carrying Wolfson. His legs were rubbery.

Our seats were first row center. That meant a long downward trip of perhaps a hundred steps. As we made our entrance we were cheered. Guns were fired in the air and there was a chant of, "Dallas! Dallas! Dallas!"

The "Star-Spangled Banner" was played and the entrants made their appearance. The first few were really crows, then came Miss Dallas. By the noise from the audience you would think she was the Messiah in female garb.

To be fair, Miss Dallas wasn't a bad looker, she wasn't good either. She kind o' got mixed up foot-wise when she made her complete turn to show the figure from the rear. There was a trace of a stumble. I noted a bit of a bulge suggesting a lot of sitting. Mebbe it was bar stools that created the spread, but it was definitely there. Facially there were jowls on their way to prominence. Secretly I hoped they would come all the way out before the crowning. It would make my job easier.

Into the picture came a tall, willowy blonde. This gal was really beautiful. She was frightened to death and her eyes welled up with tears. The gown she wore was ill-fitting, probably borrowed for the occasion. The high-heeled shoes seemed to bother her as she walked. With it all, she naturally was of regal bearing and to the manner born. This "agate" was going to be tough to beat. The rest of the crows wouldn't bother much.

Now came the parade down the staircase in bathing suits. I've seen a few bulges in my day, but this parade was the battle of the bulge. The Dallas dame was no exception. She had a suggestion of knocked knees that seemed to speak to each other. "You passed last time—my turn now, remember?"

Now comes the lineup for the last inspection. I gave a cursory look for my mind was made up. It would be the willowy one from Waxahatchie. I leaned over and made my decision known to Coleman and Miss Howard.

Coleman grabbed Miss Howard and said, "Let's get the hell

out of here." The gal didn't want to go but Coleman was insistent. "I'll have the car at the door," and he was gone.

Wolfson??? He left the minute he saw Miss Dallas. I saw him exactly one year later at a pub in London.

The master of ceremonies appeared with a warm smile toward the Dallas dame. Standing center stage he looked at me as much as to say, "We have already made the decision. Come up here, you peasant, and do the honors."

I was introduced, after a fashion, and made my way center stage. As I approached the mike I turned and made an Irish royalty bow to the contestants, then faced the audience. An attendant appeared and handed me a gold crown, balanced on a purple pillow.

"Goin' to look right nice on her, ain't it?" As he looked slyly toward "Bulge" Dallas.

With the pillow and crown in my hands, I went hammy. Taking a stance of feet spread apart, I let my eyes slowly rove the vast arena from the very last row, down a hundred steps to the front row, from one side to the other. Then came the ham statement of all time. Into the mike it was spoken, slowly and deliberately.

"Ladies and Gentlemen, I am deeply honored to be chosen by your chief executive to crown your Texas Lady Beautiful. It hasn't been easy," and I turned and bowed to the line of gals. Turning to the audience, I hesitated—the hesitation on my part to find a way for a quick exit after I made the presentation. It would have to be the same way I came in. After all, Coleman was up there with the car. Now it comes.

"Ladies and Gentlemen—I hereby crown the Texas lovely, Miss Waxahatchie."

I turned and placed the crown on the head of the sniffling blonde, kissed her hand, and made for the aisle and up the long flight, eight steps at a time. I was halfway up when the stunned audience realized what had happened. The first ten rows came after me en masse. It was a helluva situation. Maybe those guns had real bullets.

Reaching the top I found Coleman. He grabbed me by the arm and literally pulled me to the car, standing with the motor racing as though about to start the Indianapolis 500. We took off like a bat out of hell and down the hill, but where were we going? I could already hear motors being revved up for the pursuit.

Miss Howard knew of a hideaway nightclub about three miles away. It was in the form of a battleship and when we arrived we took a secluded table on the top deck. All the better to see the enemy if they decided to attack. Coleman was all for calling the police. I was against it. Mebbe the answering cop would be a relative of the Dallas cow, or maybe she was the cop's mother.

Coleman aggravated the situation by telling me that we had been invited to a victory dinner for Miss Dallas at a nightclub in Dallas. I was to repeat the crowning there. I was in trouble.

At four in the morning, after dropping Miss Howard at her home, Coleman delivered me to the hotel and wanted to stay the night. He was afraid to return to Dallas. The bulldog edition of the Fort Worth paper was on the street. It carried a small block on the front page. It said, "An individual from California came to the Casa to crown Miss Texas. The only good judgment he used was to take the first available transportation back to where he came from." And I'm still in Texas.

Coleman called the desk to say, "Mr. Grady left early this A.M. for California. Please send his bill to the studio."

We sneaked to the airport.

Miss Waxahatchie?? I never heard from her. Not even a card. I did hear that she didn't make Atlantic City because she couldn't stand wearing shoes and, anyway, that she was needed on the ranch.

The governor?? Oh, yeah, L. B. Mayer heard from him. The guy lost the next election. The overwhelming vote against him from Dallas did the trick.

Thirty-Two

I HAD an experience with a moppet that was a lulu.

The late John Considine was a successful producer at MGM. His *Johnny Eager* and *Boys' Town* were money-makers. John had a brother-in-law who was an agent, and said brother-in-law brought in a picture of a four year old. She was on the cover of a national magazine and was shown having a conversation with a famous industrialist. She was a beautiful child named Mary Agnes Fogarty, and a subtitle said she had an I.Q. of 150.

The fact that she had an Irish name heightened John's interest. He called me to his office and asked if I had seen the magazine cover. I had seen it and so told him.

"And you're not doing anything about it?" said he.

"What should I do, John? Admitted this is a highly intelligent child of four, but we have Margaret O'Brien and Juanita Quigley on the lot now and we are looking for vehicles for both of them. What will we do with another child, and an inexperienced one at that?"

"Then I infer that you are not interested."

"That's about it, John."

"Okay," he snapped, and I took my leave.

On the way out of Considine's office I met his brother-in-law,

Tom Conlan. Seeing him confirmed my original thought. It was Conlan who had brought the Fogarty child to Considine's attention.

About an hour after my session with Considine, I received a flash over my intercom from L. B. Mayer. "Come to my office on the double."

Arriving at Mayer's office, I found Considine displaying the cover picture and making the pitch that beauty like this, even in a child, should not be overlooked.

I repeated to L. B. what I told Considine: "So she is beautiful —what about the idle beauty we already have under contract?"

Mayer was a smart operator. He rarely crossed his successful producers. That was left to the likes of me. Deep down he might differ, but if it came to an issue, the producer won out and I took orders.

The Fogarty child lived in a small town outside Cincinnati. L. B. ordered me to go there and meet the child and make arrangements to bring her to the studio for a test. Considine had really made a pitch.

I arranged it. Inasmuch as Conlan had brought the child to Considine's attention, he should accompany me to Cincinnati and do the legwork. This would be a trip deluxe.

The Santa Fe Chief. A drawing room for Grady and a bedroom for Conlan. Same arrangements out of Chicago to Cincinnati. Arriving at our destination I went to my penthouse hotel suite, Conlan to a smaller suite below. A chauffeured limousine awaited my pleasure during my Cincinnati stay.

I told Conlan to contact the Fogarty family, go to their home, and talk with them about going to California. If the child turned out to be a monster, she would still be taken West. Once and for all, I was determined to stifle this haphazard interest in children just because of a pretty face.

The Fogarty home was a two-hour drive from Cincinnati. Conlan phoned to advise me that it was a very small town with wooden sidewalks. Father Fogarty was a bricklayer and by the looks of his face, a bottle man. They lived in a small frame cottage on the outskirts of the town.

Conlan made his pitch and Fogarty said he and his family would come to Cincinnati to meet me, but I would have to pay him the daily wage that he would make as a bricklayer. I agreed to everything, anything they wanted.

Bright and early Saturday A.M. the Fogarty group arrived in my limousine. The old man had had a few beers on the way up, and was not backward in loud belching.

The child, Mary Agnes, was beautiful. Typically Irish. Black hair, large blue eyes, and well formed. She idolized her old man. As for her mother? It seemed the child could take her or leave her, and most of the time she left her.

Mother Fogarty would admonish the child with, "Leave that be, Mary Agnes." Little Mary Agnes would give her mother a look of contempt and do as she pleased. Bleary-eyed Fogarty, after a while, would speak to the child, repeating the mother's "Leave that be, Mary Agnes," and the child would obey.

I started the discussion re the trip to California. I knew that Fogarty already had his other shirt packed, but I thought I would let him be important. "Do you think you could get away from your business, Mr. Fogarty?"

Conlan called me to one side. "This guy hasn't worked in several weeks."

Dennis Fogarty looked out the window in deep thought, turned, and said, "Well now, Mr. Grady, I'm a pretty busy man. I'll have to give this some thought."

Conlan was making signs behind the man's back that he was a little daft. He didn't have to tell me. While Fogarty was "giving it some thought," I looked for Mary Agnes. She was not in the room, but I did hear running water.

Spencer Tracy had given me a very beautiful and expensive pigskin toilet case. It was not on my dresser and upon investigating the running water, I found our little darlin' sailing my toilet case in a bathtub half full of water. I could have brained her. Her mother gave her a slap across her little fanny. The little angel literally spit at her mother and ran to her father. Lovely child.

To sum up the arrangements: I would bring the family to California. I would pay Fogarty $11 a day beginning from the time of departure. I'd bet all the tea in China that he'd never earned more than seven. I would also supply a nurse-teacher for Mary Agnes. Conlan said that the kid did not go to school, but I was determined to pile it on to forestall any more of these useless trips.

Train accommodations? Drawing room for Grady, drawing room for the Fogartys. Bedroom for the nurse. By the way, she was Fogarty's sister-in-law. Conlan had a bedroom. As for food, they ate as though it were going out of style. Fogarty didn't draw a sober breath from the moment he noted Conlan picked up all the tabs.

In Los Angeles, the family had a suite at the Ambassador Hotel. They were instructed to get a good night's rest and a studio car would call for them in the morning for a trip to MGM.

The next A.M. I got a call from the studio driver. Fogarty could not be found. I had an idea where he was, but ordered the group out without him. When they arrived at the studio I had Conlan take Mrs. Fogarty, the sister-in-law, and the moppet to make-up. I was going to shoot the test that afternoon.

By 11:30 we were ready to go. Little Miss Mary Agnes and her high I.Q. was comfortably seated in a big chair facing the camera. I was going to try and converse with her and record the conversation as we photographed.

We were ready to go. "Turn 'em over," and the camera turned and the kid ran like a bullet to her aunt, not her mother. Five times we tried it and five times she bolted out of the chair as the camera turned.

From the moment she left Cincinnati this kid gabbed incessantly. She would talk to anybody and everybody. Now not a yipe. I'm a very patient guy with kids, but even Considine, who visited the set, thought the kid should be belted. He left the set before I could speak my mind about him, Conlan, and kids in general. I ordered the crew to break for lunch. Mary Agnes, the little angel, was yelping for her father. I dispatched Conlan to the Ambassador to bring him out. The child was to take a nap until he arrived. If he could be found.

At 2:30 Conlan phoned that he couldn't find Fogarty. He had looked in every gin mill in the Ambassador area. I knew he must be in the hotel, since he had no money and would have to sign the checks for the drinks. The driver found him sitting with a construction gang in the rear of the hotel. There was Fogarty seated next to a mortar mixing tub, a case of beer at arm's reach. He and the workers were having a ball.

Conlan loaded him into the car and arrived at the studio at 3:30. I'd been at it five hours and not one foot of film of the little darlin'.

Fogarty arrived on the set. He had a "leaner" that had him walking to the starboard side as he walked. The child ran to him, delighted.

I sat him in the big chair, with Mary Agnes comfortable in his lap. Fogarty was sound asleep. Cameras rolled and as I talked to Mary Agnes, the large orchestra in the next studio gave a resounding whack on the cymbals and Mary Agnes was off like a bolt of lightning.

It took some time to catch her and get her back to her old man's lap. We had brought black coffee to him and he was now awake. Mrs. F. started to bawl him out for his drinking, and the child kept belting her in the leg as she talked, then threw a tantrum. Come hell or high water, I was going to get this kid on film. Back in her old man's lap and, "Turn 'em over." BOOM, she's off again. Five times I tried and five times she ran. I finally gave up.

What a day—what a week, beginning at Cincinnati!

Next day I brought Considine to the projection room to show him the film shot of his discovery, his little Irish prospect. Do you know what he saw? Fifteen hundred feet of film showing the fly on old man Fogarty's pants.

Needless to say, the Fogarty family went back to Cincinnati, the whole thing a fiasco. Fogarty wanted to stay in California for a vacation. What a freeloader! The parents of the child and the sister-in-law never had it so good, and childwise, the studio never had it so bad. The Fogarty venture cost MGM $5,600. That included test and crew. $5,600 for the pictures of Fogarty's fly.

Thirty-Three

LOUIS B. MAYER, guiding genius of Metro-Goldwyn-Mayer Studios, was a super-salesman. All his waking hours, when not otherwise engaged, he "sold" MGM productions to all and sundry. His pitch would be all the more eloquent if his office was visited by an exhibitor aligned with another studio.

Very, very VIPs, hoping to meet L. B., would give MGM ample notice that their California schedule included a visit to the studio. Rest assured a reception, commensurate with the importance of the visitors, would be arranged by the very capable Howard Strickling, L. B.'s public relations man, and his right arm.

Before visitors arrived, L. B. liked to be briefed. He wanted to know the guest's importance and background. Did he control theaters? Was he a family man and working at it? Was he a churchman and what were his politics? Usually a picture of the important guest would be supplied so that L. B. could single him out for special attention. It never failed to flatter.

Eddie Mannix, studio general manager and my Irish pal, together with myself, was in on one of the VIP receptions. Not long after it started, Mannix and I wished there was a rock to hide under.

On this particular day, the very important visitor was a major exhibitor from the Midwest. His theater holdings numbered several hundred, and when Mayer heard he was aligned with Paramount, he planned a super-pitch.

The briefing on Mayer's desk said the visitor's name was Jimmy Costigan. He preferred to be known as Jimmy rather than James. The brief said he was a churchman of importance, having been instrumental in building a cathedral in his home-town. A good family man, three sons, very important theater holdings, and a leader in politics in Cook County. He had emi-grated to this country in 1919.

Now everybody knows Cook County is in Illinois, including the Chicago area. Mayer, in his zeal to make a good pitch, hastily misread Cook County, Illinois, as Cork County, Ireland. To Mayer, the name of Jimmy Costigan and County Cork went hand in hand.

L. B. requested his number-one girl, Ida Koverman, to get him a history of the Catholic Church, together with data on County Cork, its industry, population, and native sons of importance. Mayer would show Costigan he was well versed in things Irish and Costigan's way of life.

Costigan, a dapper little guy of a little more than fifty years, arrived in Mayer's office with four companions. Mayer's greet-ing was something to observe. Because of the photograph on his desk, Mayer knew which was Jimmy. He didn't wait for Strick-ling's introduction but bounced over to Costigan, threw his arms around his shoulders, and affecting an Irish brogue, came out with: "Jimmy, m'boy, it's a pleasure to meet you and your friends."

Costigan looked at L. B. strangely and proceeded to introduce his companions, and peculiarly they were all of Greek extrac-tion. This didn't stop Mayer, he went into his planned routine.

"Jimmy, I know all about you, and a credit you are to the Irish. My good friend Cardinal Spellman will be pleased to know we have met. And to think you come from the beautiful County Cork, where most of the great Irish statesmen first saw the light of day. And that cathedral you caused to be built in Cork will be your lasting monument when you and I are dead and gone."

Mayer now introduced Mannix and myself as his two Irish

staff-members, telling how important we were to him. Costigan didn't seem impressed, he seemed ill at ease. Mayer went on:

"Jimmy Costigan, I know you are a good family man. I would wish that if I were a Catholic, and had sons such as yours, one of them would take holy orders and be dedicated in priestly robes. Tell me, Jim, are your parents still living in County Cork?"

That's as far as Mayer got. Costigan stopped him.

"Mr. Mayer, I think you have been misinformed. I am a Greek. My Greek name is Tanapoulous. Costigan is a name I have been using for years in business. I'm not from County Cork, I'm from Cook County, Illinois, and my parents are still in Greece."

I felt sorry for Mayer. All his research and planning for naught. I knew poor old Ida Koverman was going to catch hell and unjustly so. I read the brief on Mayer's desk. It distinctly said "Cook County." L. B. wanted so badly to impress Costigan that he had rushed things. Eddie Mannix explained to Costigan.

Mayer retired in embarrassment to his anteroom, there to have a heart attack or to throw up. The Costigan party had a hearty laugh when Mannix finished explaining.

Mayer reentered the scene looking sheepish. Jimmy Costigan greeted Mayer with the richest brogue, saying, "I learned that Irish brogue from the Irish neighborhood I lived in in Chicago.

Know something?? Mayer's pitch was not in vain. We ended up with the Costigan account.

Much has been written about Louis B. Mayer in books and magazine articles. Evidently each writer thought it better to dislike the man even before they met him, and cut him up unmercifully.

The writers said he was stubborn, quick to anger, unforgiving, and capable of holding a lasting "hate." It was written that he was tyrannical, overbearing, and a "consummate ham." To a degree I will go along with this, but goddamn it, not one writer gave the man his just due as a showman. In my opinion, he was one of the great showmen of our time. Not a writer gave him credit for that.

I first met Mayer in 1908. He owned a small vaudeville theater in Haverhill, Massachusetts, and was interesting himself in the new entertainment medium, "moving pictures."

In those days of struggle the man was a human dynamo in every phase of the business. Any observer would have been convinced that Mayer was destined for greatness.

Having all the faults that the writers enumerated, Mayer had to be a helluva man to go as far as he did in the amusement world. I believe that L. B. Mayer's influence made the motion picture industry the respected giant that it became. Now that he's dead we should call him the "spinner," because seeing to what depths his beloved industry has fallen, he must be turning over in his grave.

L. B. Mayer talked big, he thought big, he acted big, he was big. It was he who was responsible for the star system. It was his foresight that made Metro-Goldwyn-Mayer Studio the most envied in the business, the largest and best operated. It was also his foresight to have under exclusive contract a fantastic roster of stars. Read and be impressed, and compare with what is around today. Greta Garbo, Norma Shearer, Joan Crawford, Rosalind Russell, Jean Harlow, Myrna Loy, Ethel Barrymore, Donna Reed, Elizabeth Taylor, Margaret O'Brien, Billie Burke, to name a few on the distaff side.

On the male list, John Gilbert, Jack and Lionel Barrymore, Clark Gable, Robert Montgomery, Wallace Beery, Spencer Tracy, Jimmy Stewart, Robert Taylor, William Powell, Gene Kelly, Walter Pidgeon, Lew Ayres.

There were many others in the featured-player class, and all under exclusive contract in the same period. Mayer was greatly aided by that genius of production, Irving Thalberg, in administering to these world-famed personages. After Thalberg's death, it was all in the hands of Mayer and the very capable assistants with whom he surrounded himself.

Knowing the value of the spoken word for his artists, Mayer had the world's best writers and creators under contract. An imposing producer and director list were Mayer's charge. To keep his studio in the forefront of world entertainment, his artists and creators were concerned only with the best: the best plays were made into pictures, together with best-selling books and outstanding original stories. The studio's overhead was enormous, and there could be no such thing as a losing picture. Studio earnings were great. All this was in the hands and under the guidance of the man with many faults.

The only word Mayer knew was "BIG." He wanted a big, successful studio, he got it. He wanted a big, successful stable of thoroughbred horses, he got it. The L. B. Mayer colors were familiar sights in every important racetrack winners' circle throughout the country. L. B. Mayer was a helluva man in my book. I had great respect for him as a showman, but though I knew him long before many of those with whom he was associated, I never felt close to the man.

L. B. and I were in continual conflict. He was utterly devoid of humor. The Good Lord blessed me with a sense of humor and I took advantage of it. L. B. did not appreciate a funny story. Anybody who did not know about this and related one of the humorous stories of the day would get a cold, unappreciative stare. The effort was never repeated.

It seems he always had a chip on his shoulder around the studio and would argue any point at the drop of a hat. If he wound up on the short end he would have the sulks, and it always seemed to be my fate to have some dealings with him at such times. A point to illustrate:

In New York I was the eyes and ears of the studio for several years before being sent out as casting director. Like the late Mark Hellinger, famous columnist and Mr. Broadway himself, I affected gray suit, gray fedora hat, black shirt, and white tie, with a carnation in my lapel buttonhole. Somewhere along the line I picked up a rattan swagger stick. I carried it continually. It served as a release for nervous energy.

Grady, in his New York attire of gray, black shirt, and white tie, appeared at the studio to take up his new duties. The second or third day I was walking down a studio street, and Mayer saw me out of his office window. It was one of his days with the sulks. Seeing me in my New York attire, he turned to his intercom and called his studio general manager, my good friend of many years, Eddie Mannix.

"Mannix, look out the window and see your Irish friend, Grady. He is dressed like a gangster. If he wants to stay around here, get those clothes off him."

Not a very pleasant introduction to studio life, and if I hadn't had the shorts I would have chucked it and gone back to New York. I stayed on to have many, many difficulties with the great man.

As quick as he was to anger at me, he was just as quick to do an about-face and compliment me for something he thought well done. He was often heard to say publicly, "That Irishman certainly knows talent. He ought to, been at it long enough." If it hadn't been my good fortune to be blessed with the talent appraisal stock in trade, I'd have been given the heave-ho many times, contract or no contract.

L. B. had few intimates outside the studio. He did have several of *his* selection, who danced attention on him, realizing that by doing so they would profit. I felt he was a lonely man.

There was a period of several years that he was dance crazy. About five nights a week he would be at the Old Trocadero, or the Mocambo, or Ciro's with a beautiful dancing partner. Since he was a married man, though not working very hard at it, it was always arranged that he would be the odd man in the table group. He wasn't fooling anybody—it was the same gal every night, though he danced with others in the group.

Mayer would anticipate the downbeat of the orchestra and be on his feet raring to go. He didn't miss a dance from start to closing. I watched him many times. He seldom looked at his partner while "terpsing." He looked like he was counting the house, but it was really the man's vain habit to look at the ringsiders and hope they were remarking the vitality he had at his age. There might have been a few making that remark, but some made cracks that I'm glad he did not hear.

On several occasions I would be called to his office the morning after a dance session, there to meet some gal he had met the night before. It was the usual routine. "This is a beautiful girl, Mr. Grady. I'd like you to make a test of her."

I never voiced an opinion whether the gal was worthy of a test or not. It would be a waste of words. I'd have to make it anyway. I had been through the same routine so many times in his ornate office.

In his office, introductions would be in order, then the routine. With his hands he would adjust the girl's hair into several makeshift styles. High, low, over one eye, gather a handful and make a psyche knot on the top of the head. The young lady

would be taken to the large window and her profile reviewed
in the light, then to a dim spot and inspected again. What the
hell that was for, I've never been able to fathom, but it was part
of the routine. A quick inspection of calves to the knees, and
then came the "walk-around." Circling the lass, deep in
thought, he was much like a sculptor preparing to sculpt a
"sculpt." I sat bored stiff. He would be trying to impress the
young lady, and the presence of his casting director helped the
importance.

When Mayer was finally unattached, he had a dinner dance
about once a month at his large home behind the Beverly Hills
Hotel. I would arrange the entertainment program—happy to
do so, because it gave me a chance to show off some of the new
musical talent we had at the studio, and some I hoped to sign.

On one occasion I saw the host paying marked attention to a
lovely brunette. I recognized her as the niece of a very prominent writer under contract to the studio. The young lady was
well set up, nice face and figure, but unfortunately she had a
rather large mouth that showed a lot of semibuck teeth when
she smiled. I sensed that I would get the usual call to L. B.'s
office the next morning. I wasn't wrong.

The brunette of the night before was getting the routine.
Hair, profile, legs, the walk-around, and the "sculpt" concentra-
tion, but Mayer was pouring it on a little thicker than usual. It
dawned on me. He was trying to make a new deal with the girl's
writing relative, and giving the extra attention to the favorite
niece might help in the negotiations. L. B. never missed a trick
when it came to studio business, and I went along with him.
Came the instructions.

"Mr. Grady, I want the best cameraman on the lot, Irene must
go all out in clothes, and makeup and hairdress must use their
top people. The minute the test is ready, call me, no matter
where I am. I'll come to see it."

Couldn't get better instructions than that. I carried out everything to the letter. Each department connected with the test did
a great job. The gal looked lovely as long as her face was in
repose, but the moment she smiled the buck teeth offset everything.

When the test was ready for L. B. to see in a projection room,
I called his faithful executive secretary, wonderful old Ida Kov-

erman. I advised her of L. B.'s wishes and it wasn't long before she called me back. She had contacted L. B. in the dentist's office at the studio. He would be right over.

L. B. came into the projection room with a blood-spattered towel over his mouth. He gestured to start the test. As it rolled on the screen he gave grunts of approval, but when the girl smiled he grunted. "Jeez, look at those teeth."

Me, without thinking, and Mayer just having teeth pulled, I replied, "Yeah, L. B., but those teeth are all hers."

If looks could have killed, my throat would have been cut. Mayer stomped out of the projection room, raging inwardly. How did I know he only had one tooth left in his head, how did I know he was holding his lower bridge in his left hand?

Mayer didn't speak to me for several weeks. I was rather surprised; for saying much less at other times I had been fired.

One of L. B.'s inner circle of intimates was an agent. This man accompanied Mayer everywhere throughout this country and Europe. He did a lot of the travel arrangements and gained first-hand knowledge of what MGM would be interested in for future picture-making. It was a very profitable association, being constantly in Mayer's company. They both had a few interests outside the picture business.

The agent had a big home in Bel-Air and many times, with Mayer as guest of honor, he entertained lavishly, and at times, quietly. Only guests that the agent felt would interest L. B. were invited. Rest assured, rival agents were not present, though some of their clients were. If the host noted that Mayer was showing more than passing interest in a rival agent's client, negotiations would be entered into, either to split commissions or in the event of an MGM deal, an outright buy of the agent's contract. This host agent didn't miss a trick.

Mayer liked to play cards—pinochle, gin, or the German game of klob. An opponent was conveniently provided, and it just happened to be a little wide-eyed writer the agent represented. Naturally the little man wound up with a writing contract at MGM, though he did precious little writing. Most of his time was taken up playing cards with the boss.

The agent was a bachelor, the little writer married. Mayer

had trouble with insomnia and would call the little man at all hours of the night to rush to his house and help him while away the sleepless hours playing cards. When L. B. fell asleep, it was the little man's cue to go home.

The writer's wife was a timid little homebody who was never on the agent's invitation list. She would sit at home and wait for her little man to return. They received a modest salary from the studio, but the wife complained. Meeting Mayer one evening, with a couple of drinks aboard, she let out a beef. Next day her writing spouse was out of a job and the agent got another card-player for Mayer.

I received a call one afternoon to come to Mayer's office. There I was introduced to a busty blonde. Her name was Concannon. Now Concannon is an Irish name and I thought to myself, "If this big amazon is Irish, I'm a Chinaman."

The busty balloon smuggler was getting the usual Mayer routine, the "sculpting of a sculpt" as it were, and I received the usual order to make a test, though this was different—there was to be sound. The gal, I was told, was an actress. (God forgive her.)

Mayer's instructions included that the scene should be a sexy one, a love scene. I winced. The costuming had to be as revealing as possible. Her curves were to be stressed. Looking through the costume she wore in Mayer's office, her curves were wide arcs. There *had* to be an angle as to the why of this test. Outside the office the agent friend tipped me off. He and L. B. were trying to buy some ranch property the gal's father owned in the Valley. I went along with the routine. I selected a sexy scene and assigned one of our young stock company players to play opposite her. It was a hopeless task. Three weeks of rehearsals and the result? Nothing. I decided to make it a silent test.

In wardrobe, in keeping with Mayer's instructions for sex, I selected a very sheer, lacy nightgown. It was all-revealing and exposed cleavage almost to her navel. I'd give them sex.

The stage crew, very inattentive to their usual routine, found it most convenient to do their work very close to Miss Concannon. They were continually setting lamps behind the girl, and then rushing forward to check their handiwork. Soon Stage 18 was crowded with onlookers who had never taken the time to watch a test being made before . . . or since, I guess.

The background scenery selected for the test was a boudoir in a castle high in the Bavarian Alps. A large picture window permitted a view of a winding road leading to the valley below. A divan was conveniently placed before the window so that its occupant could see the scene deep in the forest. So far, so good.

While Miss Concannon reclined on the divan, the personable, velvety-voiced young actor told her the story that MUST run through her mind as she was being photographed.

"You are a royal princess. Your lover is a captain in the royal army and because he is a commoner, your family objects to the romance and will not allow you to see or communicate with him. You last saw him nearly two years ago and in all that time you have been faithful in thought, word, and deed. A trusted maid smuggled love missives in and out of the castle. Princess, this day your wonderful lover is returning from the front; your stored-up love will have its outpouring. You will clasp him in your arms at last."

Pretty good, huh? Our busty Miss Concannon liked the story and liked the way the story-telling young actor related it. The test was to be made with separate picture and sound track. Miss Concannon's makeup was freshened and her locks brushed; she wet her lips and we were ready to roll.

If the lady had uttered one word with her raspy sinus voice it would have spoiled everything. As the story of her love life was being repeated to her, she visualized all too vividly. Evidently her frustrations had been aroused.

She writhed, she heaved the "busties" until I thought any minute they would come out into the open. Her arms waved from side to side as she crossed and uncrossed her legs. Now the big moment. Her young actor assistant said:

"Princess, look down the mountain, the road to your castle, your lover is there, home from the wars. The king and queen are in the village. This is your day, your day with your lover."

Wow! Did she twist and turn, heave, and wet her lips. She was living every minute of it, we thought. The crew loved it, the gals left the set.

"Now, Your Highness, your lover is in the castle . . . He is in your boudoir . . . He is in your arms. Princess, what is it you most desire at this moment?"

To our utter amazement the "princess" rolled over on her

side and spoke for the first time. "Could I have a glass of tea with lemon?"

That test made the rounds of the private home projection rooms. It was a must-see for months to come. The tea and lemon line was hysterical.

Mayer and the agent saw the test and gave up on the real estate deal. Just as well, the state took over the property for a freeway. Never a dull moment.

L. B. Mayer liked to see his name in print, but whatever article it was connected with had to be of importance—nothing inconsequential. My good friend and his constant companion when Mayer traveled was Howard Strickling, publicity chief for MGM. Howard saw to it that all Mayer's publicity was top-drawer.

An important syndicate writer for a chain of Southern news-papers came to Hollywood. An appointment was set up with L. B. The day she appeared for the interview, Mayer was in a reminiscing mood, and repeated statements he had made to other writers. The old gal wasn't interested. She wanted a state-ment of importance from the great man and asked an impor-tant question.

"Mr. Mayer, who is the greatest star you have ever known, past or present?"

This could be an embarrassing question; it could have reper-cussions if answered by Mayer. With fifty top stars on the studio roster, if he mentioned just two, he would have forty-eight on his neck. He ducked the issue very gracefully by advising the writer to come to see me, "an authority on such matters." Gra-dy's opinion would be his, said Mayer, or vice versa.

Putting me in a spot like that would be more vice than versa. Mayer was a smart studio head. He wanted names mentioned that were in current MGM pictures. Greer Garson had just finished *Mrs. Miniver.* It was a big success. Surely I would be smart enough to mention Miss Garson as my number-one choice for women. Spencer Tracy and I were very close at the time. His *Captains Courageous* was an all-time great. Tracy had to be my male choice. So thought Mayer.

When the lady asked for my choice of the greatest male or female star I had ever seen, I did not hesitate.

"A star to my mind must be all-embracing in the art or arts. Their talents must be such that they are unforgettable, they must inspire." I was very definite in my opinions on this subject, and though I knew whom I was going to name, I found it difficult to make my words descriptive enough. Getting in deeper, I named my all-time greats.

"The greatest woman star I have ever seen, past or present, is Judy Garland."

Judy's name was unexpected by the writer. Her poised pencil went from her pad to her mouth as she leaned back in her chair and meditated. I felt she was disappointed.

"Why Judy Garland, Mr. Grady?"

"You, as a motion picture and drama critic, have probably seen everything that Judy Garland has done. Am I right in assuming that?"

"I am a great admirer of Judy's."

"All right. Have you ever in your career heard a song sung to equal her rendition, be it comedy or a lilting ballad? Judy Garland can do and has done dramatic scenes that will tear your heart out. She can do comedy that compares with the best comedienne in the business. She can dance. Remember the tramp number with Fred Astaire? That great specialty was planned, rehearsed, and photographed in its entirety all in one day. She will go into Carnegie Hall, amphitheaters, arenas, anywhere—and keep an audience spellbound for two or more hours, and she does it alone. Where this frail body gets the stamina to do it is a mystery. By accepted standards, Judy is not beautiful. She has physical stature imperfections that you are unaware of when she is in action. Let her sing a love song, or do a scene that involves sentimental expression, you forget imperfections. She is beautiful. Judy Garland excels in everything she attempts, and I means excels. Madame, I will go on record as saying the greatest star I have ever seen is Judy Garland."

There were moments of silence. "Mr. Grady, I have been sitting here reflecting. I have seen everything that Judy has done, either stage or screen. I feel like apologizing for not thinking of her in the terms you express. You know something? I agree with you. Now for your choice in a male star?"

It wasn't going to be easy to refrain from mentioning my friend Tracy's name. He was and always will be a great, to be sure, but I was asked for my opinion. My answer had to be from the head and not from the heart.

"I hope you know the French theater and the French cinema, because my male star choice is French. The greatest male star I have ever seen, Spencer Tracy notwithstanding, is Pierre Fresnay."

"I am an admirer of Mr. Fresnay."

"My knowledge of the French language is very limited. Just looking at Fresnay, his facial expressions, his hand movements, his eyes, I knew every word he was saying both in the theater and motion pictures." I had seen Fresnay on the French stage and in motion pictures. I saw him in drama and comedy. He excelled. He came to New York and did a play called *Noah* at the Longacre Theater. He was in the title role.

In the second act, Noah was pleading for a cessation of the rains. He walked to the stage footlights, stared out over the audience into the recesses of the top balcony. His plea was so moving and so realistic that I found myself, in my second-row seat, turning my back to the stage and Fresnay, and staring into the balcony, fully expecting to see the gods to whom Noah was pleading. Finishing his speech, Fresnay moved upstage, the curtain was lowered, the audience sat for several moments spellbound before rising and showering this great actor with shouts of "Bravo, bravo." I have yet to see a more moving performance. I name Pierre Fresnay as the greatest male star I have ever seen.

After telling her about this experience, I received a look from the lady that told me she was in full agreement with my choice. I had won her on both counts.

In her widely read column, she credited Mayer with these two choices. There was hell to pay. He denied that I had any right to speak for him. The controversy received more space than the selection. I was really in the doghouse, so much so that a free-lance writer who had spent three weeks with me night and day preparing a magazine article about my life, was denied the right to have it published, a denial Mayer had a right to make because of my studio contract.

I still stick to my guns. The greatest stars I have ever seen are JUDY GARLAND and PIERRE FRESNAY.

Thirty-Four

A LASTING memory in my life will be my meeting with the most beautiful woman who ever graced the stage of the Metropolitan Opera—Madame Maria Jeritza.

I was never an opera lover, but a friend in the Green Room Club invited me to the Met to see and hear this new operatic sensation. She was a Viennese who had supplanted Geraldine Farrar in the hearts of all Europe and the Americas.

My friend had standing-room tickets and the opera was *Tosca.* Standing there enthralled throughout the long evening, I developed a case of goose pimples. Jeritza was a tall statuesque beauty with a wealth of blonde hair—a great actress. Curtain call after curtain call greeted this great star at the opera's end.

Years later I was in Toronto attending the premiere of Keith Winter's play *The Shining Hour.* It was directed by a present-day great of Canadian origin, Raymond Massey. When I returned to the Royal York Hotel, I found an urgent message to return to New York as quickly as possible. A planned trip to Detroit and Cleveland canceled, I was in New York the next afternoon. J. Robert Rubin, my boss and L. B. Mayer's partner, called me to his office.

He told me that Jack Cummings, Mayer's nephew, and a director named Chuck Reisner had been sent to New York from the studio to make a movie test of Maria Jeritza. Each day they went to the St. Regis Hotel where she lived, they were announced then invited into her apartment, but Madame Jeritza would not make an appearance. They had already spent three days waiting in the apartment without meeting the lady. I was dispatched to the St. Regis.

Like the others, I was announced and invited to the Jeritza suite. There I found Cummings reading a magazine, and Reisner looking out the window at Fifth Avenue below.

"What's going on, Jack?" I asked.

"You tell us. L. B. wants us to make a test of Jeritza, and this is as far as we get. She won't come out of her room. Her maid says she is shy."

"Which is her room?" Chuck pointed to a door.

I knocked on the door . . . No answer . . . I knocked again . . . No answer. Opening the door slightly, I looked in. Madame Jeritza was sitting on the edge of her bed, fully clothed and nervously wringing her hands. I noted a slight smile on her face as I spoke.

"What's going on, Daisy? Those men out there have been waiting three days to see you. I have just arrived from Toronto to take over. Be a nice lady and come out and meet the boys."

I took her by the hand and entered the drawing room. Cummings and Reisner nearly collapsed when I presented Madame Jeritza. Again that mischievous smile on her face. This gal had a sense of humor.

After murmuring an acknowledgment of the introduction, she released my tightly clasped hand and went to a divan at the extreme end of the long drawing room. The divan was atop three steps and directly under a life-sized painting of the beautiful Jeritza at the time she made her Metropolitan debut. The painting was as beautiful as its subject.

As we sat looking at her, we were unconsciously compelled to look above the lady on the divan at the painting over her head. It was the greatest trick I had ever seen. The lady on the divan gave me the illusion that she was just as beautiful as the painting, though there was a difference of nearly twenty years.

I was seated on the floor of the large room, my arm resting on a low backgammon table. To ease the prevailing silence, I grabbed a pair of dice and invited the lady on the divan to shoot craps.

"Come on, Daisy, try your luck." Perhaps it was the familiarity of "Daisy" or that she was in the company of someone who baffled her. Ignoring Jack and Chuck, she came down on the floor. We shot dice. In a short few minutes, she had lost and I won $80.

From Cummings and Chuck I got, "Well, I'll be goddamned!"

I repeated to Jeritza what she already knew. Mr. Mayer wanted a test of her. Jack and Chuck had been sent to New York for that purpose, and the test was to be made as quickly as possible. She wanted to wait three days, I presume for physical reasons, but Cummings and Reisner had to return to the studio. I took over.

Inasmuch as this was a photographic test, no sound, interest would be centered solely on her, photographically. No dialogue to divert from her errors or imperfections. Wardrobe was an important factor. I asked to see what she intended wearing for the test.

In her dressing room there were walls of wardrobe closets. Her clothes were magnificent, made by the best houses in New York and Paris. The gowns were all sleeveless and after selecting several, I had to level with the woman. It was best that she wear some jewelry on her very long arms. Jewelry would be to her advantage. After all, the gal was in her forties, and cameras are cruel and tell all. A very agreeable gal, she promised to take care of the jewelry end and be at the Fox Studios, 54th Street and Eleventh Avenue three days later at 8:00 A.M.

The star was at the studio at the appointed time for makeup. Two hours later we were on the set and ready to go. A quick glance through the camera finder and she looked okay, except for a few crow's feet that lights could correct, but New York cameramen at that time did not have the craftsmanship of their West Coast counterparts. I had her moving around the living room set, rather than the standing pose that makes one so self-conscious. Silent photography is a tough assignment for the uninitiated. The first shot finished, I asked Madame to change to another gown and, if she could, to change her costume jewelry.

"By the way, Madame Jeritza. That costume jewelry you have is very beautiful. Did you buy it in Europe?"

She let out a yelp. "Lisa, Lisa—come quick!" Lisa was her secretary. Lisa and the personal maid came on the double, the secretary carrying a carved wooden case the size of a shoe box. Circling the box were wide brass bands.

"Lisa, 'Beelee' thinks this is costume jewelry. Please open the case and show him."

Lisa and the maid gave me looks of semicontempt that I could think of such a thing. The box was opened and Grady nearly collapsed. That case contained an assortment of jewels that Tiffany's would like to have in its showcases. Since we were on an open stage with strangers all over the studio, almost in panic I shoved the three women into the portable dressing room erected for her convenience. There I took a closer look at the contents of the jewel case.

Only in Rome's famous house of gems have I seen a more beautiful collection. There were diamond tiaras, necklaces, rings, brooches, sunbursts, bracelets, these pieces inlaid with diamonds, emeralds, and the most vivid pigeon-blood rubies I have ever seen. Most every royal house in Europe, as well as world-famous personages, had gifted this woman—all in appreciation of her artistry. I was alarmed and thoroughly frightened. I instructed the three women to latch the room door and not to leave until I returned.

I sped to the telephone and phoned my friend, Detective McGann of the New York Police safe and loft squad, and formerly of the Fifth Avenue jewelry detail.

Mac came post haste, took one look in the jewel case, and proceeded to give Madame a mild and corrective dressing down. Here she was on Eleventh Avenue near the river, the heart of New York's famous Hell's Kitchen, among strange people, strange surroundings. She was tempting fate.

The detective, a jewelry expert, appraised the collection roughly at a million dollars. He would not allow anyone to leave the dressing room until he had brought two men from 47th Street to stand guard. While awaiting the policemen, Mac reexamined the collection.

Represented in the fabulous jewel case were the royal houses of Great Britain, Germany, Italy, Greece, Spain, Portugal, and Sweden, together with the Netherlands and Austria. In addition, Madame Jeritza's former husband, a famous European, had showered his wife with priceless examples of the jeweler's art.

It was very relieving to close up shop after the final shot, and see that the policemen accompanied Jeritza to her bank vault to deposit the treasures. WOW! What a day!

Maria Jeritza could have been a twin of my friend Garbo when it came to shyness. She disliked crowds. In restaurants she was always inconspicuous in a secluded corner. Chauffeur-driven during the day, she took long walks at night, unnoticed, as she preferred.

There seemed to be rapport between us. She had never known a Broadway sense of humor, and she wanted to know everything about the picture business and the life of a Broadway agent. My story of the Silver Slipper crowd fascinated her, as did the private-party business. We had dinner several times in out-of-the-way spots, preferably places where they had string music. She was a very pleasant companion.

The word from the studio: Jeritza's New York tests did not show her to advantage. The photography was disappointing and the lighting left much to be desired. I wasn't surprised, though it would be a body blow when I told my friend. To be truthful, the lady was in her mid-forties and only for very short moments were there signs of her once-great beauty. In several angles she looked like Jean Harlow.

The camera is a cruel instrument. You can think horses and talk cows, but the camera tells. It will add from one to two inches on the hips. It takes an expert to photograph *any* beauty, I don't care who it is. One mistake and a damaging imperfection will appear on the screen. With dialogue, photography is a talking picture; silent photography is a series of paintings for the eye only.

Chicago and reviewing a new play. I had heard from Mayer on Jeritza's test. He agreed that the New York cameramen had failed the woman. I was to use my own judgment as to how to proceed.

Jeritza was in Houston doing a concert. I phoned her and

gave her the not-too-pleasant news, but softened the blow by saying we were unfair with the photography and if she would come to the studio, I would make another test, using only the tops in cameramen and the last word in equipment. I would also make it a sound test that would help greatly.

Maria Jeritza arrived in Los Angeles and took the top floor of the Beverly Wilshire Hotel. She had many friends here in the opera world and planned to entertain royally, as only she could do. I, in the meantime, was upset. I had seen the New York test again and, even overlooking the mechanical imperfections, I knew the inevitable results; still, I'd give this wonderful lady a run for the money.

Just a few short years in a woman's life can make all the difference in the world, camera-wise. Cameramen today are artists, their camera and their lights are brush and palette. In the thirties, there was less than the perfection there is today.

I had written some dialogue that I hoped would help. The scene was an inn in the Bavarian Alps, costumed accordingly. Jeritza looked very charming in the atmospheric costume. Behind the camera we had Charlie Rosher, one of the best photographers of females, and we also had Jack Dawn, a master at makeup, plus Lillian Rozine, tops as a hairdresser. All connected with the test fell in love with this remarkable woman and never did a better job with a subject.

Jeritza, a very liberal woman, appreciated the crew's attention and rewarded everyone with substantial gifts, unexpected and accepted with thoughts of remembrance rather than as a reward for services rendered. If the woman had been Mrs. Joe Doakes, she would have gotten the same attention. My secretary and assistant, Marcella Knapp, received a very beautiful wristwatch, and to my astonishment I was presented with a very expensive gift. I couldn't accept and so told Madame. She understood.

Every department connected with the test went all out, and when it was finished and developed, L. B. Mayer and I saw it together. It was as anticipated . . . a once-beautiful young woman, now a beautiful character woman, again showing traces of Jean Harlow features.

We had no vehicle at that time for the great lady's talents and it was with heavy heart that I told her there was no studio interest at the moment. She took it like a soldier, but I felt that inside her heart was broken. She had never known defeat and for it to come at this time of life was difficult to accept.

Jeritza continued to reside at the Beverly Wilshire. To her many friends she was just waiting for the studio to come up with a vehicle. I confirmed whatever she said.

At a gala one night in the hotel suite, Winnie Sheehan, former head of Fox Studios, was a guest. He was trying to make a comeback and threw hints at Jeritza. She would be good subject matter. To the surprise of the town, the short, rotund Winnie married the tall, statuesque Jeritza, and went to live at his large estate in Bel-Air. The entertainment of local society continued. I attended a sit-down dinner one night for ninety-two people—a Who's Who of the industry.

Mayer arranged for Winnie to do a picture at MGM . . . the story about the Lippizan horses with which Madame was very familiar, having owned the finest specimens in Europe. Between the time he resigned from Fox Studios and his comeback try, the industry had passed Sheehan by. He just did not keep up with the trend. Autocratic at Fox, he tried the same tactics at our studio. It didn't help. The Lippizan horse picture was just so-so, and the Sheehan comeback just didn't materialize. His spirit broken, Winnie Sheehan died a few years later.

Madame Jeritza? I hadn't seen or heard of this great lady for years, but recently I learned that she was married and living in New Jersey. Still a radiant and talented beauty, vivacity and personality unsurpassed. I wish that her defeat at MGM had not materialized. It would have been an industry asset if she were part of it. My salute to a great lady.

Thirty-Five

I ASSUME that you have heard the well-known New England saying, "The Cabots speak only to the Lodges—and the Lodges speak only to God." It was, and is, the code of the old-line "Codfish aristocracy."

I would like to relate an incident typifying the above.

I have written that I was born in the "Brickyard," an across-the-tracks section of Lynn, Massachusetts, the habitat of the proud and struggling "shanty Irish."

The opposite of the Brickyard was Ocean and Nahant streets, the bailiwick of the city's very proper upper-crust, and never the twain shall meet. A resident of Nahant and Ocean who was seen in the company of, or speaking to, a Brickyarder, would have been ostracized.

I was on the boat train to Paris. If one knows the ropes at the Channel port, you tip the platform man and your luggage is placed in your compartment. No tip, and it goes forward into the baggage car, resulting in delay and confusion on your arrival in Paris.

Seated comfortably at a window seat, my bags beside me, I was joined by two ladies and a gentleman who were to be my compartment companions for the trip to Paris. I could hear

grumblings from the dowager-type old gals because my baggage was with me and theirs was in the baggage car ahead. At
the time I was reading the Paris edition of the *Herald Tribune;*
I noted the broad A, typical of Boston, in their remarks.

Pleased at the sound of hometown folks, I lowered my paper
and said smilingly, "Boston—yes?"

"No," replied the man, "just outside Boston. Lynn."

"Well," I replied. "Proof of a small world. I'm from Lynn."

"What part?" asked the elder of the dowagers, as she peered
over the tops of her spectacles at me.

"The Brickyard," I said proudly.

"Oh?" and I detected a nudge and her sister handed over her
smelling salts. Not one word was spoken to me all the way to
Paris. Wow, was I ignored!

I thought of William Anthony McGuire's great line: "Always
speak to a man going *down* Sixth Avenue, because tomorrow
he may be going *up* Fifth."

My favorite hotel in Paris is the Ritz. My nightly hangout, the
Ritz bar, is a gathering place for Parisians and world-traveling
Americans. At least once during their Paris visit, your friends
will show up at the Ritz.

The most important man in all Paris for the traveler to know
is Georges Scheur, manager and majordomo of the Ritz bar. He
knows all, yet will not tell. He knows the whereabouts of everybody and everything. Truly a remarkable and well-liked man.

I had my favorite table in Georges's room, and on the day of
my episode with the Codfish Aristocracy on the boat train, I was
at my usual table, imbibing my favorite nectar, Old Forester.

Glancing toward the waiting line at the entrance, I saw my
boat train hoity-toities awaiting a table. I called Georges and
related the incident of the afternoon and pointed out the three.
Georges wanted to know if he should not see them.

"On the contrary, Georges. Invite them and seat them at my
table here." Georges is evidently an eye-for-an-eye man because he looked at me unbelievingly. Nevertheless, he invited
them out of line and ushered them to my table. They were in
a state of bewilderment. I was in dinner clothes and they did

not recognize me. I called Marceaux, the waiter, while the gentleman whispered "Thank you."

"Marceaux, service, please, for my guests and bring me the bill." As I rose to go to the bar I said to the three, "Be the guest of a Brickyarder." You could have knocked them over with a truffle when they recognized me.

I'll give the man credit. He came to me at the bar and apologized for their earlier conduct. I repeated Bill McGuire's philosophy: "Always speak to a man going *down* Sixth Avenue—because tomorrow he may be going *up* Fifth."

Thirty-Six

T HIS is about a popular and beloved guy, the studio chief of police, who acted also as chief of the studio fire department, the late Whitey Hendry.

Whitey was everybody's friend. All hours of the day and night he would be called upon to aid some studio employee, executive, actor, or one of the back-lot crew. The occasion might be an accident or difficulty with the police. Whitey could always be relied upon to lend a hand.

If it were a matter of serious proportions that would not look good in the public prints, Whitey and his influence would have it played down. The same influence in many cases changed police blotters.

Our man Whitey was very proud of his two departments— with one exception. His fire apparatus was antiquated. He pleaded with the powers that be to purchase modern equipment. His pleas were so convincing and frequent that the powers gave in. A beautiful engine pumper was on its way to the studio in exchange for $40,000. Fire Chief Whitey was in his glory with the old piece gone and the bright new pumper in the firehouse. He stroked it as one would a pet.

Queen Wilhelmina of Holland was a studio guest. Stage 28

had been transformed into a beautiful banquet hall, complete with entertainment stage. On the dais with the royal personage was a Who's Who of Hollywood. Executives, stars, and important newspaper people. With so many famous guests it was to be an important day in industry history.

Nicholas Schenck, MGM president, shared the hosting spot with L. B. Mayer, seated on the queen's right. Whitey and his police force were complimented by everyone for their efficiency in handling the crowds and traffic. The queen sent Whitey an autographed photograph. A great and proud day for the chief.

In the midst of the festivities, the frightening sound of the studio fire alarm rent the air. Whitey, the fire chief, rushed to the scene of the fire, with Nick Schenck and Louie Mayer, forgetting all about their royal guest, at his heels.

The blaze, a serious one, was in the storage sheds at the rear of the lot. Unless contained quickly, the fire could take on serious proportions, spreading and destroying valuable scenery and properties.

The queen, like the commoners, was curious. She came to the fire on the arm of the genial Irishman and studio general manager, Eddie Mannix. The new pumper was on its way to the scene, and when it arrived there were cheers from the onlookers and applause from Her Highness.

Quickly hose lines were spread and the all-important work of the pumper was to begin. I could have cried.

The fire was raging out of control. Mayer was screaming, Schenck yelling. Whitey didn't know how to operate the pumper. The factory instructor had gone to his hotel just as the queen business started. Whitey and his men had to be in attendance, thus missing out on his instructions.

Mayer and Schenck were frantic. Eddie Mannix laughed so hard the tears streamed down his face, joined by the queen. Poor Whitey, never did he have a more embarrassing moment.

The Culver City Fire Department finally put out the blaze.

Whitey Hendry took a week off and watered his rose garden.

Thirty-Seven

T HE "loose and plenty" period of the twenties gave impetus to the custom of having Broadway stars and vaudeville headliners entertain at private parties in the home. It was a very profitable sideline to my agency business.

A host or hostess would phone and advise us of their type of function and how much they wanted to spend for the entertainment. The amount of money governed the caliber and importance of the entertainers. My clients were select, but I often received calls from the johnny-come-latelies of the moneyed world. When I told them the cost of the type of entertainment they wanted I would hear a THUD—it would be the caller falling to the floor in a dead faint.

My favorite hostess was Mrs. Graham Fair Vanderbilt, a very gracious lady in New York and Palm Beach society. She was known as Birdie to her intimates and I have never known a daintier, more democratic and beloved lady in that social world. Ours was a very successful entertainment association. She never questioned my judgment in the selection of entertainment, or music for dancing. That was my end without interference.

There were several incidents that were humorous but at the

same time embarrassing for me during our long association. It is easy now to look back and have a laugh.

Mrs. V. was entertaining the prince and princess infanta of Spain. Something new and in Latin motif was requested to entertain her royalty.

At the Palace Theater in New York, a famous South American orchestra was playing as the headline attraction. The organization had been brought to this country by the State Department for a six-week goodwill tour. An enterprising agent prevailed upon the government to extend the tour to include some U.S. vaudeville theaters. The orchestra consisted of thirty-five musicians, a leader, and a girl singer, and was in the twelfth week of its extended tour.

The musical organization had left its native country with just the costumes its members would wear on the six-week tour. One costume for both stage and street wear, good for publicity and propaganda. With the tour extended, I can assure you ample ventilation was provided wherever they appeared.

I described the musical aggregation to Mrs. V., ideal for the entertainment of her distinguished royal guests. I invited her to the Palace Theater to see the orchestra and confirm my judgment. She thought the outfit wonderful and said she had to have them at her home at all costs. I quoted what I thought was the price I would have to pay, plus 10 percent for my services: $150 for each musician, $200 for the lady singer, and $250 for the leader—the total $6,500. Mrs. V. thought it a bit expensive but she wanted them.

I advised her of the one-costume situation and suggested that her butler have all the windows of her large drawing room open wide for the occasion. Thirty-five, under the circumstances, could make the room a bit stuffy, to put it politely. Mrs. V. promised to have the windows open throughout the house for the proper ventilation.

The agent for the South Americans was named Fitzgerald. In my previous dealings with him, I had found him to be a very sharp trader. I called Fitz and asked him for a quote on the price for the orchestra at a private function. He wanted to know where the affair was to be held, but I wouldn't tell him. All I had to do was to mention the name Vanderbilt and the price would be astronomical. He finally quoted the price of $750. I was so surprised I yelled, "WHAT!?" I thought it would be a great deal more.

Fitz, not knowing the reason for my loud "WHAT," said, "Okay, $500, and you pay the transportation." Would I pay the transportation! For a $5,500 profit, I'd carry them up there in my arms.

My assistant had rented chairs and music stands for the aggregation. All would be in readiness when we got there. I hired two Fifth Avenue buses and my organization set out.

Mrs. V., I found on our arrival, was a bit under the weather; shall I say, indisposed. She was sitting by a large window, but to my consternation the butler had failed to heed my warning and all the windows were closed.

In looking around, I noted an absence of guests on that floor. The prince was present in a small group, but they all had handkerchiefs to their noses. It took the orchestra about ten minutes to tune up and when they were ready to play, the guests, in a body, were in the driveway below. The music was sweet but the atmosphere was sour. I was relieved that M'lady was indisposed. Price: $6,500, for an audience of two—Mrs. V. and myself.

My check, as usual, was there the very next day. I put it in the bank and then pondered—should I go to confession?

Mrs. Vanderbilt called from Palm Beach. There was to be an important deb party at her New York residence. It was for her daughter. She inquired as to the cost of Maurice Chevalier, then appearing at Ziegfeld's Midnight Frolics. He was the toast of New York at the time.

Knowing the Frenchman's love of the dollar and his unwavering bargaining manner, I quoted a rather high price, anticipating difficulty with him: $10,000. Reluctantly she agreed. Chevalier demanded $3,500, and I closed the deal.

At the party, Chevalier was in his element. The young ladies and their escorts screamed and applauded in ecstasy. From another part of the house I heard the applause, but curiously enough no singing or music. I went to investigate.

As I approached the drawing room, I saw Chevalier in Inverness cape and opera hat going down the stairs, leaving the house. I called to him.

"Hey, Maurice, they are still applauding. Come back and do an encore. You've only sung three songs."

"Mr. Irishman, you want Maurice for an encore? You pay me $1,500 more."

From the drawing room there were cries of, "We want more! We want more!"

"You hear that, Maurice? Come back."

He rubbed his forefinger and thumb together. "Non, $1,500," and he was gone, and me after him. He was too quick. He got away. Fool that I was to give him his $3,500 check before the finish.

I returned to the upper floor and had Harry Rosenthal, the orchestra leader, play dance music with the announcement that Chevalier would return later. Thank the Lord, Mrs. V. was in Palm Beach.

Several years ago, I was in Paris. I had taken a former client and French musical comedy star to dinner. After a pleasant couple of hours, Mlle Aubert suggested we go to Monseigneur's, the nightclub famous for its sixteen violinists.

As we entered the club, and I was trying to adjust my eyes to the very dim lighting, Aubert followed the captain to a ringside table. At the table I found her in animated conversation, in French, with the occupants of an adjoining table. I was presented.

"Monsieur 'Beelee,' please meet my good friend, Maurice Chevalier. This is my former New York manager, Maurice, Beelee Gradee."

"Oh, oh, my goodness, I know Beelee from New York," he chuckled. "Remember the party at Mrs. Vanderbilt's?"

"I certainly do," I replied.

The great Chevalier turned to his young girl companions, and included Aubert in his statement.

"I sing for the very 'reech' Mrs. Vanderbilt's young guests. I make my Irish friend Beelee pay me $3,500. Ho—Ho—Ho." He laughed, and the others joined in.

"Ho, Ho, Ho, yourself, Frenchman, and a couple more Ho, Ho's. Yes, I paid you $3,500 that night, but do you know what Mrs. Vanderbilt paid me to bring you there? $10,000. You make $3,500, I make over $6,000, and I don't sing. Ho, Ho, Ho."

His consternation at my statement can well be imagined. I

was "included out" in any following conversation. He left with his gals soon after.

In passing, I must tell of an eerie climax to my evening with Mlle Aubert. She had told me that her aged mama had heard so much about Beelee Gradee that she wanted to meet me, and would I go to her home that night to meet mama?

Jeanne Aubert had had a very deep but frustrated love affair with a French gentleman. Unfortunately he was married to a wife who would not understand and step aside so that he could marry Jeanne. Many years of the affair and Aubert's lover and benefactor died suddenly. She was grief-stricken.

It must have been a helluva love affair because to perpetuate her sweetheart's memory, Aubert had his body photographed while it was stretched out on its bier. The photograph was enlarged to life-size and hung across a wall facing her bed. A red light illuminated the macabre scene.

I had to pass through Aubert's room to meet mama abed in an adjoining chamber. To view the remains of the dead lover stretched across the wall was frightening, and it was a very clammy handshake I greeted the old gal with as she lay in bed. I didn't sleep for a week.

Of course I had to get in dutch by remarking to Aubert, "Is that thing up there to discourage romantic advances?"

Oooooooooh—what she said!

M'lady Vanderbilt liked first-nights at New York openings. If there was anyone in the cast whom she thought might fit into her scheme of entertaining, I would receive a phone call with the message to have the specialty she liked at her home on a stated night.

One of her selections was from George White's Scandals. It was a comedian named Lester Allen. I was a bit surprised at her choice since Allen was also a nightclub comic and was prone to off-color material, but he had redeeming features as a dancer and could do comedy songs and above-the-waist stories if he chose.

In engaging him for a Vanderbilt party, I warned him—no off-color jokes. He was to conduct himself in a manner beyond criticism. He promised.

I was watching other acts on the program in the ballroom when Mrs. V. came to me in a bit of a dither. A complaint.

"That man Allen is at the bar telling some very dirty stories to my guests. I want him out of the house immediately."

I went to Allen holding court at the bar. Surrounding him was a large group of the Vanderbilt guests. He was in his glory with the off-color jokes.

"Hey, Allen, I told you there were to be no off-color jokes. Madame V. wants you out, and out quick. Get going!"

Allen gave a shrug of the shoulders and was on his way— OUT. To my surprise most of his listening group at the bar went with him. He was to continue his recital at a nightclub where he was appearing.

The next morning I went to Mrs. Vanderbilt's house, as was my habit, to pick up my check. Her comment about Allen the night before floored me: "I was a bit disappointed in that little man Allen last night. The dirty stories he told were unbelievable. There was one particularly dirty one—I wish I could remember it. It was so funny . . ."

Thirty-Eight

*M*ORRIE WISEMAN was a tailor of sorts. We who patronized him called him Little Morrie; he was a little rotund man with a heart as big as himself. Though Morrie wanted more than anything in the world to be recognized as a maker of men's clothes, the nearest he came was pressing and repairing, always a rush job. He did the pressing of theater usher uniforms in the Broadway district, as well as the uniforms of policemen on their lunch hour. The one-suit actor set, out of work, came to the shop because our little man would put it on the bill until they got a job. Most of the day there would be a group of men walking around the store in their underwear while Morrie and his assistant did the pressing.

Almost all of Morrie's work was on the cuff, so to speak. "You can't pay now? Okay, pay Morrie when you can." The little man helped many an actor make a well-pressed and groomed appearance at managers' offices when he applied for a job. I don't think Wiseman had what he called "no-pay stiffs." The only "no-pays" were the cops. It seems nobody believed that Morrie could make a suit. It was either mistrust, or because of the $35 tab that Morrie insisted had to be paid COD.

Borrah Minnevitch, long before his fame with the Minnevitch Harmonica Rascals, was a solo harmonica virtuoso. I booked him into the Strand Theater, 47th and Broadway. He was part of the show preceding the picture. Elsie Janis was casting her Elsie Janis Puzzles Revue, a musical. I took her to see Minni at the Strand. She liked him and I made a deal for him to appear in the revue at $350 a week. Quite a jump from his vaudeville and picture house salary of $135.

Now that my harmonica client was in the money, he wanted some walking-around tailormade clothes, not at cello prices but for harmonica money. I recommended my friend, Morrie Wiseman.

Minnevitch had a double-jointed body. He could control every muscle. A shrug of his right shoulder and a hump the size of a small watermelon would appear. Another shrug and it would disappear. He would shrug the left shoulder, and boom —there would be the hump on that side. He could produce them on both sides at the same time. Minni could distend his stomach so that he looked seven months pregnant. From a thirty-inch waist, he would blow it up to forty-six inches. We determined to have a li.tle fun with Morrie.

At Wiseman's shop, I introduced Minnevitch with the news that he wanted Morrie to make him two suits. One would think Morrie had just been told he was the father of a child by Lillian Russell. He waltzed around and rubbed his hands with glee. He rushed for suiting samples from which Minni selected material for the suits.

Morrie called his assistant, another frustrated tailor, to assist with the measurements. As Morrie and his aide went for the tape measure, Minni gave a shrug and there was a hump on the left shoulder blade. Wiseman seemed surprised; he stood back and surveyed, then he rubbed the hump for luck and proceeded with the measurements, his assistant taking the inches down.

The assistant wanted to rub the hump for luck also, but Wiseman pushed him away with a caustic expression in Yiddish. "Don't get so friendly with the customers, Meyer. Excuse this, Mr. Minni, he is full of Jewish superstition. Pleez, Mr. Minni, this is Tuesday, come back Thursday for a try-on. Meyer, let's measure the pants."

Minni's waist was thirty-two inches on the nose. We took our leave, and would be back Thursday.

At the Friars' Club, we let a few of the gang in on the gag, and five of the boys came with us for the Thursday fitting. To Wiseman they would be prospective customers. As we walked into Wiseman's shop, Minnevitch gave a shrug, and the hump that was on his left shoulder at the measuring was now a beautiful little melon on his right shoulder blade.

Morrie had made provisions for it on the left side. He was full of apologies and blamed his stupid assistant. "With new customers looking on yet," he said angrily.

"Please, Mr. Minni, I'll stay up all night. I'll fix the coat. That stupid Meyer. A butcher he is, a tailor he ain't." We were to come back Saturday.

Saturday added more Friars to the spectator group, and to Wiseman they were prospective customers. As we walked in, Minni gave a double shrug, and the humps were on both sides of his shoulder blades. There was a deathly silence. Wiseman reached for a large pair of cutting shears and looked around for Meyer. We, the spectators, had a helluva time stifling our laughs.

Morrie and Meyer went into a back room. The argument was in Yiddish, and it was loud and long, climaxed by a scuffle; a table was tipped over and Meyer ran hell-bent for election out of the place, yelling to Morrie that he was going to the cops. Wiseman was now brandishing a sink plunger. He chased Meyer into the street. I stepped in.

"Forget it, Morrie, it was an honest mistake. Let's try on the pants."

As Morrie went for the trousers, Minnevitch threw out his stomach. The waistline was more than a foot from meeting. Poor Morrie, I thought he was going to have a heart attack. To save the little guy's life I explained the gag. He just fell into a chair and watched Minnevitch blow up and deflate his stomach. Minni tossed the shoulder humps around like basketballs. Morrie was fascinated but came out of his wonderment when Meyer returned to the shop, followed by two cops.

Meyer insisted that Wiseman be arrested for assault with a dangerous weapon. Nothing but arrest and the electric chair would satisfy him. We explained the situation to the police. Another demonstration to the cops by Minni and the episode was over.

We took Meyer and Morrie to the Friars for some schnapps. Wiseman came out all right. He took orders for six suits from Friars. At last he was "WISEMAN—TAILOR TO THE PROFESSION."

I had one other amusing caper with Wiseman. It concerned Mack Gordon and his partner, Harry Revel, a song-writing team, who at the time, though very capable, had yet to make their name on Broadway and its Tin Pan Alley. My office represented them. From the talents of these two gentlemen came songs that are heard time and again even today. Among them: "Did You Ever See a Dream Walking," "You're Such a Comfort to Me," "Stay as Sweet as You Are," "Time On My Hands," "Love Thy Neighbor," "You Can't Have Everything," "Never In a Million Years," and many others.

Mack Gordon was the lyricist and the best delineator of a song in the business. He was a round, fat man—five-feet six-inches tall and about 250 pounds in weight. He was a native New Yorker, and a resident of the Bronx. Mack had the shorts and was a one-suit man. This suit was made of well-worn blue serge. The seat of his pants were so shiny that when he walked down the street he looked like a low lighthouse. He was quite a man with the knife and fork, and not overly careful when using them. The coat was well covered with stains from slobbered food. If a cook had seen the coat he would have sent it to the kitchen to be breaded.

Harry Revel was a little Hungarian and quite a contrast to Gordon's poundage. Quiet and mousey-like, he was dominated by Gordon. Such beautiful lasting melodies came from this little man.

When my office took over their representation, I determined that they should have an important hearing. An appointment was set up with the great Florenz Ziegfeld, who was preparing another Ziegfeld Follies. Gordon and Revel were to play and sing their melodies for the great man. The appointment was made for 5:00 P.M. the following Thursday.

The boys realized this was their big chance and were on pins and needles. They showed up at my office at two in the afternoon to go over the tunes they would demonstrate for the great man. We had three hours to wait.

I got one look at Gordon's blue serge suit. It was a mess. I couldn't take him to the fastidious Ziggy looking like that. The suit would have to have a quick sponge and press, and by the one-and-only reliable Morrie Wiseman. I prayed Gordon wouldn't get a desire to eat before the audition.

A call to Wiseman and he came running. I told Morrie the importance of a quick top job and he promised faithfully to have it back in an hour, "a practical new soot, so help me."

Gordon walked around the music room in his rather worse-for-wear underwear while rehearsing the numbers and waiting for the return of the blue serge.

In the midst of a beautiful love song, I heard Fire Department sirens going up Broadway. Mebbe it was a bit of the Irish witch in me, but something whispered in my ear—Wiseman's.

I dispatched Clarence, my handy man of color, to the roof to ascertain the location of the fire. We were in a building on 46th Street next-door to Dinty Moore's. Clarence yelled down from the roof that he could see a cloud of smoke over on 47th Street near Sixth Avenue. Holy jumping bedpans, that's where Wiseman's shop was located.

The phone rang, it was little Morrie. He was in tears. "That no-good Meyer, my helper, put too much cleaning fluid on the serge suit. A hot iron and there was a big flame. I'm out of business."

The 250-pound Gordon was without a suit to go to Ziegfeld's office. Oh me, oh my!

Frantic phone calls to stores. No one had a suit for our fat man. It would be a novelty for Ziegfeld to listen to beautiful songs by a man wrapped in a few bath towels. That would go for Earl Carroll, but not the great Flo. Downtown in New York was Louie Guttenberg's. Dealer in second-hand clothes for the theatrical set. If we went down maybe they could find something.

Gordon was wrapped in two raincoats and the drapery for the piano. To the street to grab a cab and downtown. Cabbies took one look at Gordon and passed by like a bat out of hell. Finally one cab stopped, the driver interested more from curiosity than in a fare. Gordon jumped in and was off to Guttenberg's.

At 4:45 Gordon returned. He was attired in a loud checked suit worn by a burlesque comedian the season before. He was a frightening sight. I called Ziegfeld and explained.

Up we went, but the doorman was for calling the police when he saw Gordon; thought he was a crackpot.

Well, they played and sang. All the numbers that they played for Ziggy he turned down. The numbers he frowned on were later hits. But Gordon and Revel got a contract for a new show on the strength of what they demonstrated. They were on their way to fame and fortune.

Thirty-Nine

THE majority of visitors to Los Angeles request a visit to a motion picture studio. MGM seems to be the one they prefer.

Visitors are grouped, and with a studio messenger as guide, they are rushed around the lot. They visit the property room, Lot No. 2 for the exterior sets, see a small portion of a picture being shot. Everybody walks, and it is not unusual to see a couple of gals in the group carrying their shoes and walking in their stocking feet. A quick luncheon or tea in the studio commissary, and the tour is over.

VIPs get special treatment—no groups for them. Some executive or his assistant will do the guiding honors. If they prefer, they can ride in a studio limousine. The VIP tour is deluxe.

Nicholas Schenck, then head of MGM with his offices in New York, phoned L. B. Mayer. Some very important European exhibitors were arriving in Los Angeles. Schenck wanted them to have red carpet treatment at the studio, meaning all doors open and a special luncheon with stars in the studio commissary.

Mayer called his right arm and studio publicity head, Howard Strickling. Strick was to assign one of his staff to guide the important visitors. He nominated an assistant, Bill Newberry, for the chore.

Newberry did a bang-up job. To his surprise he received a letter from Nicholas Schenck commending him for his outstanding job as host. Everybody with whom he came in contact got a look at the letter.

Several weeks passed and Newberry was still showing the—by now—well-thumbed letter. He further bragged that all future Schenck visitors to the studio would be in his charge.

Another letter arrived from Schenck. The Chinese ambassador to the United States was sending two of his top aides back to China for conferences. They would like to spend a few hours in Los Angeles before their long journey to China. A request for Schenck for a studio visit by the Chinese. Inasmuch as MGM was about to release *The Good Earth*. Schenck realized the value of good public relations and publicity. The studio visit, by all means, and Newberry was delegated as studio host to the important Chinese. He walked around eight feet tall.

The Chinese visitors arrived, elegantly attired in formal clothes topped by silk hats. They came in a chauffeured limousine with State Department identification plates and flag. Two Secret Service men also were in attendance. These men presented Newberry to the visitors with some instructions.

Because of their inability to speak English, the Chinese preferred having lunch at an inconspicuous commissary table, and requested that the luncheon consist of the Maryland fried chicken they had heard so much about. They had spent four days en route to California on a train and preferred to walk around the studio.

Newberry assured the Secret Service men all would be in order and said he would phone their office at the end of the tour so they could call for their charges.

There was to be nothing that the Chinese were not to see. Lot No. 1 and its many stages, Lot No. 2 with exterior sets depicting streets representing all parts of the world. Newberry hoped the Chinese would not request a visit to Lot No. 3. It was three miles away and contained hot, dusty Western frontier sets.

Several hours later the Chinese were really enjoying their tour. There was one thing Newberry could not understand. His guests could never pass a men's room without entering. Newberry, to insure them privacy, would stand outside and warn everybody away. They would be walking around the lot, the

Chinese would say something that sounded like "scuse" and duck into a men's toilet. Seven toilets on the morning round and Newberry was worried. Were the Chinese sick?

By 1:30 P.M. Newberry was dead on his feet. He was hot, his clothes were dusty, and his feet hurt. The Chinese were as fresh as daisies. Luncheon would be a welcome end to the long walk and toilet waiting. With gestures, Newberry suggested lunch. The Chinese smilingly nodded in agreement. One more trip to the men's room, their eighth, and they were ready.

As Newberry and his guests entered the commissary, everybody present stood and applauded, a respectful gesture. The visitors gave a low bow in acknowledgment and Newberry smiled gratefully. It was a big day for him.

The lunch was a fiasco. Instead of an inconspicuous table, they were seated in the middle of the large room. Instead of Maryland fried chicken, they were served chop suey. Newberry raised hell with commissary manager Frances Edwards, accused her of insulting Mr. Schenck's and the State Department's visitors. Frances cried copious tears and pleaded that she not be reported to Mr. Schenck.

The Chinese, unperturbed, pointed to sandwiches being served at the next table. That's what they wanted. The three had ham sandwiches and tea for lunch. Newberry was livid. He hated tea and ham.

The luncheon over, all present rose as Newberry and his charges made their exit. Gad, was he mad at Frances Edwards.

Once outside, the Chinamen made a beeline for the men's room and again guard duty for Newberry. Fifteen minutes in the privy and they emerged. Newberry had visions that his day with them was finished, but little did he know. The Chinese made circular motions with their arms. They wanted to go around again. Oh, brother!

The afternoon tour was longer. It included Lot No. 3. Yup, they walked. Kids in the street outside the studio followed the strange-looking trio. Passing drivers hurled insulting remarks. "No starch in the collar . . . Have my laundry back Friday," etc. Newberry, embarrassed, was thankful the Chinese did not understand English, but he did have trouble with the pesky kids.

On Lot No. 3, the usual walk around Western street sets, numerous trips to the men's room, and Newberry was almost in a state of total collapse. The hell with Schenck, the State Department, and these G.D. Chinamen. They would ride back to the main studio and like it. When they emerged from the toilet and saw the waiting car they protested, but Newberry insisted. They rode.

Upon arrival at the main lot, it was Newberry's intention to call the Secret Service men, advising that the visit was over. While awaiting the State Department car, he would have publicity pictures taken.

The last men's room visit was of short duration. The Chinese emerged smiling and looking at their wrist watches. They produced a piece of paper from a pocket, handed the paper to Newberry, and said, "Cripes, we're tired. Where do we get our money? We want to get the hell out of here."

Newberry nearly fainted. The Chinese visitors were bit players and extras.

Danny Gray, head of the editorial department and a pal of Newberry's, was a bit tired of his friend's continual bragging. A group of us got together and planned the Chinese gag tour.

The letter from Schenck and the signature was a product of Strickling's office. The extra bit-playing Chinese were selected by my office. They were wardrobed at night so that Newberry would not see. The Secret Service men, as well as the chauffeur, were bit players. The car license plates and State Department banner were made in our prop shop. Frances Edwards was instructed to serve the chop suey instead of chicken, and in order to be tearful when she approached Newberry with an apology, she peeled three onions in the kitchen.

Why so many visits to the men's rooms? Both Chinese were chain-smoking cigarette men. One of them rolled his own—one hand yet. They used the toilets to sit and rest their weary feet.

Newberry went on a drunk. He didn't show around the studio for a week. To this day he detests anything Chinese. Do you blame him?

Forty

W E HAD an assistant director at MGM named "Potsy" Sloop, a lumbering hulk of a man who walked like a bear looking for a place to fall down. Potsy had three acres over in the Valley— in the town of Encino. He was a turkey fancier and couldn't get home quick enough at day's end to fuss with his prize birds, which were comfortably housed in a kind of enclosure turkey people call a "run."

Potsy had been having trouble with four-footed night marauders that were molesting his pets, thirty beautiful gobblers. He determined to put an end to these night raids.

It was a very warm summer night and Potsy slept on the screened porch. He was wearing just his pajama tops, no bottoms. Ponchartrain, his Great Dane dog, slept beside him on the floor, and a double-barreled shotgun was within easy reach, fully loaded.

Potsy Sloop was sleeping the sleep of the just at about 2:00 A.M. A rustle in the turkey run roused him. Grabbing the shotgun, and followed by the Great Dane, Potsy, with all the stealth his great frame could manage, slowly, but slowly, crept toward his birds and their enemy.

Slow—slow—hesitate—slow—slow—hesitate, Potsy approached the enclosure, gun at ready, Ponchartrain one pace to the rear.

Suddenly a surprise rustle. Potsy stopped short. The Great Dane didn't stop and the beast's cold nose touched Potsy in his long-hanging vitals. It scared the hell out of him to the extent that both barrels of the gun went off and eight of his prize gobblers bit the dust.

Potsy has been wearing the bottoms of his pj's ever since. As for Ponchartrain the Dane? Sloop wrote to his brother in northern Minnesota to send a nose warmer for the animal.

Forty-One

*Y*OURS TRULY, the Irish Peacock, has strutted quite a span of years in this telling of his life in the wonderful, exciting world of show business. And so it was—the Golden Years. Irving Berlin said it—There never was and never will be any business like show business. I was lucky to be part of it, to know and to have as my friends and associates the all-time greats of the entertainment world.

New York—Broadway—was my life for more than forty years. There I met the royalty of the theater onstage and off. Names—where do I start? Van and Schenck, Lillian Russell, W. C. Fields, Al Jolson, John Steele, Ethel Merman, Belle Baker, Flo Ziegfeld, Sophie Tucker, Billy Burke. All giants in their own right, living up to every tradition that the show must go on.

Then in 1931 the call was, "Go west young man," and along with stars, writers, directors, producers, and men and women from all branches of show business, I headed for the film capital of the world—Metro-Goldwyn-Mayer.

MGM, the greatest entertainment empire in the history of the world. I was a part of and saw it grow to the worldwide greatness it attained in the forties, fifties, and mid-sixties. In front of the camera and in back of the camera were the men and women and boys and girls who made the slogan come true: "More stars than there are in the heavens."

Louis B. Mayer, Irving Thalberg, Clark Gable, Spencer Tracy, Greta Garbo, Joan Crawford, Norma Shearer, Robert Taylor, Jimmy Stewart, Eleanor Powell, Joan Blondell, Lionel, John, and Ethel Barrymore, Mickey Rooney, Judy Garland, Myrna Loy, Rosalind Russell, Gene Kelly, Fred Astaire, George Murphy, Walter Pidgeon, Jean Harlow, and Greer Garson were just a few of the greats it was my honor to have as friends and fellow workers.

It was the Golden Era. The glamorous and exciting years that made the dreams of the Irish Peacock come true.

Index

(Pages in italics refer to a photograph of the subject.)